TWO WHEELS
TO FREEDOM

ALSO BY ARTHUR J. MAGIDA

Code Name Madeleine

The Nazi Séance

Opening the Doors of Wonder

The Rabbi and the Hit Man

How to Be a Perfect Stranger

Prophet of Rage

The Environment Committees

TWO WHEELS TO FREEDOM

THE STORY OF A YOUNG JEW, WARTIME RESISTANCE, AND A DARING ESCAPE

ARTHUR J. MAGIDA

PEGASUS BOOKS

NEW YORK LONDON

TWO WHEELS TO FREEDOM

Pegasus Books, Ltd.
148 West 37th Street, 13th Floor
New York, NY 10018

First Pegasus Books cloth edition September 2024

Interior design by Maria Fernandez

Map on page ix by Gene Thorp

Library of Congress Cataloging-in-Publication Data is available.

ISBN: 978-1-63936-722-1

10 9 8 7 6 5 4 3 2 1

Printed in the United States of America
Distributed by Simon & Schuster
www.pegasusbooks.com

"The real damage is done by those millions who want to 'survive.' Those who don't want their little lives disturbed by anything bigger than themselves. Those with no sides and no causes. Those who live small, mate small, die small. If you don't make any noise, the bogeyman won't find you. But it's all an illusion, because they die too, those people who roll up their spirits into tiny little balls so as to be safe. Safe?! From what? Life is always on the edge of death; narrow streets lead to the same place as wide avenues, and a little candle burns itself out just like a flaming torch does. I choose my own way to burn."

—Sophie Scholl, executed by the Nazis
for her non-violent resistance to the
regime. She was 21 years old.

Contents

A Note from the Author

Without stories, we'd be adrift in a constant now, a blur with little meaning and little purpose as we struggle to make sense of what we've done, or what we think we've done, or what we're sure we've never done because that's just not the kind of person we are. Or so we think. Stories illuminate and punctuate, entertain and amuse, instruct us about how to better ourselves and how we can learn from our past or learn from others. In the end, stories—our great teachers—tidy up the busy parade of our lives, that messy procession we craft and enjoy and endure, from our birth through our death.

That's why the story here—the story of Cioma Schönhaus—is worthwhile. By now, we've heard many stories about World War II and all that came with it. Most are depressing and dreary. That's the way of war, and especially the way of this war. Indeed, part of Cioma's story is depressing. That should be neither ignored nor suppressed. We are not allowed to look away, hoping we won't be mired in the bleakness that we already associate with this conflict. Flinching is not an option and who would want to, anyway, when it comes to Cioma's story—one so fresh, so out of the ordinary that, on its own, it defines "extraordinary." It's also so unexpected, so beyond what we know or beyond what we think we should know, that it's best you accept now that this is no feel-good yarn sprung from an overwrought imagination. (Cioma's imagination, that is. Not that of the author of this book. Let's leave him out of this, for now.) Nor did this book spring from overworked, misplaced hope (again: Cioma's). It rests on fact, on truth, on life. On Cioma's life.

A young Jew hiding in Berlin during the war, Cioma somehow retained his sense of self and, more unlikely, his sense of fun. Determined to meet the Nazis on his terms, Cioma dined in swanky restaurants, drank in trendy bars, kept up more than a modicum of a social life with girlfriends aplenty—all while thumbing his nose at the Nazis around him. In late 1942, Joseph Goebbels, humiliated that almost sixty-five thousand Jews still remained in Berlin, ordered transports to take every Jew who still resided in the city to destinations that have burdened us forever with what it means to be human. Throughout the winter of 1942–43, as most of Berlin's Jews were sent to their deaths, roughly seven thousand went into hiding. Miraculously, by the end of the war, almost two thousand "U-boats," as they called themselves, would still be alive. Cioma, a U-boat himself, was not among them. By the end of the war, he was somewhere else.[1]

Read on, if you will, for tales of courage and charm and pluck.

Read on, even if you think you've heard it all before and you don't want to hear it again.

Read on, for Cioma's exuberance doesn't correspond to the usual story of Jews—or of anyone—in Europe during World War II. His joys and pleasures, sorrows and sadnesses, were shaped by knowing what we can do when no one expects we can do anything. Through persistence, determination, and a spunky delight in defying the odds, Cioma's spirit was free and expansive: a light on a continent in which most of the lights had gone out.

For Cioma, for everyone in those years, there were losses. Many losses. Cioma offset these with his audacious adventures, never ceasing to continue on his way—spirits high, chin up, and rarely looking back.

As should we, if only we can learn from the stories we haven't heard yet, the stories that, out of nowhere, engage, charm, and broaden us. Like this one.

A final note to readers: Throughout *Two Wheels to Freedom*, "camps" and "transports" are in quotation marks. Ordinarily, quotation marks do not surround these words. I'm using them so no concessions are made to the Nazis for the vocabulary they chose, deliberately and menacingly. "Camps" were not camps. "Transports" were not transports. Each was part of the Nazis' horribly efficient killing system. The euphemisms adopted by the Third Reich should not disguise, or ameliorate, that gruesome, shuddering, and terminal fact. Eighty years after the Holocaust, it's time to put this linguistic charade to bed.

Cioma

Dramatis Personae

The Schönhauses

Cioma Schönhaus: Our hero. Bon vivant, romantic, artist. Resists Nazis with his art and his spunk. Cioma had many names. Even Cioma—a nickname since birth—wasn't his real name. That was Samson. He had at least four fake names during the war: Peter Schönhausen, Gunther Rogoff, Peter Petrov, and Hans Brück.

Boris and Fanja Schönhaus: Cioma's parents. After moving from Russia to Berlin, then to Palestine, and back to Berlin, they refused to move again, despite Cioma's many urgings.

Meir and Sophie Bermann: Cioma's aunt and uncle. Refugees from Russia, they lived a few blocks from the Schönhauses, and they took in Cioma and his mother when their apartment was bombed in an Allied attack.

Marie Bermann: Cioma's grandmother. Also from Russia. Kind, doting, and loving toward Cioma, her only grandchild.

Rosmarie-Susanne and Rigula Schönhaus: Cioma's first and second wives, respectively.

Michael, Sascha, David, and Beat: Cioma's sons.

Cioma's Girlfriends

Renate Klepper: Cultured, modest, curious. Attended art school with Cioma. Daughter of a renowned novelist.

Dorothee Fliess: Smart, pretty, spirited. Went to movies, museums, and galleries with Cioma. Biked with him to the countryside. Daughter of a prominent lawyer.

Tatjana (last name unknown): Russian immigrant. Courted Cioma with caviar and champagne, and with nights at the theater and films. Sewed a small pouch for Cioma in which he kept maps and ID.

Lotte Windmüller: She and Cioma had crushes on each other at the labor camp in Bielefeld. Both were too shy to do anything about them.

Gerda: Last name she used with this alias unknown, though other names she used were Ellen Scheuer and Ellen Dimsack. Real name: Ellen Hirschfeld. Pretty, sultry, tempestuous. Cioma broke up with her when she foolishly flirted with an SS officer.

Anti-Nazis

Franz Kaufmann: Lawyer, bureaucrat, Jewish convert to Christianity. Persuaded his Bible study group to hide, feed, and provide fake IDs for Jews in Berlin.

Helene Jacobs: Carried IDs Cioma faked to Kaufmann. Hid Jews, including Cioma, in her apartment. Ashamed of Germany: "I lost my homeland."

Ludwig Lichtwitz: A forger in Kaufmann's circle. Became close friends with Cioma. Provided advice and money for his escape.

Ernest Hallerman: Carried IDs between Cioma and Kaufmann. Betrayed some members of Kaufmann's circle to the Gestapo.

Edith Wolff and Jizchak Schwersenz: Formed only Jewish youth group in Germany during the war. Cioma faked his first ID for Jizchak.

Kurt Müller: Pastor in Stuttgart. Brought some of Cioma's fake IDs back from Berlin for local Jews who were hiding. Hosted Cioma for several days in September 1943.

Det Kassriel: Taught Cioma how to behave like a non-Jew while hiding. Helped sell furnishings from Cioma's family's apartment so the two of them could afford to live underground.

Karl Barth: Internationally renowned Protestant theologian residing in Basel. Prevented the Swiss government from sending Cioma back to Germany as it had with tens of thousands of other Jews.

Prelude

C ioma Schönhaus's most memorable outing in his boat was the first time he took it out. The day he bought it was the same day he lied about his boating experience to the man who sold him the dinghy. Cioma (that was his nickname; Samson was his real name) didn't use his actual name that spring day in 1943. Partly because he was twenty years old—young enough to think he could get away with almost anything and still naïve enough to try. And partly because, with people like him not safe in Berlin, it was a good idea to trust hardly anyone. So he told the man working the small dock on Lake Stössensee in western Berlin that he was "Peter Schonhausen" and he'd come to buy a small sailboat. Aside from the name he was using that day, Cioma had another problem: he had to convince the man who was selling the boat that he knew his way around one. That wouldn't be easy: Cioma had been on a sailboat only once before and then as a passenger, not a sailor. But now, almost a year after he'd gone into hiding, Cioma was reasonably sure he could fool just about anyone about anything. His blend of charm and bluff rarely failed him. Today, it held once more.[1]

After paying for the boat, Cioma took it out by himself. He had no idea what he was doing. This boat had a life of its own, and it careened from one side of Lake Stössensee to the other. Soon, Cioma learned to control it, steer it, and adjust the sails for wind and for currents, feats that would have enraged Adolf Hitler. Jews were supposed to whimper and cower and die, not enjoy themselves like men of leisure on boats where they didn't belong. This brashness and confidence were the key to Cioma's character. His ease had let him slip into a life that he should not have been living in this year and in this city. Cioma's most reliable weapons were his happy-go-lucky disposition and his smile, which made the day worth living for anyone who was on the receiving end of it. That smile endeared him to friends. It also disarmed his enemies, of whom there were many.

When a friend—another Jew who was hiding from the Nazis—gave Cioma the white turtleneck sweater and white trousers he'd worn when cruising on a motorboat he'd owned before the war, Cioma had the perfect cover. Between the boat and the clothes to go with it and the ridiculous fact that a Jew had the chutzpah to buy a boat in Germany in the middle of the war and sail it near the Chancellery, where Hitler lived and worked—add all that together and, as Cioma said years later, "Nobody would have thought this was a Jew in hiding. This was much better than sitting in Aschinger's" (a popular chain of beer halls) "unshaved and gaunt, and wearing a frayed, dirty shirt, and frightened that the Gestapo would grab you any minute." It was also more fun.[2]

When Cioma left the dock in Pichelsburg, where he bought the boat, he passed three piers that stretched onto the lake like long fingers walking into the water. All sorts of boats were moored here—rowboats, sailboats, canoes, and houseboats. There was also a restaurant, the Wilhelmshöhe, which was full almost every night, even during the war. The Wilhelmshöhe's four long terraces climbed the slope above the lake; each terrace was set back slightly from the one beneath it, with small lamps resembling model lighthouses secured to the wooden railings that divided the terraces from each other. At night, reflections from the "lighthouses" shimmered in the lake below, a watery penumbra that did Cioma no good the first night he took the boat out: he ended up stranded on a riverbank a few miles south of the restaurant, and nowhere near the warm, beckoning lights of the Wilhelmshöhe. This was the curse of the amateur who pretended he knew all about boats. As hungry as he was, Cioma realized he'd never reach the Wilhelmshöhe before closing time: with his skills as a sailor, he'd sink the boat before he got there. So he stretched out on the boat's mahogany deck—damp, chilly, and suddenly not too sure that a boat was the best way to get the rest he needed. His doubts got worse as bombs began lighting up the city and antiaircraft guns thrummed the air with shuddering percussions. Shells that missed the planes splashed into the river near Cioma. Open areas, he knew, were the worst place to be during an air raid. But even if he'd spent the night in the room he was renting back in Berlin, he wouldn't have gone to an air raid shelter. If someone examined his papers too closely—papers he'd faked: Cioma was one of the best forgers in the city—he could be thrown onto the same trains that had taken his parents to "the east."[3]

At dawn, Cioma rowed back to Pichelsburg, annoyed that oars, not sails, were taking him back to where he started. Cioma took the subway home. That afternoon, he bought a book he should have read before taking out the boat. The book was titled *Sailing for Beginners*.

Before too long—though not without a fair amount of trial and a lot of error—Cioma taught himself how to sail. That was a blessing. On the boat, Cioma relaxed as much as a Jew could in Berlin in 1943, and the sailing outfit his friend had given him made him look debonair and polished, almost like sailing was in his blood and he was a veteran seafarer, an old salt just back from the seven seas. That wasn't Cioma, and that was fine with him. Sailing gave him what he asked of it: it kept him awake and alert and reminded him he was still his usual cocky self. At the same time, behind all this bravado, Cioma harbored the saddest of sorrows. Sometimes, these stared him right in the face, literally, like the pillows he used aboard the boat that his mother had embroidered to liven up the couch in their apartment: bright flowers and birds and fanciful designs. Cioma used the pillows as a makeshift bed. After spreading them out on the bare wooden hull, he'd think of the life he'd had with his father and his mother, the life they would never have together again. And he'd think of other relatives, and of too many friends: all too young not to be alive. The boat carried Cioma away from this pain, and toward his life that could have been and might still be, thanks to his grand gestures (like sailing a boat) that, if nothing else, were giving him a hell of a good story to tell after the war, and a hell of a good way to survive it.[4]

PART ONE

THE WANDERERS

1

"You Better Go Back"

Cioma Schönhaus's parents, Fanja and Boris, immigrated to Germany from Russia not long after the Russian Revolution. First, Fanja moved to Berlin with her wealthy parents. There was no place for them in Vladimir Lenin's utopia, not with the Bolsheviks nationalizing everything—factories and generating plants, stores, and businesses, large and small. Hoping to continue their lucrative clothing enterprise in Germany, Fanja's parents—Mr. and Mrs. Bermann—shipped the expensive fabrics from which they tailored fine suits for men from their shop in Minsk to Berlin. Soon, Boris deserted from the Red Army, in which he was a company clerk, and moved to Berlin as well: he wanted to be with Fanja, his sweetheart and fiancé. Her parents paid for their wedding in 1920, planned everything, and invited most of the ninety guests. The bride and groom were young: Boris was twenty-two—nineteen months older than Fanja. Fanja wore a large brooch that sparkled under the chuppah, and Boris, poor Boris, was very much the odd man out. He knew few of the guests, and he had so little money that, to look respectable, he had to borrow a pair of shoes that were too small for him and pinched his feet all day. An unabashed Socialist, Boris rankled at the wedding's expense and at all its hoopla. He knew he wasn't quite right for the crowd he was now moving in.

Fanja's parents were bourgeois and proud of it. Boris, despite fleeing the Bolsheviks, saw himself as a man of the people, and he wanted to be with the people.[1]

Still, Fanja and Boris were reasonably comfortable in Berlin. So many Jews had recently moved there from Russia, Romania, Lithuania, and Bulgaria, as well as from other parts of Germany, that, by the early 1920s, Jews made up 4 percent of the city's population. By 1925, there were thirty thousand Jews just in the neighborhood where the Schönhauses lived. The number of Jews rose so fast that many Gentiles were sure Jews were taking over. They certainly weren't, but Cioma's parents had reason to hope Berliners would be friendlier to Jews than Gentiles in Russia had been. Over the centuries, Minsk, the city where they'd lived, had treated Jews miserably one year, decently another, and despicably a third. It was all very confusing. In 1495, Jews were kicked out of Minsk. That pleased the Catholic Church, which had never liked them, and it especially pleased the nearly bankrupt city government, which robbed its way back to solvency by confiscating Jews' money and property as they were being forced out of town. Eight years later, when Jews were allowed to return, their land, homes, cemeteries, and, of course, their synagogues were restored to them . . . except for what their Christian neighbors refused to surrender. Soon the old animosities were relit—ancient conflagrations that had simmered and churned and had never really been snuffed out—and new laws required that Jewish men wear yellow caps and Jewish women wear yellow kerchiefs: anything to distinguish them from Christians. In their heartache and their stubbornness, they persevered and, by the late nineteenth century, half the city's population was Jewish, almost 90 percent of its merchants were Jews, and Jews controlled Minsk's lumber trade and owned its largest industries. Yiddish culture thrived. Jewish religion flowered. Then came the Russian Revolution, and the Bolsheviks closed all the synagogues and religious schools, turned the Jews' cemetery into grazing grounds for goats, limited Jews' access to food and housing, and disenfranchised 40 percent of them. Many of them moved to Germany—so close, and so safe. Or so it seemed.[2]

The Berlin the Schönhauses encountered was full of artistic optimism, nasty political grudges, novel architecture, and dyspeptic critics. In the late nineteenth century, Berliners were determined to outdo Paris and Vienna in culture, wealth, and luxury. Villas sprang up in chic neighborhoods, their ceilings dripping with plaster cherubs and their grand rooms groaning under the weight of dark, heavy furniture and thick, plush carpets. Fountains in the villas' courtyards spurted champagne during receptions as small ensembles played Bach and Beethoven, the twin jewels in the crown of Germany's musical heritage. The glamour distracted from the poverty that sprawled all over Berlin, then the largest industrial city in Europe and the city with the most tenements in the world. All those workers had to live somewhere, with sometimes up to thirteen people sharing a room. At the same time, some villas were providing more than two thousand square feet for their servants to live in. Several working-class families would have gotten lost in all that space.[3]

Most of the Jews in Berlin, including the Schönhauses, lived in a neighborhood called the Scheunenviertel. (Its name derived from the *scheune*, or wooden barns, that flourished here.) By 1920, over forty thousand Jews lived here. A babel of languages—Yiddish, Hungarian, Romanian, Russian—filled the air. Shops sold schnapps, brown bread, smoked fish. One block alone boasted nineteen prayer rooms and several synagogues. A small restaurant—really, more of a hole in the wall—showcased a model of Solomon's ancient temple in Jerusalem. Though made of cardboard painted red, white, and gold, it was treated as if it were the real thing, one that made its owners a pretty penny: two marks let you enter the room that housed this Lilliputian homage; two more marks got you a brochure; another two marks got you a brochure in Hebrew. The temple was an homage to an ancient past;

everything else in the Scheunenviertel, as Boris and Fanja Schönhaus would discover, was a re-creation of a more recent life left behind.[4]

Eventually, Berlin's Jews became slightly less impoverished, and more of a community, with Jewish community centers, Jewish hospitals, Jewish nursing homes, Jewish theatrical and musical programs—all of it enriching everyone's lives, all of it announcing that Jews were a part of the city and they weren't leaving. But success made Jews conspicuous, just like in Minsk. By 1930, half of Berlin's lawyers and doctors would be Jews, and Jews would own half of the city's banks and almost three quarters of its department stores. Outsiders saw only Jews' wealth and success. Most didn't know that 75 percent of shops owned by Jews barely broke even and 15 percent of Jews were so poor they couldn't survive without help from the nineteen soup kitchens run by Jewish-sponsored welfare agencies.[5]

This was the world Cioma Schönhaus was born into on September 28, 1922. His legal status was tentative. He wasn't a citizen. Communists back home had stripped Russian citizenship from anyone who left the country after November 1917 "without the authorization of the Soviet authorities." Cioma's parents hadn't asked anyone if they could leave: Fanja left with her parents to escape the revolution; Boris was a deserter from the army. All of them were stateless and, under international law, a child of stateless parents was stateless, too. No government anywhere protected Cioma, and no rights or benefits were conferred on him. He and his parents were "guests" of Germany, sometimes barely tolerated guests who chafed at being called "unprotected persons" and "outlaws." Though they were safer than if they'd stayed in Russia, they weren't even second- or third-class citizens in Germany. They weren't citizens. Anywhere.[6]

Cioma's timing wasn't great. Ten days before he was born, a barely known rabble-rouser had shrieked out the latest of his incoherent speeches. In Munich, Adolf Hitler had attacked bankers, politicians, and the "few dozen Jewish bankers" who, the future

führer claimed, were controlling every German, all sixty million of
them. Hitler demanded that every Jew who'd moved to Germany
after 1914 be deported and their money and property be seized. That
was the only way to save Germany from this "Jewish pestilence."
Anyone who disagreed, Hitler warned, would "feel how life tastes
in a concentration camp."[7]

Though Cioma's parents had moved to Germany after 1914,
they were staying. They'd already left behind friends, relatives, and
possessions once. Here they'd remain: Berlin was their new home.
Or so they thought, until a few weeks after Cioma had his first
birthday. On November 5, 1923, more than ten thousand out-of-work
laborers, furious that they'd been denied unemployment benefits,
took to the streets in the worst antisemitic riot of the fragile, unstable
Weimar Republic. Police looked on as Jews—veterans from the recent
war—tried to turn the rioters back with the few pistols they owned.
Only after one rioter was shot did the police intervene. By the time it
was all over, 1 Jew was dead, 129 people injured, and more than one
thousand shops ransacked and looted—all within a few blocks of the
Schönhauses' apartment.[8]

The riot forced Fanja and Boris to make a decision about a land
that was even more foreign to them than Berlin had been when they'd
moved there from Minsk. Berlin and Minsk were European, with
vaguely similar music and literature, and streets laid out in broad
boulevards and slightly more narrow avenues, and the smell of boiled
cabbage and freshly baked challah, kugel, and knishes spilling out into
the streets from every apartment. Fanja and Boris' possible destination
would be more of a challenge than moving to Berlin had been. And
yet, as Zionists and as Socialists, only one land made sense: a nation
that was not yet a nation; a sandy spit of land that appealed to refugees,
pilgrims, and dreamers who were streaming in that direction from
many places, a land with many languages, customs, destinies, and
visions—political, messianic, mystical, utopian—that would, somehow,

have to be consolidated and massaged if this Jewish back-to-the-land enterprise had a reasonable chance of succeeding. For many Jews, Palestine was a dubious proposition to begin with, full of camels and donkeys, and settlements that could barely be called towns or villages and certainly not cities, and seven hundred and fifty thousand Arabs who easily outnumbered the seventy-five thousand Jews, who often disagreed with each other about why they had come, and what would emerge from all of this. Theodor Herzl, the father of modern Zionism, once said, "If you will it, it is no dream." Boris and Fanja were ready not to dream, and to will this place into being.

In 1926, the Schönhauses left Berlin for Rishon LeZion, a settlement four miles west of the Mediterranean, ten miles south of Tel Aviv, and thirty-five miles west of holy, sacred, volatile Jerusalem—also known as Gan Adonai, "City of God"; Kiryah Ne'emanah, "Faithful City"; Ir Hatzedek, "City of Righteousness"; Gei Chizayon, "Valley of Vision"; and another sixty-four names that glorified a city that had been changing hands for more than three thousand years. Israelites, Jebusites, Hasmoneans, Egyptians, Romans, Philistines, Babylonians, Mamluks, Turks, Christians, Jews—almost everyone in the ancient and modern world wanted to possess Jerusalem, rebuild it, refortify it, defortify it, pray in it, or prevent others from praying in it. Life in Jerusalem was never settled; never without various faiths, all competing for truths and revelations; and never without conquering powers, all determined to keep the city theirs forever, a miracle that never happened. Jerusalem was destroyed twice, attacked fifty-two times, captured and recaptured forty-four times, and besieged twenty-three times. Jesus was crucified, was resurrected, and ascended here; Muhammed visited Jerusalem on his night journey from Mecca, carried by his winged horse, Buraq; and here Jews were buried on the Mount of Olives, certain that this was where the Messiah, whom they'd long awaited, would first appear and, when that happened, those who were buried here would enter heaven before anyone else on earth.[9]

Boris and Fanja never visited Jerusalem; traveling in Palestine was almost as hard as getting there from Berlin. There was no flying horse for them, no quickened path to heaven, no Messiah whose mother was named Mary and whose father was God. Mostly they remained in Rishon LeZion, which had been founded forty years before by ten Russian Jews. The town was distinguished more by its patron—Baron Abraham Edmond Benjamin James de Rothschild, scion of the legendary banking family—than by its population (1,373 Jews and twenty-three Muslims when the Schönhauses arrived). What awaited the Schönhauses was a remote, secluded outpost, one that Rothschild had uplifted by paying for a synagogue, a community hall, a park, vineyards, almond plantations, the first Hebrew-language kindergarten and elementary school in the world, and a boulevard bordered by tall, stately palm trees—all reminders of Europe amid drifting sand dunes and the grating, jarring braying of donkeys and camels. This wasn't what the Schönhauses had dreamed of, but it was what they had to accept. Moving to Berlin with its ready-made culture was one thing. Creating a home from sand, sweat, and the long-ago promises of patriarchs and prophets was quite another.[10]

Getting through the day—any day—was hard. One settler called Palestine "a wild country. You must open your eyes and guard your life. Be aware of this. Life here is transitory, and people are affected." There were snakes and scorpions, and the scorching heat of a sun the likes of which Boris and Fanja had never encountered. Sand was everywhere—in clothes, food, machinery, cars. Sand, in fact, was all Cioma would remember about Rishon LeZion. Seventy-seven years after he'd been there, he'd recall the "sand between your teeth." Not donkeys or camels or the blistering, desiccating, unrelenting heat. Only the sand. That was either his only memory of Rishon LeZion or his most memorable memory, for surely more happened to him while he was on the settlement than encountering sand. Sand may have stayed with him longer than anything else because he felt it the most and it bothered him the most. Donkeys and camels were wonders. Sand was an irritant, an aggravation, and aggravations can stay with us longer than pleasures. The sand may also have stayed with Cioma because it introduced him to the grittiness of life, a grittiness that would haunt him as a teenager, as a young adult, and as a much older adult who was forever stunned and dismayed at the losses he'd suffered over the course of his life. The losses rarely failed to make him cry or call out for those he missed, and who had been missing for much too long. These were the circumstances that defined and shaped and molded him. They were the sand between his teeth.[11]

Boris, more dedicated to Socialism and Zionism than his wife, liked the land and its challenge and its history. Fanja—usually the optimist in the family—did not. After barely a year, they faced a dilemma. When he was five years old, Cioma contracted dysentery. In Palestine, medical care, and especially medicines that were effective against the severity of Cioma's illness, were both scarce. "If you want the boy to survive," their doctor advised, "you better go back."[12]

The Schönhauses had moved from Russia to Germany, then from Germany to Palestine. Now they'd relocate back to Germany. They couldn't risk their son's health. Sometimes the Promised Land didn't keep its promises. And sometimes people drifted with the wind, light as feathers, while their eyes didn't stir from their prize, as righteous as it might be. Fanja and Boris hadn't found theirs yet, and after three major moves—Minsk to Berlin, Berlin to Rishon LeZion, Rishon LeZion to Berlin—they were still hoping to settle into a land and a home and a life from which they'd never have to pack their bags again.

2

"In Earlier Times, They Would Have Burned Us"

B ack in Berlin, the Schönhauses first moved in with Fanja's parents at Hirtenenstrasse 41, then to an apartment of their own at Würzburger Strasse 17, and finally to a two-room flat at Sophienstrasse 32–33, a few blocks from a large square—Hackescher—where, in warm weather, customers ate sandwiches or drank beer at tables spread over broad patios, and where a welter of bus, subway, and tram lines met, finding their way through a complicated maze of an intersection. Here, four streets—An der Spandauer Brücke, Rosenthaler Strasse, Gross Präsidentenstrasse, and Oranienburger Strasse—converged briefly before going their separate ways. Despite the potential for mayhem, the chaos was organized, and the buses, subways, trams, automobiles, and pedestrians that came within inches of brushing up against each other avoided accidents and other havoc—a miracle of city planning, or maybe a miracle of imposing order (no matter how jumbled) in a city, and a country, that was experimenting with democracy, vaguely hanging on to its aristocracy, and barely warding off militias from the left and the right that were eager to topple the closest thing Germany had to a legitimate government.[1]

Hackescher Market was a buffer, a transition, between the bourgeoise—or those who aspired to be bourgeoise—and the bustling, struggling Jewish Quarter only a few blocks away, which was crammed with peddlers, shopkeepers, beggars, shuls, Jewish community centers, a Jewish home for the aged, and a Jewish cemetery: a Jewish world oriented around this life and the next. Sophienstrasse, where the Schönhauses lived, was one of the more beautiful streets in Berlin, with graceful architecture more half a century old, narrow sidewalks along a narrow roadway, and a canopy of trees that flowered in the spring and summer. It was out of the way, quiet, and peaceful: almost an afterthought to the bustling streets nearby.

Directly across the street from the Schönhauses' apartment building was a large Lutheran church whose trees, gardens, and meandering paths were so pastoral, such a quiet refuge in the big city, that they wouldn't have been out of place in a country village. The tolling of the church's bells woke Cioma every Sunday. For Cioma, that didn't mean people were being summoned to worship. It meant he couldn't get back to sleep.

If not for Jews, there might not have been a church. In 1712, Lutherans living outside Berlin's city walls petitioned the Crown to let them have their own church, complaining that the parish where they attended church was too far away and too inconvenient to get to, especially on roads that were icy in the winter and washed out in the spring. Queen Sophie came to the rescue, with a donation of four thousand reichsthalers, which she divided between building a church and setting aside a fund to be invested, with the interest used to pay preachers, organists, and the rest of the church's staff. The Lutherans named their church after her—Sophienkirche, or Sophien Church.

When local Jews learned that the Lutherans didn't have enough money to buy land for their church, they offered almost an acre from the extensive plot of land they'd reserved for their cemetery. The Lutherans accepted the offer, and the Sophien Church was consecrated in June 1713, the eighty-eight pipes of its organ bursting with such deep sonorities that little children were scared the earth had opened up and would swallow them. A 226-foot-tall tower was later added to the church, along with its loud and unavoidable bells that eventually ruined the sleep of young Cioma Schönhaus.

Few people who lived on Sophienstrasse knew that the Lutherans who'd accepted land from the Jews had promised "everlasting good neighborliness" toward their Hebrew friends. Nevertheless, the pact held during some of the worst moments in Germany's history, affirming that being Lutheran, being German, and being humane were not mutually exclusive.

It's hard to say why Cioma's parents moved to the Scheunenviertel. Maybe because they were left-wingers and revolution was in the air here: a quarter block from the Schönhauses' apartment was the former headquarters of the Spartacus League—Communists who'd tried to overthrow the government in 1919. It was just as likely they moved here because Judaism was also in the air. It was impossible to get away from it in this neighborhood. And while the Schönhauses were never devout, despite their Zionism, they always identified as Jews. There's also a chance, a small one, that they chose the Scheunenviertel because the oldest Catholic hospital in the city was half a block away from their apartment on Sophienstrasse. St. Hedwig's offered some of the best medical care in Berlin, and it treated everyone. Creed didn't matter, nor did faith. No one asked which God any of St. Hedwig's patients prayed to. Being this close to St. Hedwig's would have made sense to Boris and Fanja after Cioma's dysentery had caused them to leave Palestine. They didn't want to risk his life now.

Most apartment buildings in Berlin opened onto courtyards where everyone got fresh air and strangers became friends, and friends became confidants, gossips, chess rivals, and nimble debaters about politics, religion, life: anything. Some courtyards were large enough for gardens, nursery schools, or kiosks that sold coffee and pastries. Boris used the courtyard outside his apartment building for the mineral water business he started after returning from Palestine. Eventually, Boris hired seven workers and three coachmen who delivered the mineral water on horse-drawn wagons to restaurants in the neighborhood. Marginally successful, the business provided Boris enough of a living to support his small family. Being this close to poverty troubled Fanja, who'd never been denied anything as a child. Still, she did her best to make their apartment as pretty as she could, with white-lacquered furniture in the bedroom, pink curtains on the windows and, in the right season, a crystal bowl full of fresh plums on the dining room table. "The whole flat," Cioma remembered decades later, "smelled of plums."[2]

In school, Cioma got by on charm, wit, and the glib assurances he gave his teachers that he understood his lessons. Most of the time, he daydreamed his way through classes. He also got lost in his imaginings out of school, most frequently at the Berliner Schloss, a ten-minute walk from Sophienstrasse. The royal House of Hohenzollern began building this memorial to grandiosity and greed—1,200 rooms and gilded everything—in the fifteenth century. The original schloss, or palace, was baroque. A few centuries later, an even bigger schloss replaced it, this one in the Italian Renaissance style. Cioma didn't go to the schloss for a history lesson, though he could have easily gotten one if he'd been paying more attention. He went to fantasize about living there someday as a Prussian prince: a ridiculous dream for any child, especially for a poor Jewish kid whose parents were barely scraping by. Decades later, Cioma knew how absurd his fantasy had been. There was no chance, he said, that he or any Schönhaus would live in the schloss: "We were poor and we lived a simple life." Too simple and too poor for the schloss. Which was exactly why Cioma's dreams about living there were indispensable. Without them, Cioma risked repeating his parents' poverty. Imagining a life grander than his gave the impossible a chance to be real, even in a small, modest way. Played well, the imagination can be a gateway to possibilities;

ignored, it's stunted and eschewed, a waste of a rich and bountiful facility.[3]

Adolf Hitler came to power when Cioma was ten years old. Hardly anyone, especially anyone abroad, knew what to make of the führer. To them, he was a buffoon, a joke, a no one who had come from nowhere and would soon go back there. The Nazis did their best to placate jitters about their chancellor. In Berlin, "Hitler's friends" were telling foreign journalists that Germany's "friendship" toward the United States wouldn't change. It worked: news reports from Washington, DC, professed that the city showed "little apprehension" that Hitler threatened international relations, particularly since Hitler, now that he was surrounding himself with "more experienced and more conservative politicians," would have to be more docile than when he'd been a "free agent," screaming about Jews, Socialists, Communists, and anyone else he didn't like. The *Boston Herald* was one of the few papers in the United States that, bravely, and sometimes subtly, warned readers not to trust the führer: "Hitler Pledges to Rule Sanely . . . ," "Promises To Govern Constitutionally," "Will Steer Clear of Anti-Semitism." Between the lines, the *Boston Herald* was whispering: this man—a walking cyclone of power, hate, and fury—meant no good.[4]

Hardly anyone was listening. They should have. While the world wasn't taking Hitler seriously, Hitler was.

Some children in Germany were dazzled by Hitler's strutting, huffing, and puffing. They knew this bully. They'd seen him on their playgrounds or on their way home from school. But when he was on the playground, Cioma preferred to be by himself. Never an athlete, he was happier making up his own not-too-demanding games than trying to keep up with other children. One day, Cioma heard someone shout "Attention!" He then noticed that most of the kids around him had stiffened, happy to be playing soldier—everyone's heroes in this drab world of the Nazis even while they understood none of it. The boy who'd called everyone to attention "inspected" their "uniforms" (no more than their everyday clothes) and their pretend rifles (sticks, branches, poles), and he slapped a "private" who was slouching. The boy didn't flinch. In this new world of brown shirts and men knocking on your door in the middle of the night, the sting of a slap, even for a child, was trivial compared to the good of the nation. The rules of the new regime were seeping into the lives of everyone, even of ten-year-olds.[5]

Another day, Cioma and some friends had fun playing their own version of Cowboys and Indians: the "Cowboys" were Nazis; the "Indians" were Communists. The head of the "Nazis" wanted Cioma to join them. "You must be a Nazi," he argued with half-baked logic. "Your parents escaped from Russia. They didn't want to stay there." For the rest of recess, Cioma, a nice Jewish boy, was a "Nazi"—fighting the Communists who were swooping down from their workers' paradise in Russia, ready to vanquish their Nazi foes and make the world safe for Karl Marx, Vladimir Lenin, parades in Red Square, and starving workers everywhere.[6]

That was also the year the book burnings began. They continued for the next six years, pausing only in 1936 to convince the rest of the world that Germany was a great place to host the Olympics that summer. Though Cioma lived less than a mile from the burnings, he knew nothing about them. If he hadn't been so young, he might have wanted to go. Many boys like to play with matches, and this was one of the more notorious blazes in history. Cioma's parents, we can be sure, wouldn't have let him out of his room.

The book burnings—organized by students, not the German government or the Nazi Party—were first dismissed as college sprees run amok. "Beer-inspired student pranks," sniffed upper-class Germans. "Excessive student zeal," cabled a foreign reporter back home. Oddly, Sigmund Freud (whose books had gone up in smoke on May 10, 1933, the first of the burnings) shrugged them off. "Only our books?" taunted this sage who specialized in deciphering human nature. "In earlier times," Freud continued, "they would have burned us with them." Was Freud challenging the book burners to do better? Soon, they would.[7]

Quickly, the book burnings were assailed as attacks on thought, on freedom, on civilization itself. One of their most cutting critics was Helen Keller, whose *How I Became a Socialist* was burned the same year as Freud's books. Keller viewed the burnings with less whimsy than Freud. "History has taught you nothing if you think you can kill ideas," Keller charged in an open letter to the "Student Body of Germany" from her home in New York. "You can burn my books and the books of the best minds in Europe, but the ideas in them . . . will continue to quicken other minds. Do not imagine that your barbarities to the Jews are unknown here. God will visit His judgement upon you. Better were it for you to sink into the sea than to be [the most] hated and despised of all men."[8]

Helen Keller could see what was happening better than those with sight.

Twenty-five thousand books were burned that first year—books by Karl Marx and Friedrich Engels, Albert Einstein, Ernest Hemingway, James Joyce. This was a night for ancient madnesses, for pagans and infidels. Definitely a night for a ten-year-old boy named Cioma Schön-haus to stay home and sleep through the night.

More books were burned the next year, and the next, and on through a good part of the 1930s. Novels, and pacifist tracts, and Charles Darwin's breakthroughs on evolution. One hundred and seventy thrillers by the British writer Edgar Wallace went up in smoke for "promoting the English way of life and manners in an irresponsible way." More than two hundred of G. F. Unger's books were burned—dime-store novels about cowboys in the American West that glorified individualism and self-reliance, dangerous traits in Nazi Germany. Unger's books were the most popular novels among children in Hitler Youth.[9]

If Cioma had been older, and more aware, he might have paid particular attention to a certain book the Nazis burned, one regularly dismissed as a simple fable for children, with animals frolicking in woods and meadows, and a father and mother worrying about their son who was too easily distracted from learning how to survive in the forest, and happy chatter between deer and rabbits and squirrels. But *Bambi* wasn't simple and it wasn't a fable. Its real meaning, once the cuteness was brushed away, was that the world is a scary place, and you stayed alive only by knowing, relentlessly knowing, everything that's going on around you.

Siegmund Salzmann, a Viennese Jew better known as Felix Salten, published *Bambi* in 1922—his response to antisemitism in Austria. By the end of the book, Bambi learns that he can never relax, never let down his guard. His mother pleaded, "No matter what you see or hear, run as fast as you can." A grasshopper warned, "You never know who's coming." Of all the dangers in the forest, man was the worst. Man killed for "sport," murdering animals who'd never harmed him with weapons as loud as thunder. "He's murdered us since I can remember," an older deer taught a fawn. "He kills us whenever we show our heads." Life was a constant, never-ending flight from man's slaughter, from his delight in maiming, killing, and destroying.

Most deer survived by running. Bambi's father taught him another way. If he lived alone, Bambi could "listen to anything that moved" and "sniff the air" or "put his nose to the ground and examine everything thoroughly." Bambi's life depended on letting nothing escape his attention. Nothing was insignificant only if Bambi was alert and conscious and awake enough to detect it. No one would come to his rescue. He had to rescue himself.[10]

If Cioma had any idea what the future held for him, and of course he didn't, he might have known that *Bambi* wasn't a charming story for sweet little boys and girls. Rather, it was almost a manual about how Cioma should behave once the Nazis really cracked down, and his parents boarded trains to "the east" and be was left behind. These were the precise moments when he had to be alert and know, like Bambi, that surviving meant he'd always be on the run, always be hunted, always be scared, and that if he let down his guard, even for a moment, he'd hear the thunder of rifles, and see lightning bursting from the barrels of weapons, and stiffen his posture not like he did with his friends when they pretended to be Nazi soldiers rigid at attention on their school's playground. Rather, he'd stiffen with shock, and horror, and death.

Cioma never read *Bambi*. He couldn't. It was burned in a massive bonfire an eighteen-minute walk from Sophienstrasse. Cioma was thirteen that year. Anyone who owned a book that had been burned could be charged with "high treason."

Cioma was too young to be a traitor, but his parents took that risk. They kept books that had been burned in their apartment. When Cioma's older cousin, Morris Gorelik, had immigrated to Jersey City, right across the river from Manhattan, he'd left his canoe and bicycle with Cioma, and his books, all of them banned, with Cioma's parents: *The Communist Manifesto* by Karl Marx and Friedrich Engels; *Mona Lisa's Smile* by Kurt Tucholsky, an intellectual, a pacifist, and a Jew; plays and satires by Alfred Polgar, another Jew. There were also bound volumes of *Die Weltbuhne*, "The World Stage," a weekly magazine about politics and art. The Nazis hadn't burned *Die Weltbuhne*. They simply put it out of business a few weeks after Hitler became chancellor in 1933. The Schönhauses kept all of these in a bookcase next to their dining room table.

Eating so close to these so-called dangerous books excited Cioma. He knew they were contraband. He didn't know why. As Cioma got older, he understood the risk: "Just having books like this in your possession could prove fatal—if certain people came across them, that is." Boris and Fanja didn't associate with those people. They bargained they never would. Their unobtrusive lives were not likely to arouse the suspicions of men who dragged you away in the middle of the night.

Admittedly, keeping banned publications was daring, and Boris and Fanja didn't ordinarily engage in anything close to daring. They were too protective of the little they'd accomplished in life to risk all for a few books. Their behavior reflected a hope that the coming storm wouldn't touch them—or maybe they willfully refused to believe that anything worse was coming their way. After returning to Germany from the Promised Land, Boris and Tanja had placed their faith, and their lives, in what they assumed was the basic goodness of many of their neighbors. Now that goodness was fraying, and the wisdom of returning from Palestine was dubious. The strain of being both German and Jewish was exhausting each of the Schönhauses.[11]

3

Hitchhiking
on the Autobahn

Cioma Schönhaus's mother worried about him. Her son was a loner. Not every child is. Cioma's kind of solitude often happens with only children, a kind of reflexive self-reliance that turns inward, not protectively, but more instinctively. It was all he had. Fanja wanted Cioma out of the house, learning how to be with other kids, how to play with them, have fun with them, jostle and argue and laugh and run with them. That was as much a part of life as staying inside and being by himself. A better balance of an inner and outer life, Fanja believed, would help Cioma discover more within himself, and beyond himself.

"Cioma," Fanja firmly told her son one day, "you *have* to meet other children." After hearing good things about a Jewish youth group that an older cousin of Cioma's belonged to, Fanja signed him up for it. She didn't ask if he wanted to do this or if he'd rather stay home and, say, make model airplanes. Fanja simply exercised her maternal authority and sent him on his way.

Cioma remembered this quite clearly. "My mother took me by my hand and said, 'You'll be part of this group.' I didn't choose to be. My left-wing consciousness [that emerged from the youth group] was mere coincidence and certainly not of my own choosing." He was also lucky that Hashomer Hatzair, the youth group in which Fanja enrolled him, was not as far left as other groups in Germany. "A little more left-wing," Cioma said, "and Hashomer Hatzair would have been Communist," an ideological cul-de-sac that could have been fatal in Nazi Germany.[1]

Hashomer Hatzair boasted that it championed "progressive Zionism and revolutionary socialism." It would build a nation in the Middle East with the Palestinians who were already living there. At the same time, it would peacefully change the rest of the world with Socialism, idealism, and compassion. Hashomer Hatzair—Hebrew for "Young Guard"—looked toward a day with no private property and no social classes, a future informed by what Judaism taught about each of us being responsible for others. Also by what Judaism taught about faith, though Hashomer Hatzair's faith had little to do with God. It focused more on faith that, someday, the world would redeem itself and there would be no pogroms, no Nazis, and no slandering of Jews as "Christ killers," or bankers, merchants, and captains of industry, all without scruples, decency, or honesty: a greedy and shady lot. This version of what traditional Jews called *olam haba*, "the world to come," would be a certain type of heaven: heaven on earth. Or as close to it as the worldly pioneers in Hashomer Hatzair could imagine.

The youngsters in Hashomer Hatzair sang and hiked, studied Jewish history and literature, and dreamed of a future, and a place, where they would belong and not be outcasts. They were exuberant and high-spirited. They were also prudes. Everyone in Hashomer Hatzair, the group's charter stated, had to be "clean in thought, words, and deed" and avoid jazz, flirting, and drinking—habits that corrupted revolutionary zeal, and could distract the boys from working toward the glory that lay ahead. Hashomer Hatzair expected its members to follow these "laws"—that's what they were called—for "all the days" of their lives. Maybe so, but not Cioma. In a few years, he would love wine and jazz. Eventually overcoming his social reticence, he'd also learn to love flirting, a hobby that never tired him.[2]

Part Boy Scouts (without the knots and merit badges), part fraternity (without beanies and other frivolities), part Hebrew school (without rote learning and scolding), Hashomer Hatzair was Cioma's extended family. But Fanja may have had Cioma join for another reason than getting him out of the house. Germany had the largest youth movement of any country in the world. In 1932, more than ten million children belonged to dozens of groups. The Nazis' own youth group—the Hitlerjugend, Adolf Hitler's personal juvenile delinquents—soon absorbed all the other Aryan groups. By 1938, eight million youths belonged to the Hitlerjugend. That pleased Hitler. He didn't believe public schools were capable of turning children into miniature imitations of himself. Hitler Youth was his solution.[3]

Noting that many of Cioma's Christian friends were in Hitlerjugend, Fanja may have wanted Cioma to know that he, too, could be in a youth group. Just not the one that was getting all the press.

Hashomer Hatzair taught Cioma about courage and community and cultivating his own version of fun. When he was around fifteen years old, Cioma joined a field trip that Hashomer Hatzair organized. The boys broke two laws on the trip. For camouflage, they wore boots, white socks, and brown shorts—the uniform of Hitler Youth. This was illegal: only Hitlerjugend were allowed to look like Hitlerjugend. And no one, especially Jews, could hitchhike on the autobahn. Hitler's "Roads of the Future" hadn't been built so Jews could hitchhike all over them. Yet Cioma and his friends easily fooled a Storm Trooper. Spotting Cioma's group trying to hitch a ride from the side of the road, the Storm Trooper pulled over his Mercedes and asked, "Where are you going?" "Cologne," the boys answered. "Pile in," the Storm Trooper called out, happy to help young Nazis get from here to there. Soon, four Jewish boys arrived in style in Cologne, their outfits proclaiming they were "Hitler Youth" and a certain private part of each of them proclaiming they were Jews. Their subtle joke—more of a practical joke—worked. It could have landed them in jail.[4]

What Cioma learned from Hashomer Hatzair extended beyond hitchhiking. Hashomer Hatzair's core creed—service, courage, community—emboldened its members into exercising a triumph of a certain kind of will. Cioma learned to use that will in his all-Jewish high school, where he hated most of the teachers. To Cioma, too many of his teachers were suspiciously eager to comply with the Nazis' demands about what to teach, and why, and how. That came to a head when Cioma's class began learning Sütterlin—the baroque, convoluted handwriting that in 1935 the Nazis decreed was the only script that could be taught anywhere in Germany. To anyone outside of Germany, even to many Germans, Sütterlin was illegible, an indecipherable nightmare. Many students wanted to learn the style of writing common in the rest of Europe so they could get jobs when they emigrated—the dream of most German Jews by then. In class one day, Cioma complained that Sütterlin was useless, a sop to the Nazis and their goose-stepping ways. "No!" his teacher yelled. "You must write Sütterlin! Germans write Sütterlin!"

The teacher, Cioma concluded, was a "good German"—a *Jewish* good German who was dutifully doing what the Nazis demanded while doing nothing to help his students. "Pure schizophrenia," Cioma reflected. "These German Jews were more German than the Germans. Hitler needed them to put his craziness into practice."[5]

Cioma was such a bad student that he almost had to repeat a year. He graduated, thanks in no small measure to the kindness of some of his teachers. Now he had to figure out what to do. Hitler annexed Austria in 1938, the year Cioma left school. Everyone knew war was coming, and everyone knew Jews, particularly, would suffer. They already were. An idle Jew, like Cioma, could end up in one of two camps—a labor camp or a concentration camp. Or in both: first one, then the other. Over the next few years, Cioma would bounce around from one job to another, one school to another, one girlfriend to another, all while trying to find himself. In that, he was the same as teenagers everywhere—all looking for themselves, for questions, for answers. But where Cioma differed is that, in his mind, he had two jobs. He had to slip away from Germany, with all its horrors and all its dreads, and its worsening, hardening war on Jews—these "dregs," as Hitler called them almost every day, these "subhumans" who had preyed on the good people of the earth for much too long. Separating them, or worse, from decent men and women was overdue. This would be Hitler's gift not just to Germany, but to all of humanity. The führer lacked many things. If anything, he never lacked grandiosity.

Cioma also had to convince his parents to leave Germany. Cioma—cagey, clever, nimble, cocky—had a chance, a slim chance, of staying several steps ahead of the Nazis. His parents were another story: middle-aged, set in their ways, and too unconcerned about much that was swirling around them. They refused to believe the warnings they heard from everyone, particularly from their teenaged son.

Still, Cioma tried.

And still, Cioma failed. His parents had their ways, and Cioma, young as he was, had his. His parents were fatalistic, or maybe just tired. Cioma was defiant, playful, and almost as often, deadly serious. Or maybe deadly scared.

In early 1939, Cioma enrolled in the private Art School For Fashion and Advertising at Bleibtreustrasse 7 in Charlottenburg, one of Berlin's more attractive neighborhoods. If all had gone well, the school would have helped Cioma realize his dream of becoming a commercial artist. All didn't go well. To cut down on expenses, the school required students to pose as models in its drawing classes. This irked Cioma. "We're paying money to go here," he complained to other students, "and we have to work as models? Next time they want us to do this, let's go on strike." The next time, students did go on strike. Furious, George Hausdorf, the artist who ran the school, called Cioma to his office.

Hausdorf knew Cioma was the ringleader. Within minutes, Hausdorf kicked Cioma out of the school. Soon after Cioma's expulsion, the Nazis closed the school. War was about to break out, and it wouldn't do to devote resources to anything as frivolous as an art school for Jews.

Without a school and without a job, Cioma was stranded in a country whose government, secret police, laws, courts, and propaganda hated people like him. Inexorably, transparently, and without shame, the regime was stripping Jews of their rights and their basic humanity. Streets named after Jews were given new names. Jewish and Christian children couldn't play together. In public parks, Jews could only sit on benches that had recently been painted yellow just for them. Jews couldn't work as midwives, doctors, nurses, dentists, or pharmacists, and they had to clear the rubble from synagogues that the Nazis had destroyed. With all that, and with parents who'd lived in Russia, Palestine, and now Germany and weren't sure where to go now, Cioma tried to get into Belgium. This was almost a prank, the sort that teenagers pull off as a dare if they get drunk one night. Cioma barely thought it through. Traveling to the Belgian border, he asked for refuge. With no passport—Germany didn't issue passports to anyone who was stateless—Belgium sent him away, the Nazis brought him back to Berlin, and the Gestapo opened a file on him.[6]

Until now, Cioma had been just another Jew. Now, he was a Jew with a record. Work, hard to find before he attempted to get into Belgium, had become impossible, particularly since Cioma really had no skills that made him attractive to an employer. His parents didn't know what to do with him. Then a youth counselor from a Jewish organization wrote to Fanja, with a blunt and truthful warning: "I can only tell you to follow my advice if your son's life is important to you. Please register him for a voluntary Jewish youth work camp. Often and randomly, Jewish young people are getting arrested. In our camps, they are safe. They work for ordinary German companies, often as laborers for road and construction projects. The camp I'm proposing to you is in Bielefeld. There are 100 boys and 20 girls. The management of the camp is very responsible. The camp is on a large farm. Cioma will enjoy it. May I register him?"[7]

Fanja said he could, and Cioma arrived in Bielefeld in December 1939. Instead of learning art—his dream!—he found himself doing manual labor in a small city 250 miles west of Berlin. That was not how he'd planned his life—if, indeed, seventeen-year-olds are capable of planning their lives.

In 1933, when the Nazis took over Germany, Bielefeld had 797 Jews—easily overlooked in a city of 129,000, though the Nazis made a point of never overlooking them. Jews had their own cemetery and elementary school and an imposing synagogue whose high, domed roof was visible throughout the city.[8]

The synagogue's prominence declared that Jews belonged in Bielefeld; its heavy stones and sandstone pillars declared they'd never leave. Then the town's Jews watched the synagogue go up in smoke on the night of November 9–10, 1938—Kristallnacht, the same night hundreds of synagogues all over Germany were burned, thousands of Jewish businesses and homes plundered, ninety-one Jews killed and 30,000 sent to concentration camps. Months later, Bielefeld's Jews were herded into "special" housing—their new ghetto—and forced to do manual labor. The Gestapo now knew where every Jew lived, their age and occupation, and the size of their family. When the time came, no Jew would escape. The Gestapo would know where to find everyone.

Cioma's work camp in Bielefeld was sponsored by the Reich Association of Jews in Germany. The Nazis had ordered the association to make sure every Jew in Germany was busy—an idle Jew was a worthless Jew. Until the Nazis banned Jewish emigration in October 1941, there was a tacit agreement between them and the Reich Association: as long as the group helped Jews get out of Germany, its farms and labor camps were acceptable as alternatives to prisons or concentration camps. By giving this job to the Reich Association, the Nazis could pretend Jews were leaving Germany on their own.[9]

The association's camps had another function: what Jews learned in them would make them attractive in Germany if they stayed, or attractive to other countries if they left. In fact, Jewish leaders were encouraging Jews to get into any field but banking, industry, science, publishing, or education—standard occupations for Jews, occupations that Nazis were sure Jews controlled. If Jews used their bodies more than their brains, maybe, the reasoning went, there'd be no more hate against them. Cioma understood that: his high school diploma and a few months spent at a defunct art academy qualified him for nothing. And the Gestapo's new file on Cioma marked him as someone who needed watching. With banned books squirreled away in his parents' apartment, and several years in a youth group that had taught him "revolutionary socialism," the Gestapo didn't know what it had on its hands.

4

"This Business Could Have Gone Very Badly"

Cioma's group in Bielefeld consisted of men and women in their late teens or early twenties. Cioma was the youngest. The males slept on what had been the dance floor of a now-closed restaurant—the Palace Garden—until recently, the place in Bielefeld for fox-trotting, but definitely not jitterbugging. The Nazis banned that as too "modern," too "Negro." From a second floor gallery that extended around the perimeter of the dance floor, mothers used to watch their daughters below: there would be no hanky-panky in this palace, a proper establishment of small-town decency and propriety. All that was before the Jews came. Now, there was no dining, no gallery (it had been ripped out), no anxious mothers, and no dancing. In place of the stiff, chaste dancing that the Nazis approved, there were rows of gray army bunk beds where Jews snored all night, dreaming, among other things, of the young women in their work crews who slept upstairs. The young men would know the women romantically only if luck, chance, and time came their way.[1]

Time, in fact, was what Bielefeld was all about.

These Jews were playing for time: stretching, as best they could, the sparse amount of time that had been allotted to them, hoping they could modify it in their favor. Not much else was. Meanwhile, the men could flex their muscles at work and show off for the women, and the women could be coquettish, and everyone could do what young men and women do when there's some degree of freedom though, in their case, "freedom" could be snatched away from them at any moment. That, they knew, was why they were there: to get more freedom, and more time. Once they gained skills, they'd be sent somewhere, maybe to a real job. Or to a job that wasn't real and where the Nazis would work them to death. Or in their wildest fantasies, the world would come to its senses, and they'd return to their villages or cities and use the skills and talents they'd honed in Bielefeld and have a life and a future. But that would take time, and time, these young Jews knew, was beyond their control. For them, Bielefeld was both in time and out of time: a stasis of the past, of the present, of a future that Cioma and his new friends did not know and could not know. The camp was a whispering of what awaited these young men and women who hadn't yet glimpsed their own futures. Some of them, somehow, still retained faith in the goodness of others, and in the delicate and tenuous balance between good and hope and reality, and their tragically lamentable opposites.

In Bielefeld, the Jews cleared forests, dug trenches, laid pipes—work none of them had ever done before. In their spare time, they played Ping-Pong, threw parties, celebrated the Jewish Sabbath, or played operettas, popular music, or modern dance tunes on a piano. The most popular tune—a bitter Zionist lament—surveyed the ever-narrowing world of the Jew, with one door after another slamming shut as the world looked the other way, pretending it either had no idea what was happening in Germany or it was none of its business:

> *A door is still open,*
> *But closed for you,*
> *Since you are a Jew.*
> *Every people in the world*

has its own country
and its home.
The world is big,
but for you it is small. . .
No place in the world,
for you are a Jew.[2]

This cheered up no one. For that, they had dating. Cioma wasn't good at it. He'd always been comfortable with girls—if they were friends and no more than that. And though it was time he had a girlfriend—most of the guys at the camp had one—he was skittish about what you did with one. Just knowing that someone found him attractive made Cioma nervous and tongue-tied, and he'd stumble over his words and emotions. A clumsy suitor was as good as no suitor. Cioma later told of how Gunther, who bunked with him, put his arm around him one day and asked, "Cioma, are you blind? Can't you see that Lotte is crazy about you?" Cioma's response was as simple as could be: "Who's Lotte?"

Cioma's fog about girls was so thick he'd never noticed that Lotte Windmüller had her eye on him. Everyone in the camp admired Lotte. She was kind, caring, and outgoing, and always looked out for her friends. Her oval-shaped face, dark hair, pert mouth, and clear eyes behind rimless glasses lent her a warm and welcoming presence. Everyone agreed about that. Everyone also agreed that Cioma was a jerk not to notice she was stuck on him.[3]

The more attention Cioma paid to Lotte, the more he noticed she had a roving eye and, maybe, wasn't the best match for him. "I have a sweetheart, but not for me alone," he wrote to a friend. "For Lotte, the many boys in the camp are a constant temptation to lose your head over. Though Lotte, indeed, makes my head spin."[4]

This churning of desire and uncertainty and jealousy culminated when some of the workers in the camp visited the Hermannsdenkmal—a

mammoth statue of Arminus, a warrior-chief whose army had stopped
twenty thousand Roman troops who were invading Germany in 9 c.e,
located forty miles from Bielefeld. Nothing about the statue was
modest. It was taller than the Statue of Liberty and weighed thirteen
tons, and its hero, Arminus, thrust a twenty-three-foot-long sword into
the air. The sword alone weighed more than 1,200 pounds.

The Hermannsdenkmal served numerous functions over the years,
most of them tuned more to the immediate moment than to the glories
of Arminus. First, it served as a place to celebrate Germany's victory
in the Franco-Prussian War, which had ended a few years before
the statue was erected. During World War I, the statue embodied
Germany's certainty that it would defeat the Allies. And during the
Third Reich, two hundred thousand tourists visited the statue every
year, transmogrifying it into a towering tribute to Adolf Hitler—like
Arminus, the Nazis crowed, Hitler would raise Germany to new
glories, transcendent heights, inconceivable conquests. Things didn't
quite work out.

Cioma and his friends didn't visit the Hermannsdenkmal to honor
Hitler. They just needed a break from work. When they got there,
Cioma couldn't keep his eyes off of Lotte, who was walking slightly
ahead of him, with a guy on each of her arms, laughing, giggling,
pleased with herself, and almost taunting Cioma that if he didn't pay
more attention to her, she'd find someone who would. Fuming with
wanting and with regret, Cioma stomped into the woods that were near
the statue, charging past birds, flowers, and butterflies that he barely
saw, blindly trudging for an hour, maybe more, until a soldier, coming
almost out of nowhere, asked for his name and ID. Cioma had blindly
wandered onto an airfield where the Luftwaffe was training pilots and
technicians. Large hangers and maintenance buildings and rows of
barracks fronted onto runways. Cioma had no business being there.[5]

The soldier took Cioma to his superior officer, a captain whose
office was in the airport's main building. By then, they knew Cioma

was Jewish. That didn't help him. "Do you know where you are?" the captain barked at Cioma. "This is a military airfield. I could have you shot for spying." The captain ordered some of his soldiers to take Cioma to the police. "Have them find out what's up with him. If he's in the clear, let him go."

Cioma barely slept that night at the police station, frantic about what might happen. Not helping was his wristwatch. He watched the second hand crawl excruciatingly slowly across the face of the watch. Every second was an hour, every hour a day. His night was a collection of fractions of fractions of time, each inflated beyond its true measure of Cioma's duration in the lockup.

The next morning, the police took Cioma to the Gestapo's local headquarters. The Gestapo was better at interrogating spies than the police. Cioma was ordered to sit across from a desk, where a muscular, square-shouldered agent was typing a report about him. The agent handed it to Cioma to sign. He began reading a few lines before the agent grabbed him by the collar and threw him out of the room. Cioma didn't know he was supposed to sign it without reading it—proof of his blind faith in a blind regime.

Luckily for Cioma, the Gestapo agent who'd driven him from the police station appeared out of nowhere, muttering under his breath, "Come along with me. Come, come." Cioma did.

The next day, his third in custody, Cioma was taken to Wilhelm Pützer—the Judenreferent—or head of the Gestapo's Jewish bureau in that region. Cioma later told his family that, while he expected the worst, he got the best. From behind his desk, Pützer, sporting a narrow little mustache that must have been inspired by the Adolf Hitler School of Good Grooming, smiled at Cioma. "So, you're Lotte's friend," Pützer said with a laugh. "My dear Schönhaus, this business could have gone very badly if I hadn't been Lotte Windmüller's godfather. Give my love to Lotte, and tell the camp leader to keep a better eye on his people."[6]

Pützer was the kindest Gestapo agent Cioma ever met. He sent Cioma home for two weeks, figuring he needed a vacation after getting the scare of his life. On September 24, 1941 (four days shy of his nineteenth birthday), Cioma boarded a train to Berlin. At this point in the war, trains were safe: the United States was neutral, Great Britain was alone, and the few bombers it had were limited in range. So far, Britain's only attacks on Berlin from the air had been over two nights the previous August—twenty-two bombers killed ten people, injured twenty-one, and slightly damaged buildings and streets. Since then, the skies over most of Germany had been clear and safe, and trains were running on time, their tracks intact and serviceable.[7]

Cioma had a compartment all to himself. Stretching out, he skimmed the newspaper he'd bought at the station. Most of it was about the war in Russia, then in its third month. Headlines proclaimed that Germany had taken another three hundred thousand Russian prisoners. Extraordinary, Cioma thought. No one had done that before. Maybe Hitler was invincible. He'd already swallowed up one country after another, from northern Africa to northern Europe to eastern Europe. Now he'd pounced on Russia, the prize that had eluded princes, kings, and emperors. The world's largest country with a population three times that of Germany (195 million versus 70 million), Russia, over the last five hundred years, had turned back invasions by Mongols, Poland, Sweden, and France. If anyone could beat Russia, it was Hitler. He was more ruthless, vicious, and determined and better equipped than anyone who'd tried before.

In June, three and a half million German troops had poured into Russia: 153 divisions, 600,000 motorized vehicles, 3,580 tanks, 7,184 pieces of artillery, and 2,740 airplanes. Their front line was the longest in history—1,800 miles. The Luftwaffe had wiped out half of Russia's 10,000 warplanes in one day. In another, it crippled 1,000 Russian tanks. In a week, 600,000 Russians were taken prisoner; in August and September, another 665,000 Russian soldiers were captured. Stalin, shocked and dazed, confessed to his closest confidantes, "We have lost forever everything that Lenin has created." He wasn't far off. For now.[8]

While riding that train from Bielefeld to Berlin, Cioma figured that Hitler just might pull this off. Then he picked up *War and Peace*, which he'd brought along for the ride. It brought him down to earth. Napoleon Bonaparte's disaster in Russia could have been a rehearsal for what would happen to Hitler. In 1812 the French army got stuck in Russia's brutal winter. Frozen corpses littered the rutted roads, their faces tilted upward for rescue that never came. Bodies were wreathed with icicles. Many of the icicles were red from blood. This was a cold the French had never known, a cold that prohibited a retreat because most of the French army was frozen, literally, in its tracks. Russia's winter had stopped the French. It might stop Hitler, Cioma considered—a sage doubt from an adolescent, a doubt that should have been voiced by his elders.

When Cioma, her beloved son, opened the door to his family's apartment on Sophienstrasse, his mother could barely contain her joy. The same with her incredulity. Cioma was always getting into the craziest of jams, and somehow he always had a way of getting out of them. "So, Cioma," Fanja said, with concern and some amusement, "they let you out of prison because the godfather of your non-Aryan girlfriend"—Lotte Windmüller—"is a Gestapo boss? For heaven's sake, that's no ordinary event. It's a miracle. But don't rely on miracles. Be careful. Don't play with fire."[9]

Fanja should have known better. Not playing with fire was not in Cioma's nature.

It might have been to Fanja's benefit to press Cioma a bit more on his story. In Cioma's telling, Lotte had been born Jewish. Her parents, Jewish owners of a flour mill, had asked a good friend, Wilhelm Pützer, to be her godfather. This was 1922, before there was a Gestapo for Pützer to join. As conditions for Jews deteriorated in Germany, Lotte was baptized. The Nazis sent her to the work camp in Bielefeld, anyway. To them, any conversion was bogus—their antisemitism was of the flesh, not the spirit. Anyone with Jewish grandparents was as Jewish as they were.

The truth is that Lotte's parents didn't own a mill, she was never baptized, her godfather wasn't a Gestapo agent, and Pützer wasn't friends with Lotte's parents. Most likely, he never knew them: Lotte's mother died in the late 1920s, her father died in 1937, and Pützer didn't arrive in Bielefeld until 1935. If he'd ever heard of Lotte, it may have been through Johanne Peppmoeller, the Windmüller family's devoted housekeeper—a Christian—who cared for Lotte after her parents died. Possibly, Johanne pleaded with Pützer, who ran the Gestapo's Jewish bureau in Bielefeld, to be kind to Lotte. If he'd helped Cioma by giving him two weeks' leave from the work camp, it may have been only because he was amused by a nineteen-year-old Jew accidentally wandering onto a Luftwaffe base. Pützer was under less pressure then, a full year and a half before he was ordered to make sure every Jew in Bielefeld boarded trains to "camps" in "the east." One less Jew in the work camp for two weeks wouldn't make much difference.

What is certain is that Cioma permanently left Bielefeld in late 1941 to move back to Berlin. Around the same time, Lotte fell in love with Paul Hoffman, a Jew who was also at the labor camp. In the fall of 1942, Lotte and Paul applied for a license for the wedding they were planning for the next summer.[10]

These stories—Lotte converting; having a crush on Cioma; asking her godfather, Pützer, to be easy on her boyfriend—come from Cioma's imagination. They appear in his writings about his life and he told them to me during several interviews. But extensive research and discussions with historians prove them to be fabrications of his imagination. They may have stemmed from a faulty memory, or maybe his own memories had mingled with what he half heard from other people, then what he half remembered after that. The land of the mind is a peculiar terrain, and no less peculiar when it belongs to someone who'd seen as much as Cioma, and who'd suffered as much as he had.

Let us not judge Cioma harshly. A born raconteur, he loved entertaining his listeners with tales full of twists and turns that, somehow, straightened out by the end of the night. A few embellishments along the way may not have mattered if they made someone lean in closer to hear about the wonders of his life, of histories unfamiliar to them, of times and places that strain credulity, yet were real. In the end, it may not have mattered if Cioma entertained people, in his own way, as well as riveted them with what he'd seen and heard and experienced. Or what he *believed* he'd seen, heard, and experienced. That belief was as potent, and as important, as the reality of his life.

The kind of liberties Cioma took with some of his stories isn't rare among Holocaust survivors. Several survivors of Treblinka, for example, described the chimneys of the crematoria at the "camp." Yet there were *no* crematoria and *no* chimneys at Treblinka. The dead were buried in large pits. What these survivors told—what they believed—was jumbled with what they'd read or heard about other "camps," "camps" where there were crematoria, "camps" where there were smokestacks.

All this is not uncommon among people who suffer from trauma. Their storytelling lifts them, and provides details and context for what they endured.

In the best of all worlds, this helps them while not necessarily harming others. Troubled souls find refuge where they can.

5

"Nothing Ever Happened Except One Kiss"

W hen Cioma Schönhaus returned to Bielefeld from the break the thoughtful Gestapo officer had given him from the labor camp, he was assigned to dig an in-ground water tank for a civil engineering company. Joining Cioma were Jonny Syna, a twenty-one-year-old music student, and Wolfgang Pander, a twenty-four-year-old who had worked as an assistant director in his father's film studio. The water tank was next to a military hospital in a suburb of Bielefeld. The crew building it was told the water was for fires, not drinking. Though no one explained to Cioma why the hospital worried so much about a major fire, he figured it was preparing for eventual bombing runs by the Allies. For an eighteen-year-old, he was prescient: hardly anyone was talking about carpet bombing. Yet.

Cioma became more muscular, and more calloused. He felled trees with an axe that was so long it reached his chin when he stood it upright on its lengthy handle. The skin on his hands thickened. Once the trees were down, prisoners were brought in from elsewhere to hoist them onto trucks. The prisoners were wearing loose, pajama-like uniforms with wide black stripes. Cioma had never seen anything like that

before. Soon, he would. Cioma watched slack-jawed as the prisoners
lifted one tree after another like they were giant matchsticks. When
the trees were carted away, and the land was cleared, Cioma, Jonny, and
Wolfgang began digging a pit to hold water for the hospital. It would
be huge—98 feet wide, 164 feet long. Cioma, Jonny, and Wolfgang
dug, and they dug some more.[1]

Cioma amused the foreman, a Mr. Westerfeldhausen, by reading
Thomas Mann's *Buddenbrooks* during breaks from work. "I've never
seen anything like this," Westerfeldhausen groused. "You don't know
how to hold an axe or fell trees, but you read books! You'll never be a
proper worker."

"Well," Cioma replied, "I don't want to be one. I want to be a
graphic artist and immigrate to America."

In three months, Cioma, Jonny, and Wolfgang finished the water
tank, impressing themselves and even Westerfeldhausen. He'd under-
estimated the three Jews. They'd arrived in the camp with soft hands
and sallow complexions and liked nothing better than curling up with
thick books. They were still reading books, but their hands were hard
and their complexions were tan, almost swarthy.

Cioma didn't stay in Bielefeld long. His application to an all-
Jewish art school in Berlin had been accepted, and in August 1940
he moved back into his parents' apartment on Sophienstrasse. Two
painters—Jews—had recently started the school on Nürnberger Strasse,
around the corner from KaDeWe, one of the most exclusive department stores in Europe. Adolf Jandorf, the original owner of KaDeWe
(short for Kaufhaus des Westens: "The Department Store of the West")
opened the store in 1907. Its six floors displayed haute couture from
Paris, sleek styling from Italy, bowler hats from England, and fruits
from South America that Berlin had never seen, and its invitation-only
fashion shows kept Berliners chic and up-to-date.

Better heeled students at the art school shopped at KaDeWe. Most
of the students didn't. They couldn't afford it. But everyone knew about

it, and just being near KaDeWe infused students with aspirations about their own creations and heightened their dreams that they'd be among the rare artists who actually made a living at their trade.

Cioma was entering a world of serious artists and committed teachers and, not coincidentally, of lovely young women. Many of them were above Cioma, socially or financially, though he attracted a good number to him with his bright smile, easy manner, and warm sense of humor. They liked to be with him, and he liked to be with them. Cioma may have gained more from this transaction than the women. Until now, he had been afraid of women. The women at the art school helped him get over his fear.

For Cioma, two women stood out: Stella Kubler and Renate Klepper. He quickly fell in love with Renate. Almost as quickly, he developed a crush on Stella, though he didn't have a chance with her. Every boy in the school had his eye on her.

Cioma couldn't have picked two more different women to get involved with, or want to get involved with. Stella was out of his league. Her thoroughly assimilated parents, both Jews, took great pride in Stella's beauty: her blonde hair, pale satin skin, upturned nose, and azure blue eyes made her an Aryan goddess—an "untouchable masterpiece," said an acquaintance, not as a compliment. Stella's magnificence was part of her family's illusions: they were sure they were safe in Germany. After all, they were "Germans." Not Jews. Proof of that was Stella's stunning beauty. Her Aryan beauty.

At first, Stella's father, Gerhard, liked Adolf Hitler. To him, Hitler's policies toward the thousands of Jews who were immigrating into Germany every year from Eastern Europe made sense. Their superstitions and folkways, long black coats, and *payot*, or side curls, embarrassed Gerhard, who liked Hitler's idea to send them back where they came from. Gerhard shouldn't have sided with Hitler so fast. In 1935 the Nazis forced Gerhard's employer—a French-owned newsreel company—to fire him. Gerhard refused help from Jewish organizations. After all, he wasn't Jewish. He was German.

Gerhard found other jobs—a frustrated musician and composer, he taught piano to children with little talent; accompanied soloists at small, barely attended recitals; or wrote reviews of concerts for publications that underpaid him but whose assignments he couldn't turn down. He needed the money. The same year Gerhard was fired, his daughter began attending—on scholarship—a private academy for Jews that had opened after they were expelled from public schools. By the time Stella enrolled in the Goldschmidt School, it had over five hundred students, several times its enrollment when it opened in 1935: a barometer of how fast conditions were deteriorating for Jews.[2]

Stella put on airs, telling other students at Goldschmidt that, unlike them, she didn't deserve being kicked out of public school. Her mother, Stella bragged, was Christian, and that made Stella half-Jewish. Everyone knew that was a lie: Stella's mother—who was 100 percent Jewish—sang in the choir in their synagogue. Most of the girls at Goldschmidt wore modest plaid dresses and sweaters with Peter Pan collars and favored long braids that extended almost to their waists, a traditional style in Germany. Stella's wavy blonde hair brushed her shoulders and went no further, and her tight sweaters complemented her shapely figure, so shapely that her classmates, especially the boys, found it hard to believe she was still in school. Any school.[3]

Just like with Lotte at the work camp in Bielefeld, Cioma got tongue-tied when he was around Stella and his thoughts got muddled. Somehow, he hung onto his fantasy that she'd be the first girl he slept with. The closest he came was persuading her to model for him. Stella kept her clothes on during the entire session.

Renate Klepper—Cioma's "real" girlfriend at the art school—wasn't a bombshell like Stella. Renate was cultured, modest, and subtle, with a quick, discerning intelligence that she may have inherited by osmosis from her stepfather, Jochen Klepper, who adored her. Jochen was

Protestant. His wife and Renate and Brigette, the two daughters she'd had with her late husband, were born Jewish. Renate and Brigitte were baptized in the late 1930s to improve their chances of surviving under Hitler. The conversions made no difference. Under Germany's new laws about "racial purity," anyone born Jewish was always Jewish. Converting was just a Jew's way to get around the law. Nor did Jochen's novel, *The Father*, a bestseller a few years before, cut any slack with the Nazis. Hitler, in fact, admired *The Father* so much—it celebrated King Frederick William I upholding Prussian dignity and might in the eighteenth century—that he gave it as gifts to friends and required army officers to read it. Hitler's enthusiasm eased Jochen into the upper echelons of the Nazis, powerful men who did their best to ignore Klepper's "unfortunate Jewish marriage." Their tolerance went only so far: in 1941 Jochen was kicked out of the army, in which he'd enlisted because he believed his country was in danger. No one who was married to a Jew was supposed to be in the army: the institution was too "pure" for anyone who'd "sullied" himself with a Jewish wife. After that, Jochen was still torn between his country and his family. "We cannot," he insisted with misplaced patriotism, "wish for the fall of the Third Reich out of bitterness as many do. That is quite impossible. In this hour of external threat, we cannot hope for a rebellion or coup." None came. Slowly, the Kleppers watched their thin prospect of a better life, a safer life, wither and disappear.[4]

Cioma had bounced around for too long now. Like the Kleppers—Jochen, Renate, and her mother and sister—he'd foundered. He was still foundering. He'd hitchhiked on an autobahn—which was strictly forbidden—then gone from a Jewish high school, where he'd complained about the handwriting he was being taught; to an art school, where he was kicked out for complaining about modeling; to a labor camp, where he was arrested for wandering onto a Luftwaffe base; then to another art school, this one only for Jews. Along the way, he'd tried to get into Belgium, a little adventure that convinced the Gestapo to keep an eye on him. Mostly, he got into the same sort of minor trouble that a lot of adolescents did, except his was aggravated by being Jewish and living in a Nazi police state. His offenses were fairly harmless. He was a risk-taker and a rule-breaker, and who didn't have a Gestapo file these days anyway?

At the age of eighteen, Cioma's character was starting to coalesce around his most telling qualities. He was stubborn, playful, whimsical, outspoken, adventurous, and rarely shy, except with young women he had a crush on. He enjoyed tweaking authority, rules, discipline—anything that smacked of the ordinary way of doing things, though under Hitler, "ordinary" had taken on a whole new meaning.

Now Cioma faced another dilemma, the sort that would stalk him for the next few years: women. He'd reached a moment when he had to figure out whom he should pay the most attention to and court, in his own hesitant and fumbling way. Cioma's problem was that the two women at art school who'd caught his attention and, to some degree, his heart—Renate and Stella—were both pretty. Renate's beauty was quiet and subtle. Stella's was obvious and unavoidable. Cioma gravitated toward both, though beyond their appearance, there was no question who he would choose: Renate. He was more comfortable with her than with Stella. Renate wasn't a goddess, a schoolboy's vision of perfection. She was more real, with minor "flaws" that made her more human, with "intelligent eyes," to borrow Cioma's words, that were narrowed by a constant squint, and bow legs that Cioma believed were a gift from God to make Renate humble and unassuming. She was also friendlier than Stella, less self-absorbed, and more curious about the world around her. In other words, she was a good match for Cioma.[5]

After classes at the art school, Cioma and Renate sometimes walked to a nearby café and talked about art, and their professors, and about other students, and what they'd do after the war. They rarely talked about politics. Not in public. That was too dangerous. One day, a drunk policeman wobbled his way toward their table in the café. "You're a Jew," he bellowed at Cioma. "Show me your identity papers."

"No," Cioma calmly replied, not knowing why the officer was badgering him. "I'm not Jewish."

"Show me your papers," the officer repeated, louder than before. "Now."

"No, I won't," Cioma persisted.

Hearing the racket, the manager came over and told Cioma, almost plaintively, "Oh, come on. Show him your papers so we can have some peace." Cioma showed the policeman his papers. Glancing at them, the officer yelled triumphantly, "He's a Jew! Get out of here!"

Renate, more sensible than Cioma, leaned over and whispered, "Please let's go home. Come on." As they headed toward the door, the policeman swayed woozily from one table to another, mumbling, "He's a Jew, he's a Jew," while pointing at the quickly departing Cioma.

Cioma and Renate told a policeman they ran into on the street about the drunken officer who was pestering customers in the café they'd just left. "Seriously?" he asked, incredulous that a policeman could be drunk and annoy customers anywhere. "We'll sort this out."

He didn't. Cioma and Renate hoped the policeman would drag the drunken officer out of the café. Maybe press charges against him. Returning alone, he thanked Cioma, patted him on the shoulder, and walked away. Nothing was settled, though the admiring look Renate gave Cioma more than made up for that. During all the time Cioma knew Renate, "nothing," he later said, "ever happened except for a kiss." Renate's respectful gaze may have trumped even that.[6]

If this had been another country or another time, Renate and Cioma might have had a life together. But this was Germany, and they were Jews, and Jews were allotted no future here. They were barely granted a present. Whatever time they had was shrinking, shriveling. Renate and Cioma sensed that, but they couldn't quantify or enumerate it. No one could. Still, their intuition cautioned that to be young and in love in Berlin meant to cherish each moment and each touch, then release them. Holding onto them risked disappointment, despair, or worse.

PART TWO

"IT'LL BE OUR TURN ONE DAY"

6

The Butter Conspiracy

Cioma fell into a routine. At art school, he enjoyed teachers' praise, flirted, often took Renate Klepper out for coffee or cocoa, and kept an eye out for Stella Kubler. And every night he went home to his parents' apartment on Sophienstrasse, all three of them aware that, every day, Germany was becoming less their country. Jews weren't wanted here, Jews weren't liked here and, paradoxically, Jews couldn't get out of here. Until October 1941, the Nazis had encouraged Jews to emigrate. After that, they made it impossible for Jews to leave by charging a heavy tax on emigration and limiting the amount of money that could be transferred abroad from German banks. Jews had to stay, especially since almost no place wanted them. Before the war, few countries accepted Jews; with the war raging, even fewer countries were taking them in. Cioma's cousin Morris had had the right idea. He'd immigrated to the United States in the late 1930s—to 94 Audubon Avenue in Jersey City, New Jersey, to be exact. But Morris was twenty years older than Cioma and, apparently, had better intuitions than Cioma's parents about what Germany was becoming.[1]

One day, Cioma came home from art school and found his mother burning in their stove the left-wing books and magazines Morris had left with them. Plays and satires, diatribes and pamphlets, politics and art—all went up in smoke. These were some of the few connections Cioma had with a past that hardly existed now. Words, ideas, histories, and panaceas for a wayward world—all charred, blackening, and crumbling in front of him.

Cioma was furious. "What are you doing?" he yelled at Fanja. "These are irreplaceable. Are you mad?"

Fanja wasn't. A few hours before, the Gestapo had raided the apartment. Fanja didn't know what they were looking for, but she wanted to make sure they'd never find this contraband that could have gotten Boris and Fanja arrested. Fanja was burning all these publications in case the Gestapo returned. That was the least of her troubles. Boris was being charged with buying and selling butter on the black market, something Fanja had never heard about, something she didn't want to know about. The next day, he had to report to the police.

Sooner or later, Boris would have bought something on what the Germans called the *schwarz*, German for "black." He'd been struggling financially for years. In 1938, when the Nazis canceled the license of every business that Jews owned in Germany, Boris had to sell—at a major loss—all the equipment, bottles, wagons, and horses from his mineral water venture. Every pfennig from the sale went into an account the state controlled and Boris couldn't touch. He also had to pay a "Jewish property tax"—thirty thousand Reichsmarks—essentially, a fine for existing. The only work Boris could find was digging trenches for a construction company. The pay was low; the days were long, and he'd come home exhausted after barely making enough money to feed his family. Desperate, he turned to the black market.[2]

Boris wasn't alone. Half the merchandise that was sold in Berlin moved on the black market. Store shelves might be bare or their windows decorated with empty containers from food they hadn't carried in months. But on the *schwarz*, you could get almost anything—soap, coffee, cigarettes, toilet paper, alcohol, chocolate, drugs, clothing and, especially, food. With bread rations five hundred grams less a week than they were three years ago, and meat rations two hundred grams less, everyone was hungry. But if you figured out how to sell food, you made money. And if you bought food, you forgot about your hunger. For a while.[3]

Boris didn't buy butter in public. That was too risky. Instead, he bought it from a good friend, Walter May. Every week, May's father sent him a substantial amount of butter by train from Beuthen, a small city three hundred miles from Berlin. May sold small portions of this to a few friends—all Jews. They, in turn, sold smaller portions to their friends. The profits were marginal, but during this disastrous war any profit was a godsend, a blessing. In late 1940, for example, May sold butter for three and a half Reichsmarks a pound. Boris Schönhaus would then sell what he'd bought from May for five Reichsmarks a pound. A small profit, but still a profit, one that allowed Boris to feed his family every night.

Boris wouldn't have been arrested if the police hadn't found his name in a small notebook in which May kept track of all the sales of his smuggling operation. It's safe to say that keeping the names of his customers in the notebook made May one of Berlin's more careless smugglers. It's also safe to say that the butter Boris bought from May was the most troublesome purchase he made in his life.[4]

The day after the Gestapo raided the Schönhauses' apartment, Cioma and his mother accompanied Boris to the police station where he'd been ordered to report. Boris was taken into a room while Fanja and Cioma sat on a bench in a corridor, waiting for him to come out. Around noon, they realized they were wasting their time: Boris wouldn't be joining them. Leaving the station, they headed toward the offices of the Jewish lawyer Curt Eckstein. Eckstein telephoned the police and asked why they were detaining Boris for so long. He listened, politely asked again, listened some more, hung up, and told Fanja what she already knew: "Your husband is being held for the time being. That's all I can tell you." That was because Eckstein couldn't ask what charges were being brought against Boris or how long he would be

held. He couldn't because he lacked the latitude he'd had just a few
years before. In 1938 the Nazis had ruled that Jewish lawyers could
only have Jewish clients. Even more demeaning was that Jewish lawyers
could only "advise" their clients. Not represent them in court or in any
conversations with the police. Worse was that "adviser" meant anything
the Nazis wanted it to mean. Usually it meant nothing.[5]

When Cioma and Fanja returned home, dishes from the breakfast
they'd had hours ago were still on the table. Breakfast for three. "Now,"
said Fanja, "there are just the two of us." So they were, precisely when
they needed Boris more than ever.[6]

Boris and six others in Walter May's black-market ring were sentenced
in August 1941. Boris, who'd sold the smallest amount of butter, was
sent to Tegel Prison, in northwest Berlin. At the trial, everything Boris
said in his defense, the judge mocked with a coarse, exaggerated Yiddish accent. It was apparent the judge had already made up his mind
and Boris stood no chance of leniency.

Cioma's uncle Meier returned from the courthouse after dark. Cioma's mother looked at him. For a few minutes, Meier couldn't speak.
When he had no choice—Fanja deserved to know what happened
to her husband—he mumbled, "A year." Screaming, Fanja collapsed
onto her bed. Cioma lay beside his mother to comfort her.[7]

For decades, Tegel Prison had treated prisoners well, thanks to its
kind superintendent, Felix Brucks. By the time Boris got there, Brucks
had been pushed out by the Nazis—and Tegel was no different from
any other Nazi prison, with torture that ended in deaths more often
than in confessions. About the only thing that distinguished Tegel from
other prisons was the work certain prisoners were assigned: building
guillotines. Adolf Hitler had recently decreed that prisoners who were
sentenced to death would be executed only by lopping off their heads.
Twenty sites in Germany had been chosen for the executions. All of
their guillotines were made in Tegel.

Boris got off easy. He didn't make guillotines and he wasn't tortured. No one wanted his secrets. He didn't have any. All he'd done was sell butter. But being imprisoned shamed his family. No one he was related to had ever been locked up. Fanja and Boris were left with little honor and less pride.

The ridiculousness of the Nazi system had been exposed by three judges spending so much time on lowly butter smugglers; by the trial spreading over two months; by the government's file about the case swelling to thirty-three single-spaced pages; by the judges shaming Walter May—"the soul of the butter smuggling ring"—for "exploiting his fellow Jews' desire to eat butter."

Nazis criticizing Jews for "exploiting" other Jews was a parody of the Third Reich. Essentially, they were punishing Jews for helping other Jews who were suffering from the pain the Nazis were inflicting on them. For the Jews the judges convicted, selling butter to other Jews wasn't a matter of "living comfortably," as the judges charged. It was, quite simply, a matter of staying alive.[8]

Hitler was sure the *schwarz* that had thrived during the last war had weakened the home front. He wouldn't be so foolish this time. Yet the absurd lengths to which the Nazis went to punish anyone buying or selling something as mundane as butter were just plain stupid. There were better ways to win this damn war. All the prosecutor's victory against Boris accomplished was pushing Fanja and Boris closer to poverty. And all that Fanja and Cioma wanted was for their husband and father to come home.

7

An Act of Lunacy

Teenagers like to sleep. In the mornings. In the afternoons. In the evenings. That's their fallback, their luxury, their habit born not of laziness, but to support their developing brains and bodies, which are just finding their way in the world. Cioma was no different. He especially liked to sleep during air raids. Why get up, he figured, when it'd be over in a few minutes and, given the small odds of being hit, he'd be just as safe staying in bed? Fanja, who knew better, went to the shelter in her building as soon as she heard the sirens wail. After a particularly bad air raid, she returned to her apartment and shook Cioma awake. "So, you still think you don't need to get up?" Fanja asked, a question that wasn't a question.

Cioma looked around. Dust coated everything. The entire apartment was lost in whiteness and flecks of paint and plaster and shards of glass too tiny to see but large enough to make you bleed if you touched them. As Cioma came to, his mother told him a bomb had killed seventeen people and destroyed half of their building. Going outside, they saw people walking around in a daze, some warmed by blankets distributed by the National Socialist People's Welfare Organization. In the middle of their courtyard, an old woman lay on a bed, feeble and injured. A woman who lived below the Schönhauses and had ignored them for years because they were Jewish hugged Fanja. Both women cried.[1]

The front of the building was rubble and ruin. The rear, where the Schönhauses lived, was still standing. Wasting no time, the National Socialist People's Welfare Organization evicted the Jews who lived in the rear and gave their apartments to Christians whose apartments had been destroyed. Around three o'clock in the morning, Cioma and Fanja walked to his uncle's apartment a few blocks away, their footsteps ringing in the empty streets. When Uncle Meier opened his door, five floors up at Münzstrasse 11, Fanja tried to explain why they were there. Meier was dubious. "A bomb?" he asked. "How come we didn't hear anything? We're so close. Are you sure?"

"Uncle," Cioma replied, with more than a touch of irritation in his voice, "our building has been destroyed. We can't stay in our flat."[2]

Meier let them in, none too happily. He and his wife, Sophie, were already sharing their apartment with his mother-in-law: Cioma's grand-mother. Two more people would cramp them even more. Cioma and Fanja weren't happy about the situation either. Asking Meier and Sophie to make room for them was more than a nod that their lives had changed, much for the worse; that every opportunity for which they'd worked so hard and for so long had slipped through their fingers. Maybe never to return. Boris was in jail, they'd been kicked out of the apartment where they'd lived for thirteen years, and now they were begging her brother-in-law—whom Fanja had never liked very much—to take them in.

On Münzstrasse, where Cioma's Uncle Meier and Aunt Sophie lived, there were more empty stores than on Sophienstrasse. Cioma especially missed the bakeries that used to line Münzstrasse, filling the entire length of the street with the sweet aroma of fresh onion tarts or pastries made with goose fat. All the bakeries were closed and dark. Where, Cioma wondered, had all those Jewish bakers gone?

Münzstrasse had more crime, more bars, and more prostitution than Sophienstrasse. All Uncle Meier had to do was look out his window and see peroxide blondes in high heels, short skirts, and red leather jackets dicker with men on the street, then he'd follow the two of them with his eyes as they disappeared into a dingy hotel on the corner. There was a war going on, and the Nazis expected women to work in factories. If they were pregnant, they could ask to be excused only when their term was nearly up. Some women, apparently, like the ones on the streets of Münzstrasse, found other ways to fill their time. These desperate years called for desperate measures.

And antisemitism—common, of course, all over Berlin—was more blatant and out in the open on Münzstrasse. One day, Uncle Meier came home laughing that he'd "helped a young woman bring up her child." While out for a walk, he'd heard a mother calling repeatedly for her son, "Come here. Come here, will you." The boy pretended not to hear her. Louder and more insistent than before, she called again: "Come to me at once! And watch out! There's a Jew behind you! He's coming to get you." The boy, Meier said, "ran to his mother as though the devil was after him." With a grin, Meier posed the punchline in his story to everyone who'd gathered around him in his crowded apartment: "Do you think the mother even thanked me?"[3]

By moving to Münzstrasse, Cioma left behind two ways he could have been protected from the Nazis had he stayed on Sophienstrasse. St. Hedwig's, the sprawling hospital a quarter block from the Schönhauses' apartment, may have been Catholic, but it remained true to its mission: to care for everyone, with dignity and with love. The staff treated Jews, hid Jews, fed Jews, sometimes distracting the police by serving them coffee while, a few doors down, doctors and nurses were caring for Jews: assuring these people who were refugees in their own country that they were as human as the Nazis said they weren't.

Cioma's other harbor of protection on Sophienstrasse was the Sophien Church, the Lutheran house of worship directly across from Cioma's apartment building, which also saved and hid Jews and wasn't shy about opposing Hitler: when the Gestapo banned its pastor, Franz

Ferdinand Vogel, from leading services—Vogel's sermons often criticized Hitler—Sunday services continued to be held in the church, led by a slightly more cautious pastor. After services, congregants gathered beneath the balcony of Vogel's apartment, which was on the church grounds. As they sang hymns for him, Vogel looked down from the balcony, his shock of white hair like a cumulus from heaven, his smile stronger than any sermon he could have delivered from the pulpit.

Cioma could have walked to the hospital or the church and asked for help. But like most Jews, he had no idea that either place was a sanctuary for people like him. Knowledge about what really went on in the church and hospital was kept confidential and clandestine. These secrets saved lives; these secrets could end lives if they were known to more than an exclusive few. In effect, Sophienstrasse was wider than it seemed, with an invisible chasm of faith and silence separating Cioma from the goodness that was so close to him. Likewise, the Christians who worked in the hospital and the church had no idea that someone named "Cioma" needed their help. The tragedy of Cioma's young life was also the reality of this street: kind hearts beat, yet walls loomed where none should have been, and a young man's fear was not known and definitely not assuaged.

In Tegel, Boris wasn't doing any better than Cioma and Fanja, especially when he and other prisoners pressed a newcomer about news from the outside. He could only think of the latest British bombing, though he didn't know much about it.

"Where'd the bombs land?" a prisoner asked.

"In Sophienstrasse. Only one house was hit."

"Which one?"

He didn't know and, anyway, the bombs couldn't have been too destructive: "Only a few people were killed."[4]

That exchange ruined the rest of Boris's stay in jail: one house on Sophienstrasse had been hit. He had to know which one. For him, only one mattered: number 32–33.

On December 7, 1941, Japan attacked Pearl Harbor. Four days later, Germany declared war on the United States. Historians called this Hitler's greatest "act of lunacy," his "most puzzling" decision of the war, one that basically guaranteed Germany's defeat: the United States was too mighty to beat. Everything had to be thrown into this war now, and everyone was needed. That's why Cioma's art school closed. Jews had better things to do than learn how to be artists. They could actually produce something now—guns, uniforms, tanks, *kübelwagens* (the German version of the Jeep)—rather than indulge their imaginations: Jewish imaginations were exactly what the Third Reich didn't need.[5]

Most of the work the Nazis gave Jews was dirty and exhausting: shoveling coal, digging ditches, toiling in factories that produced synthetic rubber whose stench seeped into you and whose blackness rarely washed off. Cioma was lucky. The government's Labor Exchange sent him to a tailoring shop that specialized in uniforms for the military. Anton Erdmann's shop was located at Poststrasse 6—less than a mile from where Cioma was living with Uncle Meier and an easy ride on the bike Cioma still had from his cousin Morris. That was good. Also good was that Erdmann quickly sized up Cioma, decided he knew nothing about sewing, and put him in charge of distributing to the shop's ninety-six Jewish tailors the trimmings—gold braiding, emblems, badges, buttons with swastikas or eagles—that gave a uniform dash and élan. Erdmann went one step further, telling Cioma that, at work, he'd be known by a less Jewish, more German name: Gunther. That was fine with Cioma. He promised he wouldn't tell anyone about their arrangement.[6]

Having a decent boss gave Cioma some measure of comfort. Still, he was troubled by news that was drifting in from Bielefeld, where he'd worked for almost nine months before returning to Berlin for art school. A few months after he left, the Nazis took over the labor camp. Now it wasn't designed to teach Jews skills that would make them more attractive workers if they stayed in Germany or more appealing to other countries if they got out. The camp was now a prison. Its only purpose was to keep Jews in Germany.

In December—a few days after Japan attacked Pearl Harbor—four hundred Jews were crammed into a restaurant, the Kyffhauser, located in the middle of Bielefeld. For three days, they slept on straw, barely ate, and weren't told why they were there or what would happen to them. Local newspapers printed nothing about the situation, though everyone in town knew about it. A major tram line—number 3—passed directly in front of the Kyffhauser, and Gestapo agents who were posted outside the restaurant chased away children who tried to look inside. On December 13 the Jews were herded onto trains that were heading "east." "East," at that point in the war, was mostly a mystery, a compass point that could have been anywhere and had little meaning. Few people knew these were one-way trips.[7]

For the next fifteen months, more Jews from Bielefeld would be sent "east." The last train left Bielefeld on March 2, 1943. Aboard was Lotte Windmüller, the pretty young woman on whom Cioma had a crush when he was in Bielefeld, then stomped away in a jealous fit when he saw her with several other guys on an outing to the Hermannsdenkmal, that giant statue forty miles from Bielefeld. A year after Cioma left Bielefeld, Lotte fell in love with Paul Hoffman, who also worked at the camp. They planned to marry the next summer. The Nazis had other plans for them.[8]

In February 1943, the Gestapo announced that everyone left in the work camp in Bielefeld would soon be deported. This time, the Gestapo announced where the trains were going: Auschwitz, a name that meant nothing to Paul or Lotte. Everyone was limited to one pair of boots, two pairs of socks, two shirts, two pairs of underwear, two woolen blankets, two sets of sheets, one bowl, one drinking cup, one spoon, and one sweater. Paul gave a woman he trusted, a Christian who lived in Bielefeld, a suitcase containing his personal papers, some photos, and the rings for the wedding he and Lotte expected to have when they returned. Had he taken the rings with him, they would have been confiscated at his destination.[9]

At Auschwitz, Paul ran into Lotte on the train platform. He was "happy," to use Paul's word, that Lotte was with Johanna Kaufmann, a "resolute and intelligent" friend of hers. If Lotte and Johanna stayed together, Paul figured, they'd survive.[10]

Paul survived for two years at Auschwitz, calling out his number—104951—when the guards demanded it, and being as inconspicuous as possible when nothing was demanded from him. That was one way—maybe the best way—to make the Nazis forget he was there. In early 1945 Paul was transferred to Buchenwald, then joined thirty thousand other prisoners on a death march in early April as the Americans got closer. Paul escaped and walked, ran, and stumbled toward the advancing Allied soldiers. He spent the rest of his life in Germany—marrying in 1954, and having two children, a son and a daughter, and never forgetting his final image of Lotte standing on the platform at Auschwitz. For Paul, that image was sacred: an emanation of the life that could have been, that should have been. A few weeks after Paul last saw Lotte, she was murdered. Most likely, Cioma would have been, too, had he not left Bielefeld the year before to pursue his dream of becoming an artist.[11]

8

"Do Not Shed Too Many Tears"

Only years later would Cioma learn that Lotte Windmüller was murdered at Auschwitz. For now, he just wanted to do his job in Anton Erdmann's tailor shop, pretending he was a nice Aryan named Gunther, and keeping Erdmann's ninety-six Jewish tailors happy. As the guy who made sure every tailor had the exact accessories they needed for the uniforms they were making—epaulets, stiff collars, flat collars, and so on—Cioma was quick and efficient and the tailors liked him. They had no reason not to. To them, he was a young German who was doing his job, and doing it well. What they didn't know was that he was just like them, a Jew trying to lay low and hoping the storm outside Erdmann's shop would pass over before it devoured all of them.

Just below Erdmann in the tailor shop's chain of command was happy-go-lucky Hans Schabbehard, who had his own secret: he'd been kicked out of the German army because he was half Jewish. Erdmann didn't care. With the war going on, all Erdmann wanted was employees who sewed and made good uniforms and had no chance of being drafted away from him for the army. The army didn't want Jews. It didn't want half Jews. Anton Erdmann did.

Schabbehard kept an eye on Cioma, making sure he didn't get into trouble. Maybe he knew Cioma was Jewish; maybe he worried because Cioma was the youngest worker at Erdmann's. His motive didn't matter. His concern was real. He warned Cioma to stay away from a seamstress who worked in the shop: she was so glamorous, Schabbehard said, she'd seduce you before you knew it. He vouched for Cioma when one thousand Reichsmarks were missing from Erdmann's office. Cioma, Schabbehard told everyone, "wouldn't pinch anything." Best of all, when Erdmann's sailboat had to be moved from a dock in Wannsee to one in Pichelsberg, a popular sailing spot on the western side of Berlin, Schabbehard called out for Cioma: "You're coming along!"[1]

This was Cioma's first time on a sailboat. The first time he felt the wind pull him along the water, the first time he saw the water so close, so fast, so shiny. At that moment, he knew he would take up sailing, someday, somehow. That sailboat ride changed his life.

Some days at Erdmann's, Cioma rode along in a truck that delivered newly sewn uniforms to the army. On one of these trips, a soldier took Cioma aside and showed him photos of emaciated men—skeletons, really—in clothes that were striped and baggy and didn't deserve to be called "clothes." The men in the photos hardly looked human. Somehow, Cioma knew they were. He also knew, somehow, that those people were Jews. The soldier had taken these photos while serving in Poland. He'd seen chimneys belching smoke, and smelled burning flesh and the sulfurous stink of hair sizzling in fires that never should have been lit, and witnessed ashes drifting upward toward an uncomprehending sky and a supposedly all-knowing God who knew not what His children were doing, or why.

When Cioma got home, he told his mother about the photos. She wouldn't believe him. "You're crazy," Fanja said. "They can't kill millions of people who haven't done anything wrong. No, you can't talk me into believing that." Pointing through a window to a sky that was bright and cloudless, the kind of day that offered hope and good cheer, Fanja did her best to convince Cioma that the only truth, glorious and undeniable, was the beauty around them: the pull of the sun and the moon, the stars and the trees: the pull of life. "Look how beautiful the weather is," she exclaimed. "The Nazis can do whatever they want, but they will never stop the sun from shining."[2]

This was Fanja's prayer, a convenient truth against other, more glaring and implausible truths: a personal song of songs that celebrated the certainties in life that could not be violated, sullied, or debased. Fanja's faith was rooted in an order that was inviolable and was as permanent as the sun in the sky and the love in her heart. Her optimism would serve her well, until it couldn't.

Cioma's understanding of his mother's effort to remain bright and cheerful would serve him well, for years and for decades—an extension of his love for her and of his empathy for her insistence not necessarily on averting her eyes, but on finding some way to get through the day, and then another, in this city of the desperate, and the frantic. "When people don't want to believe that something is true," Cioma said decades after his mother refused to accept what he told her about the photos he'd seen, "then they just won't. They'll find hundreds of alternate explanations so they don't have to believe it. I think the mass of the Germans knew what was happening. My boss at the tailor shop, Anton Erdmann, once said to me, 'We will have to atone for a very long time for what they are doing in Poland.' But he would never have asked me to hide in his house. That would have been too much of a protest for him. Hitler made people very afraid."

Cioma accepted that soldier's account of what he'd seen and what he'd photographed. "In Poland," the soldier told Cioma, "they are burning all the Jews. The chimneys are smoking all the time." On some level, his mother accepted that too, despite her bromides about the sun shining and the weather always being beautiful. "No matter what is going to happen," she told her son, "I will stay with your father.

I'm not going to let him go alone. Don't make this harder for me than it is already."[3]

Fanja knew where Boris would be sent.

She knew where she would be sent.

She knew that the photographs Cioma had seen were real, that the smoke from the chimneys were real, and that the scrawny men in those baggy, striped pajamas were Jews.

Sometimes, the mind deceives us so the heart can live.

One day, Anton Erdmann called Cioma into his office and told him he had to leave his shop. "It's impossible," Erdmann said, "for a normal person to grasp what our soldiers are doing to the Jews in Poland. God help us if we lose the war. We'll all be in for it. But in the meantime, you people are catching it." Looking carefully at Cioma, he told him, "You have to start wearing a star like everybody else." At that point, Cioma was wearing his Star of David as little as possible. Then he broke his news to Cioma: "I can't keep you here any longer."

Any day, Erdmann's ninety-six Jewish tailors, and Cioma along with them, could be sent to "Poland." And any day, Cioma's cover could be blown. Snitches were everywhere. For a few Reichsmarks from the Gestapo, or just for the fun of it, people turned Jews over to the Nazis, never to be seen again.

Erdmann offered to help Cioma get a job at Wysocky's, the tailor shop where Cioma's mother worked. The owner had "better connections" than Erdmann did—"a better line to the top," Erdmann said admiringly. "How it works, I have no idea. But Wysocky's can do more to protect you."[4]

At Wysocky's, forty-eight women and four men, including Cioma, made uniforms for the German army, just like at Erdmann's. Cioma's mother kept an eye on him, teaching him about tailoring as he went along. He relished the smell of peppermint tea and real coffee that was in the air. (No one knew where Walter Prager, the owner of Wysocky's, got the coffee from—since 1940, real coffee had essentially disappeared from Germany.) And there was a camaraderie, or something close to it, that Cioma hadn't enjoyed at Erdmann's. Sometimes, Cioma joined two employees in songs from the war in which they'd served—the previous world war, the war in which they'd been respected as equal and brave citizens of their fine and learned country. "If a bullet shoots me dead," went one of these songs:

> *And home I cannot wend,*
> *Do not shed too many tears, but find yourself a friend,*
> *Take care to find a fine young lad, my lovely Annemarie,*
> *I won't mind if you don't find*
> *One from my company,*
> *One from my company.*

Or sometimes Cioma and his friends sang:

> *Stand fast, stand fast in the storm's deadly blast*
> *So the world can see, the world can see*
> *how loyal we can be.*

Paul Levi and Karl Wiesner, the veterans who were teaching Cioma these songs, had been loyal to their country during the previous war. Now, the world couldn't see, or wouldn't see, how loyal they'd been. Nor could it, or would it, stop the new storm that was washing over them, a storm whose undertow was more powerful, and more deadly, than the one they'd survived nearly thirty years ago.[5]

There was one more thing for Cioma to learn at Wysocky's other than songs he'd never heard before. Walter Prager, the owner of Wysocky's, had a pretty wife. That didn't stop him from having an even prettier mistress—an employee, Evchen Hirschfeld. And having an affair with Prager didn't stop Evchen from thinking about having an affair with Cioma.

Until now, Evchen had little to do with Cioma's mother. Suddenly, she was fast friends with Fanja, often coming to the Schönhauses' apartment after work, saying little, eating little, just hanging out, though no one knew why. One night, Cioma found out why. After everyone else had gone to bed, Evchen was still there, idly flipping through a magazine in the living room. Edging close to her, nervous and uncertain and hoping none of his relatives who were sleeping one room away walked through the living room on their way to the bathroom, Cioma began unbuttoning Evchen's blouse. She didn't resist. He continued, button by button, until all their clothes were on the floor and the two of them stretched out on the couch. Cioma had no idea what he was doing. Evchen did, guiding him as teacher, seductress, and tutor until whatever they were doing was over, which didn't take long. In fact, it ended embarrassingly too soon for Cioma, who had never done this before and had expected greater—and longer—pleasures.

Evchen stood up and slowly put on her clothes. Cioma offered to walk her home. She declined. The next day at work, Evchen was sitting next to Walter Prager, her usual place of honor. Cioma nodded as he walked by. She ignored him. She also stopped visiting the Schönhauses in the evenings. At home, Cioma withdrew, preferring to be by himself. When his mother asked why he was behaving this way, he answered in a monotone, "Nothing. Why?" That's where they left it, which was probably just as well.[6]

Evchen was a nuisance and a flirt, and Cioma knew he was better off without her. That took time. By then, he had a real girlfriend—Dorothee Fliess—smart and pretty, with blonde hair that flowed past her shoulders, elegantly arched eyebrows, and shapely legs that extended tantalizingly below the tartan skirts she liked to wear. After Jews were kicked out of public schools, Dorothee took courses in stenography and typing and worked as a secretary in her father's law firm. In 1941 the

Nazis ordered her to join the five hundred forced laborers who worked in an armaments factory in Treptow, a borough in southeast Berlin. She was nineteen years old.

The work was dirty, tiring, and grueling. Cioma and Dorothee somehow found time to visit galleries and museums, go canoeing and biking, and explore the woods that lined the edge of the city. In one gallery, the owner took them aside. He'd been eavesdropping and could tell, as the gallery owner said, that Cioma was "an artist of some kind." He led Cioma and Dorothee into a back room, where he pulled a curtain back, revealing paintings by artists the Nazis had banned as "degenerate"—Oskar Kokoschka, Max Beckmann, and Max Pechstein. Three of the leading expressionists of the day.

"It's a terrible shame our führer was once a painter," the gallery owner confided to Cioma and Dorothee. "He thinks he's an expert on painting."

Then the gallery owner told Cioma and Dorothee about an "amusing" incident that had happened recently. An aunt who made "wretched flower paintings" asked if he'd show them in his gallery. He hung them at the rear of his shop, hoping no one would see them. Not long after that, two representatives from the Reich Ministry for Public Enlightenment and Propaganda came to his gallery, seeking art for Hitler's offices in the Chancellery. "With the unerring eye of connoisseurs," the gallery owner recalled, "they picked out my old aunt's pictures. I couldn't believe my eyes. Yes," he laughed, "we live in great times."

With a hearty, "Have a nice Sunday," the gallery owner escorted Cioma and Dorothee out the door. They had much to contemplate: the gallery owner had given them new ways to appreciate the greatness of the times in which they lived.[7]

Dating Dorothee brought Cioma into the orbit of one of the more prominent Jews in Berlin—her father, Julius Fliess, had served in the German army during World War I, lost an eye in combat, returned to the front lines before he completely healed, received a medal and, after the war, became a highly respected lawyer. In November 1941 the Jewish Council of Berlin told Julius that, in a few days, he and his wife would be ordered to board a train to "the east." Dorothee—essential to the war effort, as she worked in an arms factory—could stay in Berlin. Julius appealed to a friend—Hans von Dohnanyi, a high official in the Abwehr, Germany's intelligence agency. Julius knew von Dohnanyi hated Hitler. Maybe he could persuade Adolf Eichmann, Hitler's henchman who'd been ordered to make Germany Judenfrei, to let Julius and his wife stay in Berlin.[8]

Von Dohnanyi obtained a letter from the head of the Abwehr, Wilhelm Canaris, praising Fliess's bravery during the previous war. That was easy: though he was deeply conservative, anti-democratic, an ally of Hitler's since the 1920s, and a close friend of Francisco Franco, the fascist dictator in Spain, Canaris had nothing against Jews. He'd already helped some of them: friends and neighbors, and people he never knew and never would, like the four hundred Dutch Jews he smuggled into Spain from May 1941 to January 1942, claiming they were spies he'd eventually place in countries that were fighting Germany. Maybe he'd help the Fliesses.[9]

Canaris's letter worked. For a while. Eichmann agreed to delay the Fliesses' deportation. But eight months later, Eichmann told the Jewish Council that he'd heard Jews were appealing to other officials to stop their deportations. In the future, Eichmann warned, any Jew who sought this sort of help would be promptly deported, along with his entire family.[10]

Canaris and von Dohnanyi came up with a new plan. Code name: Operation 7. They'd claim Fliess was a spy they'd eventually send to the United States, much like they'd done with the four hundred Jews they'd already spirited from the Netherlands to Spain. But Spain was too far for Fliess and his family to easily reach from Berlin. Canaris and von Dohnanyi settled on Switzerland.

Bureaucratic red tape delayed Fliess's departure. Meanwhile, the number of Jews whom Operation 7 would help increased from the original three—Fliess, his wife, and Dorothee—to fourteen. Canaris and von Dohnanyi couldn't say no to anyone.[11]

All this time, Cioma and Dorothee were going to movies and galleries, on long walks and quiet picnics: doing what teenagers in love do. In the summer of 1942, they biked to Fangschleuse, a small town eighteen miles southwest of Berlin. Along the way, they were mostly quiet, thankful for these few days that were theirs, grateful for their time together, knowing it was scarce and could end any minute. At one point, Dorothee told Cioma, "You know, you can never tell what the future holds. But if we get torn apart and I never see you again, I'll still be as crazy about you as I am now." They were learning that, although they'd been led to believe love was an effortless possessing of each other, a sweet arpeggio of longing, trust and oneness, it was more than that. They were confronting the fact that it could end sooner than it should, maybe abruptly and perhaps violently. No one had told them about the corruptions of love in a time of fascism.

In Fangschleuse, Cioma and Dorothee found a room for the night in a farmhouse. This was the first time they had been alone. They sat on the edge of the bed, lost in their thoughts and in their nervousness, eating cake the farmer's wife had kindly brought them when they arrived. After an awkward pause, Dorothee said softly, "I'm going to tell you a secret, but for God's sake, keep it to yourself: I shouldn't be telling you this at all. Next week, I'm emigrating to Switzerland with my parents. I'd much rather stay here with you, and stay in my beloved Berlin."[12]

This was not what Cioma had expected Dorothee would say. Not tonight. Not in a farmhouse in Fangschleuse on what was, he realized now, not only their first night together, but possibly their only night together. Stunned, Cioma asked how Dorothee was getting into Switzerland. She didn't answer. She couldn't.

That was the end of their discussion. But not their love.

On the night of September 30, Dorothee and her parents and the eleven others in their group boarded a train for Basel. Canaris and von Dohnanyi had provided them with falsified passports and visas—the advantage of running an agency where fakes like this were the standard tricks of the trade. As Dorothee and the others removed their Jewish stars, once they were safely in Switzerland, Dorothee regretted not telling Cioma that she'd been so determined not to leave him and her friends from the munitions factory where she worked that her parents had to spend hours persuading her to join this secret trip out of Germany. It was good they did. Five months after Dorothee left, almost against her will, the Gestapo sent everyone in the factory to "the east."[13]

Dorothee had left her beloved Berlin, and her beloved Cioma. Now Cioma had to figure out how he could leave Berlin. He was running out of friends and family who could help him. Berlin was not a city in which you wanted to be alone.

9

A Night on the Town

Wysocky's had its share of characters. There was Walter Prager, a Jew who secretly defied the Nazis' orders that Jews surrender their money and their positions, and who generously shared the coffee that he got from who knew where with his many employees. And Paul Levi and Karl Wiesner, the two veterans who boisterously sang songs from the Great War and wouldn't let anyone forget their bravery in that conflict. And of course, there was Evchen Hirschfeld, Wysocky's resident seductress and Cioma's embarrassingly brief one-night stand.

There was also Det Kassriel, a trained tailor slightly older than Cioma, who knew his stitches and the density, warp, and woof of various cloths and fabrics, and various styles of clothing, especially the style of the uniforms they were making at Wysocky's. In his off-hours, Det made two-piece suits that slimmed the figures of the stout women who worked in a nearby market, bartering his tailoring for bacon, sausage, and cheese—treats difficult, sometimes impossible, to acquire with ration coupons. They were called "rations" for a reason. There was a limit to what they could purchase, which often was nothing.

Det and Cioma got along. Maybe too well. One day, Det invited Cioma to join him for drinks at the Hotel Kaiserhof. Cioma was stunned: the Kaiserhof, a few blocks from the Chancellery, where

Hitler lived, was the führer's favorite hotel and restaurant. It had been since the early 1930s. Adolf Hitler, Hermann Göring, and other big-deal Nazis still went there for a good meal or a night on the town, undeterred by the war or occasional bombing from the British or the possibility—there was always a possibility—of assassination. *Why*, Cioma thought, *would Det go there*? It was safer to walk into a cage of lions.

Det had thought this through carefully. Just like what had happened with Cioma, a soldier who'd returned from Poland had told Det about chimneys that belched smoke and about men who were skeletons and wore uniforms that were rags. "It'll be our turn one day," Det grimly told Cioma. When that turn came, he'd go into hiding. And to survive, he'd have to act like he was confident and assured and, like any other German, was happily Sieg heil!-ing his way through the day. If he couldn't pull that off, he'd be another belch of black smoke in Poland. Going to the Kaiserhof was Det's dress rehearsal for living underground.

"As long as you look confident, you can't go wrong," Det told Cioma. "Do you think anyone asks Goering or Himmler for their ID? Anyway, there'll be four of us. Two of my sailor friends are coming in their uniforms."[1]

Cioma agreed to go. Det's sailor friends would give them good cover and, anyway, he'd never been in any of Berlin's grand hotels. That would be part of the adventure.

The Kaiserhof opened in 1875, the first of Berlin's grand hotels. Soon, there would be the Adlon and the Esplanade, but the Kaiserhof always topped the list. It was the first hotel in Berlin with electricity, telephones, and bathrooms in every guest room, and the first with pneumatic lifts and steam heating. Almost overnight, the hotel became so synonymous with wheeling and dealing that an international conference was held there in 1884-85 that gleefully divided Africa among the European colonial powers, assuring that the next century would be full of wars, all the way from Sudan and Egypt in the north to the Cape of Good Hope in the south. The Kaiserhof was so attentive to its guests that when an American returned after being away for a year, he'd barely unpacked his suitcase before a bellhop delivered a package containing a pair of shoe trees he'd left behind on his previous visit. And so glamorous was the Kaiserhof that when Hermann and Emmy Göring married in 1935, only one hotel would do for them—their führer's favorite. A wedding photo shows them here with Hitler—Hermann and Emmy beaming as Hitler glowers with his usual intensity.[2]

As the city splintered after World War I, with street fighting and political assassinations almost every week, troops from the far right seized the Kaiserhof, wrecked furniture, swung from chandeliers, flooded parts of the building, and shot at left-wing militia who were waiting for them behind barricades outside. It took years to restore the hotel, and even longer to restore its reputation. Hitler moving there in 1931 didn't help. The hotel's élan polished the panache Hitler didn't possess on his own. He had tea here with the filmmaker Leni Riefenstahl, plotted late into the night with Hermann Göring and Joseph Goebbels, and summoned government officials from the Chancellery across the square, acting like he was already their boss.

With Hitler turning the Kaiserhof's top floor into his command post and his living quarters, Jews stayed away, good citizens stayed away, foreign guests stayed away. "Monstrous losses" were mounting "by the day," a Kaiserhof executive lamented. "Why not," he asked plaintively, "close shop?"

Why, indeed? And why not evict Hitler, whose presence was contaminating the hotel? In September 1932 the hotel's board of directors convened to wrestle with those questions. It didn't work out well. One director warned that Hitler's recent triumphs at the polls would encourage more Nazis to move into the hotel, another was annoyed that "not enough" was being done to attract the hotel's more traditional clientele, and all the directors were cowed by their guest who had taken over the hotel's fifth floor. In the end, the Jewish-dominated board—five of the seven board members were Jews—voted to let Hitler stay. Maybe they were afraid of reprisals from the Nazis, or maybe they were sticking to their duty to the hotel's shareholders to stay neutral and make a profit again. Profits were good. There's also the chance that Walter Meinhardt, the chairman of the board (and a Jew), was torn between being a tolerant liberal and censoring anyone for their politics. What's important, and sad, is that a group of Jews who still had some power surrendered the Kaiserhof to Hitler.[3]

None of that stopped Cioma or Det. All that was exceptional about their night at the Kaiserhof was that they shouldn't have been there. The bar where their little group sat hardly looked like it had in its pre-Hitler days. The entire room had been refurbished to resemble a traditional German restaurant, with dark, oppressive wood paneling. All the paintings by foreign artists, especially French or British artists, had been replaced by canvases depicting Berlin's more famous landmarks. Less cosmopolitan and more "German" now, the bar had a different luster than in the past, and it attracted customers who were more strident and more masculine—closer to the image of the new Germany that was out to defeat the rest of the world.

Det ordered drinks for everyone in his group: whiskey and soda, no ice. He'd been at the Kaiserhof so often that he knew what was available and what wasn't. By this point in the war, most of the bottles the bar displayed had colored water in them, a deception that bothered the staff as much as their customers. "The old bartender," one of the Kaiserhof's regular customers recalled after the war, was in "visible pain" when someone ordered a cocktail. "Dreadfully sorry," the bartender would apologize, "but today, precisely today, we've run out of ingredients."

The sailors who were with Det stood out with their impressive uniforms and their loud bragging about recently sinking a British torpedo boat in a fjord in Scandinavia. The attention they were getting was fine with Det. It helped him practice looking like an "ordinary" German even while other people were eyeing him. If everyone in the bar had ignored him, he'd be under no scrutiny, and the night would be wasted.

Cioma did his best to do everything Det told him to do. He looked confident. He sounded confident. Det was right: the only way to pass as an Aryan was to act like an Aryan. All that the generals, admirals, and Nazis in the room saw was a self-assured young man, one who was sure that he belonged in Germany and at the Kaiserhof, the best place to be in Berlin any night of the week. Cioma was putting on a good show. What the rest of the bar didn't see was that, behind his confident facade, he was wobbly and shaky and just wanted to get the hell out of the joint.[4]

In 1942 three themes were converging in Cioma's life: escaping to Switzerland, where Dorothee Fliess and her parents had fled, thanks to Operation 7, the code name for Canaris and von Dohnanyi's sneaky ruse to get Jews out of Germany; hiding, like Det planned to do; and buying a sailboat, like the one Anton Erdmann had taken Cioma on while he worked at Wysocky's as a tailor. These three—escaping, hiding, and sailing—shared a common denominator: freedom. Freedom by living in another country. Freedom by assuming a new name and a new life and becoming so invisible (and in plain sight) that the Nazis would look right through him. And freedom by communing with winds and currents, hearing the caw-caw-caw-ing of birds, and smelling the freshness of the water and the air. Gaining that freedom, whatever form it took, required courage. Cioma knew that. Right now, he vacillated between fear and confidence. Too much fear and not enough confidence and he'd be a coward. Too much confidence and not enough fear and he'd be rash, impulsive. Cioma's spunk and zest—the enjoyment he got out of every moment—might be enough to tamp down his fear, and his cleverness could help provide his version of courage. Perfecting that equilibrium would take time and chutzpah. Until Cioma decided which of these routes was most sensible for him, he'd have to put his plans on pause. He would know when he was ready to outsmart the enemy. If, indeed, he ever was.

Meanwhile, Cioma's neighborhood was shutting down. The kosher meat shops were gone. The synagogues that had been everywhere were gutted by fires or vandals. The streets, once full of peddlers and women and children playing games were emptying. The Nazis had sent many of the adults to work in factories. The rest were sent . . . somewhere.

At Wysocky's, Walter Prager called Cioma into his office and leveled with him: "Schönhaus, I've got to throw you out. It's a shame, but I want you to survive. You've got to move to the armaments industry. If you stay here, I can't prevent you from being evacuated."

"But Herr Prager," Cioma protested, "you've got such good connections in high places."

Prager lowered his voice so no one outside his office would hear him. "Yes," he said, "and it's precisely because of my good connections that I know you'll be safe in the armaments industry. I'll try to place you with Gustav Genschow in Treptow. His factory makes small-bore arms. That's all I can do for you now."

At the Labor Exchange where Cioma went to be reassigned to Genschow's, he was told he'd be working twelve-hour shifts: alternating between the morning shift (6:00 A.M. to 6:00 P.M.) one week and the night shift (6:00 P.M. to 6:00 A.M.) the next week: dawn to dusk for seven days, then dusk to dawn the next seven days. After one week of this grind, Cioma was ready to throw himself into the Spree, which flowed through a large park near the factory—a hulking, five-story building that filled half a city block. With skylights on its modified mansard roof and rows of tall narrow windows on every floor, sunlight streamed in everywhere. Firetrucks had sprayed the outside of the building with green, brown, and black paint to camouflage it from air raids. A tram line ran down the middle of the cobbled street in front of the factory: four perfectly straight lines of track that lent order to a city that would soon be desperate for order. In less than a year, Allied bombing would hit its stride.

Cioma usually took a tram or subway to his new job. This wasn't legal. To use public transportation, Jews had to work more than 4.8 miles from where they lived. The apartment where Cioma was living—his aunt and uncle's—was 4.2 miles from Genschow's. Those six tenths of a mile disqualified Cioma from using public transit. He didn't care. He'd reached the point where his life was so untethered that great risks seemed to have little consequence.[5]

The subway was Berlin in miniature, a microcosm of all the fear, suspicion, desperation, and anxiety that were common in the streets above it. One day on the subway, a man standing near Cioma looked at him, turned around to see if anyone was looking, then turned back to Cioma. The stranger now pointed to the spot on his coat that corresponded to where Cioma had sewn a Star of David on his jacket. The man shook his head almost imperceptibly and got off a few stations later. On the platform, he turned around to see if he was being followed. He wasn't. Cioma didn't know if the man was silently sympathizing with him, or if he was one of those Jews Cioma had heard so much about: Jews who lived in the shadows and had no real home and were always on the run.[6]

On his first day at Genschow's, Cioma didn't make a good impression: he was late. That didn't endear him to his immediate supervisor, a former teacher who'd taught Cioma and had never liked him. "So, Schönhaus," he said, remembering Cioma's habits as a student, "it's always the same ones who come late. Arriving late here is not as harmless as it was at school." At Genschow's, anyone who was late more than three times had to report to the Gestapo's office on the factory's second floor.[7]

Cioma was assigned to a lathe that retooled barrels from old rifles so they'd fit submachine guns. Cioma mastered the work fairly quickly: clamping a barrel into a lathe, turning a crank, checking the measurements, clamping another one in. The routine was so mindless that, between barrels, Cioma had time to daydream, usually about being a painter after the war. Despite that, his speed and efficiency impressed his bosses. "He's got the whole thing down to a fine art," two supervisors said as they passed by Cioma's lathe one day. "He even has time to take a rest in between. Fantastic."[8]

So fantastic that, the following day, Cioma found two lathes at his work station. He now had to work two machines at the same time. Cioma's showboating had cost him any leisure on the job. He'd have been better off producing submachine barrels at the same laggardly pace as everyone else. Cioma excelled with two lathes so much that he got another promotion: filing the barrels so they'd fit snugly, but not tightly, inside a u-shaped channel in the interior of a machine gun. These had to have a tolerance of minus one hundredth of a millimeter at the front of the barrel and plus one hundredth of a millimeter at the rear. If these minuscule measurements weren't met, the barrel would be too large or too small. Either way, it would be useless. This exacting work demanded exacting concentration, and no more daydreaming. The only upside was Cioma could sit on a stool while working.

At first, Cioma filed off too much from the barrels he made: a fraction of a millimeter made the difference between a usable barrel and junk. Cioma threw the junk into a heap that was carted away at the end of his shift. A supervisor, a Mr. Ackermann, noticed what Cioma was up to. Cioma had pegged Ackermann as such an ideal-looking Aryan that he could have gotten a job as a bodyguard for Hitler. Stopping by Cioma's work station one day, Ackermann whispered to Cioma, "Lad, you're creating too much waste. It doesn't take them long around here to suspect someone's committing sabotage. It's better to give it a knock on the head."

Cioma had no idea what Ackermann was talking about.

Tap on the barrels, Ackermann explained. Make the channels fit the barrels snugly enough to constrict their movement though lightly enough so inspectors in the factory didn't see what Cioma had done—a delicate equilibrium that, done well, assured that when a gun was fired, it wasn't accurate. "And if our soldiers miss . . ." Ackermann continued, "and somebody they're trying to shoot stays alive by mistake, well, that's fine by us, ok?"[9]

That was more than fine with Cioma. Also fine was that he now knew Ackermann was not an "Aryan." But he had a new problem: between sabotaging weapons that he was making for the army and pretending over drinks at Hitler's favorite hotel that he was another German who loved the führer, Cioma had to resolve his bifurcated life. All this pretending was exhausting.

10

The Kindest Nazi
Fanja Ever Met

When he wasn't sabotaging machine guns, Cioma was worried about his father—still imprisoned and shoveling waste on the outskirts of Berlin—his punishment for selling butter on the black market. Visiting Boris one day, Cioma was relieved his father was in a small building next to the main prison. "Papa," he said, "it's so lucky you're in this little building. You could escape from here."

"For God's sake, Cioma," his father responded, "what are you talking about? Anyway, where's your star?"

"In my pocket. I couldn't have gotten in here without it."

"Cioma," Boris counseled in Russian, "*nye rush nichevo, nye boysa nikavo.*" ("If you don't make trouble, you don't have to be afraid of anybody.") In other words, behave and do what you're supposed to do.

"Papa," Cioma said, trying to change the subject, "do you know what's going on? They're sending all the Jews to Poland. They're killing them there. We should get out while we can."

"Don't talk nonsense," Boris scolded. "They can't kill all the Jews. But it worries me that you're going around without a star. Please phone the warden"—with whom Boris was friendly—"to let me know that you got home safely."[1]

Cioma not wearing a yellow Star of David should have been the least of Boris's worries. His son was right. Jews were being killed in Poland. But Cioma's plea that they leave Germany was too late. Jews hadn't been allowed to leave Germany for at least half a year. Cioma's friend Dorothee Fliess and her parents had been lucky: the Abwehr, with its money, know-how, and teams of forgers who could create fake IDs, had spirited them out of Germany. Cioma didn't know anyone in the Abwehr, or in any other intelligence service. If he ever got out of Germany, he'd have to do it his way, with IDs he'd counterfeit for himself. Right now, he had no idea how to do that.

In May 1942 Cioma and his mother were ordered to report to Burgstrasse 28. The address terrified Berlin's Jews. Previously, the home of the Berlin Stock Exchange, the stolid, graceless five-story building was now the headquarters of the Gestapo's Jewish Department in Berlin. Persecuting the city's Jews was engineered here, centralized here, executed from here. Jews were tortured and murdered in its basement, and orders to deport Jews were dispatched from the second floor. Cioma and his mother were told to go to the second floor.

Cioma and Fanja were shown into Room 23. Everything was deliberate, polite, civil. The officer behind the desk, Cioma later said, "looked like a respectable, middle-class family man" with "half-moon spectacles perched on the tip of his nose." He motioned for Fanja and Cioma to sit down. "Frau Schönhaus," he began, "you know that all the Jews are being evacuated to the east. For labor service. Actually," he demurred, in a gesture of feigned kindness, "you should have gone long ago. But I have established that your husband is serving a prison sentence. That is why I have arranged for your leaving date to be postponed." That would give this kind Gestapo officer enough time to pull some strings and have Boris pardoned. Then, the Schönhauses could travel together. The officer would go one step further and get Cioma excused from working at Genschow's. That way, the officer explained, Cioma "wouldn't have to stay behind in Berlin by himself."

In another three weeks, the Gestapo agent continued in his serene, measured tone, Cioma and Fanja had to report to a synagogue on Levetzowstrasse. They'd be reunited there with Boris and the three of them would go to the Grunewald station for their train to the "east"—a long-sought reunion arranged by the kindest Nazi Fanja ever met. She was sure he really cared about her, and about Boris and Cioma, and she was certain he wanted families to be together. This, for Fanja, had to be the true face of Hitler's regime, and all the rumors she'd heard, and all of Hitler's rules, regulations, and edicts that affected Jews, were simply aberrations and flukes. No one in their right mind, Fanja persisted, could have enacted all those horrors. Fanja didn't realize the Nazis didn't fall within any definition of "right mind."[2]

Jews were slowly learning what "east" meant. Not Fanja. For over a year, the Nazis had been telling Jews that going "east" was their chance to be productive, to stop taking everything and producing nothing. Parasites no more, they'd show they could work as hard, maybe harder, than anyone else. Somehow, despite the photos of "camps" that Cioma and others had seen, and the barely comprehensible rumors about chimneys and black smoke and ashes darkening the sky in faraway places, Fanja was among the majority of Jews who dismissed all this as the imaginings of troublemakers and provocateurs who knew nothing about the essential goodness of people, goodness that Fanja believed in, tenaciously and ferociously. Her own fantasies were essential to keep herself together. They were as essential as not knowing that, by the end of the war, the Nazis would send tens of thousands of Jews to the "east" from the synagogue on Levetzowstrasse, where Fanja and Cioma would report in three weeks. Knowing those numbers now would be too shattering, too numbing: a piercing truth that could not be grasped, that might never be grasped. For now, illusions and denials were the only routes to survival, however fleeting that survival may have been.[3]

As Fanja left the agent's office, she told Cioma, "Actually, he was quite decent." Into every Gestapo agent's life a little Jewish praise must fall. Then she flinched as an SS officer walked toward them, beating a decrepit, emaciated prisoner who was barely staggering down the corridor. When he collapsed on the floor, the SS officer yelled, "Get up! You know what'll happen if you don't. Get up!"

On the street outside, Fanja turned to Cioma, tears in her eyes, she said, "Doesn't that monster have a soul in his body? What kind of a world is it where creatures like that rule Germany?" Then she looked around. It was a beautiful spring day. The sun was bright. The flowers were blooming. Now that Fanja was back in her world, her unshakeable optimism rejuvenated her. She walked to work at Wysocky's tailor shop, certain of better days, brighter days.

On June 2 Fanja reported to the Levetzowstrasse synagogue, carrying a rucksack crammed with what she'd been told to bring:

> Two pairs of waterproof shoes
> Four pairs of socks
> Six pairs of underpants
> Two pullovers
> Two blankets
> Four shirts
> One hat or cap
> Two pairs of gloves
> One overcoat

Cioma didn't report to the synagogue. He didn't think he had to. His foreman had given him a letter requesting that Cioma remain in Berlin. Genschow's needed him. The letter read:

Gustav Genschow, Small Arms Manufacturer, Berlin

   Treptow, 31 May 1942

   This is to certify that Cioma Israel Schönhaus is employed in our firm as a precision engineer. He is an important worker. We request an extension of exemption for him.

   Heil Hitler.

   Signed: Schwarz, Foreman and SS Captain[4]

At Genschow's, Cioma worked as he usually did, hammering barrels into submachine guns. Looking up after an hour or two, he saw two men wearing fedoras and civilian suits standing over him. Escorting Cioma from Genschow's, they headed toward the Levetzowstrasse synagogue.

The shul was a madhouse. Noise and chaos were everywhere. Everyone was confused, bewildered, and hungry. No one was sure where they were going, or when, or why. Cioma's mother was completely lost when he found her. She needed someone to guide her through the mayhem. Cioma was her guide.

A Jew was shouting out names in alphabetical order. Finally, he called out, "Fanja Sarah Schönhaus and her son, Samson Cioma Israel Schönhaus." Cioma handed him the letter from Genschow's. Glancing at it, the Jew asked the Gestapo agent who was sitting behind him, "Should the young man go with the transport, or stay here?" The bored agent looked at the letter and gave the question a little thought—these people really didn't matter to him: they were just freight for the next train. Finally, he just about yawned out an answer: "Stay . . . go . . . stay . . . go . . . I don't care. Ok, yeah. He's going."

Cioma couldn't believe this. He'd almost been guaranteed he'd be exempt. He had to be. He knew about those smokestacks.

Cioma and Fanja walked down a long corridor lined with desks. At one, they surrendered whatever money they had with them. At another, they were asked where they'd been working. "Genchow's," Cioma said, adding, "Actually, I'm exempt." The woman behind the desk rifled through her files and found Cioma's letter. "Here it is," she announced. Looking up at Cioma, she declared, "Schönhaus. You're in a reserved occupation. One second, please," she requested as she walked away to find her supervisor. Suddenly, Cioma's father appeared, almost from nowhere: the Gestapo officer Cioma and Fanja had met a few weeks before had kept his word. Boris was "pardoned." They would now travel together, a family again.

Without trying, Cioma overheard a loud discussion that concerned him: "But, my girl, if everybody who comes here shows us a letter like this . . ." Cioma couldn't make out the rest of that sentence, but he didn't disagree with its logic. "Of course," Cioma thought, "if everybody carried a letter like mine, they'd never get enough people for one of their transports." Cioma's scare was unfounded. The woman returned to her desk. Smiling, she told Cioma, "You can go."

"Where?" Cioma asked, so surprised he could barely get out that one word.

"Home. You've been deferred."

Fanja looked at Boris. "What do you think? Do you think he should stay?"

"Of course he should stay," Boris answered firmly. "Maybe he can rescue us."[5]

Cioma gave his parents the sausage sandwiches he'd made for his lunch at Genschow's, hugged Boris and Fanja goodbye, and walked down a long corridor toward the street. "It was all very undramatic," he later said. "A bit like a normal farewell in a train station." He didn't look back.[6]

The Nazis were slowly emptying the Schönhauses' neighborhood. On Sophienstrasse—the quiet, almost bucolic street where they'd lived for eighteen years—neighbors were disappearing, just as Boris and Fanja had. One after another:

Jakob Bergoffen and his wife, Felli, disappeared from Sophien-strasse 6. Once prosperous owners of a paint shop, they'd fled to Prague in 1939, then to France, then sent back to Germany. Jakob and Felli were murdered at Auschwitz. Jakob was fifty years old. Felli was forty-nine.

Karl Bukofzer disappeared from Sophienstrasse 5. He was killed at Auschwitz three days later. Karl was fifty-seven years old.

Also from Sophienstrasse 5, Alfred Koh disappeared. He was killed at Auschwitz, date unknown. Alfred was forty years old.

There were others, of course. Most of the people who were sent away were similar to Boris and Fanja. They didn't know where they were going, or why, or how they could escape from this trip whose destination was a mystery. For now, the answer to that mystery was best not known.

Boris once told Cioma that he'd made two mistakes: leaving Russia and leaving Palestine. If he'd stayed in Russia, in the new Soviet state, he'd have tested the wisdom of a Russian saying: "Don't touch anything and nothing will happen to you." Boris would have seen only what he was told to see, touched only what he was told to touch, and been a model comrade in Vladimir Lenin's new paradise. In Palestine, he'd have helped build a country for the dispossessed and the expelled, the righteous and the sinful. Despite the sand that was always blowing around and his wife not being cut out for the life of a pioneer and a son who needed better medical care . . . even with all that, Palestine would have been better than the Germany they returned to. For Boris, another move would have been his ruin. "No," he said when Cioma begged him to leave Germany, "I'm not leaving. You don't make the same mistake three times."

Boris could have left the Reich when Jews were allowed to leave. Fanja and Cioma wanted to go, and their relatives who'd settled near New York City would have taken them in. Boris balked when they couldn't get a visa for Fanja's seventy-three-year-old mother. Her papers from emigrating from Russia a quarter century before were so messy and had been folded into thirds and quarters and eighths so many times that they were tattered, unreadable, and useless to the authorities. If Fanja's mother couldn't leave, Boris told his wife, he wouldn't.

"You're sacrificing yourself for my family," Fanja argued.

"No," Boris said, "if we don't do anything, if we don't draw attention to ourselves, nothing will happen. It can't turn out that bad. We won't be murdered, will we?"[7]

Boris and Fanja were sent to Sobibor, in southeastern Poland. Before leaving Cioma at the Levetzowstrasse synagogue, Fanja had given him a postcard to mail to her friends at Wysocky's tailor shop:

> *My dear colleagues:*
> *I go joyfully in the hope of being together with my husband. Farewell all! I'm looking forward to seeing you again in good health.*
> *Yours,*
> *Fanny Schönhaus*

From Sobibor, Boris was taken to Majdanek, ninety-two miles to the south. There, he sent a postcard to his brother-in-law Meier who still lived in Berlin:

> *I have arrived here safely. Have you heard anything from Fanja? I've been looking for her everywhere. Cioma was right about everything. I'm glad he's not here with us. Farewell.*[8]

When Cioma saw the postcard, he couldn't figure out how his father had gotten it, or acquired the pen and ink with which to write, or gotten the card past the censors. Cioma didn't know that the Nazis permitted some mail from the "camps." The correspondence assured those left behind that they were fine or, at minimum, still alive.

That postcard from Boris was the last anyone heard from him. Even less was heard from Fanja.

A Brainless Hitler
and a Stupid Joke

Aside from a few friends and fewer relatives, Cioma was now alone in Berlin, a city that was a shadow of its former self. Butchers closed on Mondays, bakers on Tuesdays, other merchants on Wednesdays. For food, Berliners hoarded hens, rabbits, pigs, sometimes keeping them on their balconies. When the zoo was bombed, "we had meat coming out of our ears," a Berliner later recalled. "Many of the edible animals which had fallen victim to the air raids"—deer, buffalo, antelope, bear—"ended up in the pot. Particularly tasty were the crocodile tails; cooked tender in big containers, they tasted like fat chicken." The animals that Berliners used to gawk at when they were alive "provided hundreds of meals. Bear ham and bear sausage were a particular delicacy."

The feasts, while they lasted, were a respite from what was being served in some of Berlin's better restaurants. Borchardt on Französische Strasse—renowned for its international (mostly French) cuisine—dated back to 1853, when it boasted bitter oranges from the Himalayas, strawberries from Algeria, and ostrich eggs, game, and fruit from the estates of Prussian nobility. Otto von Bismarck was a regular customer, and Borchardt's finest dishes were delivered directly to the emperor, when there was one. Now Borchardt offered one basic dish: red cabbage, a mashed potato, and an unidentified cut of meat. Two soups could be ordered: vegetable consommé and a "special" soup whose provenance was as vague as the "meat" that was served with the main course. Borchardt was no better than a restaurant on Potsdamer Platz where, a journalist grumbled, he was served "little sausages of uncertain contents, each about the size of a cigar butt. Before the meat, they gave you a chalky, red, warm liquid called 'tomato soup.' With the meat, you get four or five yellow potatoes with black blotches on them."[1]

The blotches were as black as the general mood in the city. Berliners, a Danish writer lamented, suffered "dullness, anticipation, fear. It was a soulless existence. The war seemed perpetual. The flowers had gone, the books had been burnt, the pictures had been removed, the trees had been broken. There were no birds singing, no dogs barking, no children shrieking. There was no laughter and no giggling. No face ever lit up in a warming smile, no friendly kiss or hug. There was still the sky above, but it was often effaced by stinking, greasy carpets of voluminous black smoke"—fires from the latest air strikes, which were now beginning in earnest. Every day and everywhere in this once-great and once-beautiful city, Berliners tried to avoid "the glazed fear that was in everyone's eyes." Their cause, they knew, was close to lost.[2]

People were desperate to laugh, and the Nazis, from their very beginning, had done their best to stop them. A few weeks after they took over Germany, they passed a law that punished "untrue or grossly distorted statements" about the Reich (i.e., jokes) with a fine, or up to two years in prison, or both. A year later, the law was extended to include "hostile" remarks made in private. Whoever told them should have known better, and "could or should have reckoned with them becoming public."

Officially, fun was a crime, and laughing was a sin.

A vaudevillian trained his chimpanzee to give the Nazi salute whenever he saw someone, even a mailman, in uniform. He (the entertainer, not the chimp) was sent to jail, and the authorities banned any simian from giving the Nazi salute. The chimp was killed for offending the führer. When a woman told this joke to friends—Adolf Hitler and Hermann Göring are standing atop a radio tower in Berlin. Hitler says he wants to do something to put a smile on Berliners' faces. "So," Göring asks, "why don't you jump?"—a snitch reported her to the Gestapo. She was guillotined.

Despite the laws, the jailings, and the beheadings, the jokes continued—a release from tension, fear, and a nagging, gnawing terror that the war might never end, that they might not survive the day, that they might never see their loved ones again. People learned to tell jokes under their breath or whisper so quietly they were barely audible. Jokes were passed around like small treasures—mementos— from lives that people used to live and were no more: lives of some reason, some kindness, and some chuckling. Everything was ripe for jokes as long as the Gestapo or snitches didn't hear you. There were jokes about food, and about the Gestapo, and about what Germany would be like after the war. All of them could cost someone his life:

A guy tried to commit suicide by hanging himself. The rope was so crummy it snapped under his weight. He stuck his head in the oven, but his gas was shut off between two and five in the afternoon. Then he tried living on his rations. He was dead in a week.

In the middle of killing some Jews, a Gestapo agent shouts to one of them, "You almost look Aryan so I'll give you a chance. I wear a glass eye. It's not easy to tell which one it is. If you can figure out which eye is glass, I'll let you go."
"The left one!" the Jew answers.
"How'd you know," asks the German.
"It looks so human," the Jew retorted.

One German says to another, "Tell me, what are you going to do after the war?"

"I'm finally going to take a vacation," his friend says, "and see all of Germany."

"And what are you going to do in the afternoon?" the other German asks.

In the first year of their rule, the Nazis issued 3,744 citations for "malicious attacks on the government of national renewal." A lot of law enforcement wasted on jokes, japes, and jests.

That didn't stop Cioma. He loved to retell a joke he'd heard from a friend:

A woman goes into a fish shop and asks for an Adolf Hitler herring. The shopkeeper shakes his head, saying they haven't got an Adolf Hitler herring. The woman shouts, "Surely you've got a Bismarck herring, haven't you? Just take the brains out of that herring, and you've got an Adolf Hitler herring." [3]

A brainless herring.

A brainless Hitler.

A stupid joke.

Cioma knew the risk he was taking, but he was undeterred. He needed to smile and he needed to laugh. Everyone did.

Maybe the day Cioma needed to smile the most was the day he said goodbye to his parents at the Levetzowstrasse synagogue. When he returned to his aunt and uncle's apartment at Munzstrasse 11, they weren't too happy to see him. They'd hoped for some quiet without him around. He was always coming home after Jews' curfew: 9:00 P.M. in the summer, 8:00 P.M. in the winter. He hardly ever wore his yellow Star of David. He was nothing but trouble, and if he kept acting like this, he'd get everyone into trouble. Still, he told Uncle Meier and Aunt

Sophie and his grandmother what happened at the synagogue, and they gave him a bowl of soup for dinner, and his grandmother came into his bedroom and consoled him as he was going to sleep. It had been a rough day, and Cioma had to be up early for his 6:00 A.M. shift at Genschow's. Work stopped for no one. Especially a Jew.

Cioma was bored at Genschow's. He filed rifle barrels. Some were good; he kept them. Some were bad; he threw them away. Some he sabotaged so carefully and so subtly that soldiers on the front lines could never trace their misfiring rifles to a nineteen-year-old Jew who worked in a munitions factory that they'd never heard of that was somewhere in Berlin. Cioma sabotaged sparingly, knowing that the art of the saboteur depended as much on the quality of his sabotage as on its quantity. If he sabotaged every submachine gun he worked on, he'd easily be found out. Sometimes, sabotaging a rifle barrel was all that kept Cioma awake on the job, providing the mischief he always craved.

Somehow, the mail in Berlin never stopped. Through snow, sleet, hail, and air raids, through streets that were cratered, potholed, and rubbled with bricks and mortar from buildings that had been standing only the day before, the mail kept coming, even when you didn't want it to come. Coming home one day from another twelve-hour shift at Genschow's, Cioma found two letters lying on his uncle and aunt's parquet floor, left there by the mailman who'd slid them through the mail slot on the apartment door. One letter was for Uncle Meier and Aunt Sophie: they were being sent to Theresienstadt—the "good camp," the "camp" where Jews were supposedly well fed and well treated; produced plays, music recitals, wrote dramas, and published poetry; and where a delegation from the Red Cross would be fooled the next year when the Nazis planted gardens, painted the houses and barracks in which their prisoners lived, and let them put on sophisticated performances for the visiting dignitaries. Once the guests left, the Jews were loaded onto trains bound for the killing fields. Of course, Uncle Meier and Aunt Sophie knew nothing about this.

They were pleased to board the train that took them to this so-called paradise. They were not seen again.

The other letter was for Cioma's grandmother. There'd be no Theresienstadt for Marie Bermann. Not for a while. Grandmother Marie was going to the nursing home at the six-hundred-bed Jewish Hospital at Iranische Strasse 2, three miles from Uncle Meier and Aunt Sophie's apartment. The hospital was one of the Nazis' great anomalies. It never closed during the war. (The Nazis kept the hospital open for their convenience. The only hospital in Berlin that was treating Jews, it was the one place where Jews who were forced to work for the Nazis could be treated if they became ill. Keeping sick Jews here also protected Germans from "Jewish diseases"—Nazis claimed Jews had their own diseases. Isolating them prevented ordinary Germans from being contaminated.) As food shortages worsened, vegetables were planted where the hospital once had large gardens for flowers, and as more bombs fell and not one touched the hospital, a nearby dairy farmer believed that the God of the Jews was protecting the facility. With the hospital's permission, he began grazing his cows on the hospital's broad lawn, certain that they would also be divinely protected. Even if that didn't occur, keeping the cows in what was essentially the hospital's backyard provided fresh milk for the hospital's staff and patients. That was divine protection. For the Jews.[4]

In June 1942 the Nazis began "transporting" more Jews from the nursing home. Many were told they were going to Theresienstadt. They didn't know that 89 percent of the hospital's Jews who were taken to Theresienstadt died there. And that those who didn't were taken to Auschwitz.

We can't say if Cioma's grandmother died at Theresienstadt or at Auschwitz. We can say with greater certainty that she experienced her last semblance of kindness and compassion at the nursing home. And that she would have been proud of Cioma, her grandson whom she'd consoled after he'd said goodbye to his parents at the Levetzowstrasse synagogue. Cioma was determined to elude his grandmother's killers before they became his.[5]

12

He Took the Job

Cioma's twelve-hour shifts in the armaments factory were exhausting, but there were benefits. They just weren't what everyone else was getting. Everyone doing forced labor was paid a fraction of what Aryans received, and no one got a vacation, holidays, sick leave, or extra pay if they worked on weekends or put in extra hours on a regular working day. What Cioma considered a benefit meant more to him than any of these: he was exempt from the "transports," and he felt safe enough to join his grandmother in the truck that took her to the nursing home to which she was sent. He also walked with his aunt and uncle to the "collection point" on Gross Hamburger Strasse, where they stayed for a few days before leaving for Theresienstadt.

A fifteen-minute walk from their apartment, the collection point was part of the oldest Jewish compound in Berlin: a Jewish school, the city's first home for elderly Jews, and a Jewish cemetery where some graves dated back to 1672. The nursing home and the school were now holding pens for Jews who were on their way out of the city. Euphemistically, the Nazis called them Judenlager, a "camp for Jews," though by now almost everyone knew what "camp" meant. They also hadn't scrubbed the lettering from the stones above the school's front portico: Knabenschule der Jüdischen Gemeinde (the Jewish Community

School for Boys). There were now no boys, and no school, and the tombstones in the cemetery next to the school would be removed in a year or two to reinforce air raid shelters. Rooms in the home for the elderly where most of the Jews stayed for a day or two had no tables, no desks, and no chairs. The Jews slept on floppy mattresses with no sheets or pillows. Surely some of the Jews who passed through on their way to Theresienstadt (or worse) wondered, if only briefly: If conditions on Gross Hamburger Strasse were this dreadful, what would the "model camp" they'd heard so much about be like? For now, it was better not to guess about such things. What they already knew was bad enough.[1]

Cioma now had his aunt and uncle's apartment to himself, though the only rooms available to him were his bedroom, the bathroom, and the kitchen. The Gestapo had sealed off the other rooms. In a city with a housing shortage, this was cruel. Vacant rooms were increasingly scarce as more apartment buildings were bombed into rubble and dust. Sealing off rooms let the Gestapo determine, to some extent, who received them. It also kept rooms unavailable to Jews. Every day, more Jews were going underground. With fewer rooms available for these U-boats, as the hidden Jews called themselves, there'd be no rest for them at this address, or the next one, or the one after that.

Cioma didn't have to worry about this. Exempt from "transports," he could live openly, and legally, in his aunt and uncle's apartment. Still, he was terrified that someday he might not be so well protected from the Nazis. He might be a skilled worker at Genschow's, but Jews were being picked up on the street for the smallest infraction. Or for no infraction. Being a Jew was crime enough.

Cioma's days had a routine. His alarm woke him in the morning. He went to work. He returned from work. He barely saw anyone, and there was hardly anyone to see. That changed one day as he was walking toward the S-Bahn station in Alexanderplatz to catch a train to Genschow's. Passing Hertie, a massive department store, Cioma saw someone who looked familiar enjoying the displays in the shop's tall ground-floor windows.

The longer Cioma looked at the young man, the more he realized it was Det Kassriel, his friend from Wysocky's who'd taken him drinking at the Hotel Kaiserhof. Det used to say his outings at the Kaiserhof would help him look confident and assured if he ever went into hiding. From what Cioma saw, Det's rehearsals had paid off.

Cioma walked up to Det casually, like they were old friends. Which they were. Acting like he was surprised to see Det might attract attention, and no Jew wanted to attract attention in Berlin in 1942.

"Det," Cioma said calmly, "how are you doing? What are you up to?"

Anyone overhearing this innocent greeting would have thought these were two old friends catching up with each other.

"I'm tailoring," Det said, adding in a voice so low that Cioma could hardly hear him, "and living illegally."

"Where are you living?" Cioma asked.

"At home," Det said.

"Not the best hiding place," Cioma mused.

"It's the best I've got," Det explained.

"Then move in with me," Cioma suggested impulsively. "I have a large flat. I'm by myself. No one will look for you there, and you'll be all right."[2]

Det moved in the next day. Cioma was relieved he had company, particularly as his world was shrinking. Familiar people were gone. Familiar places were banned to him. Genschow's was slowly being emptied of people he knew and people he liked. And like a blessing, one of the few times he'd wandered around Alexanderplatz, he had bumped into an old and trusted friend, a sign that coincidences still happened, and many remained capable of gladdening and delighting him.

Cioma was one of the few Jewish workers left at Genschow's. Sometimes, that didn't work out too well for him. One guy picked a fight with him: he didn't like Jews. Other workers were always telling Cioma to work faster. To them, Jews—" slow and lazy"—were taking their time with everything. But then there was Cioma's supervisor, Mr. Ackermann, who'd taught him how to sabotage the rifle barrels he was making. And there was a Jew, Walter Heyman, who never sabotaged anything. Heyman had another specialty, one that was his own peculiar secret. In Berlin, certain secrets meant certain death.

A former journalist, Heyman was a head shorter than Cioma. A missing front tooth caused him to lisp, and his hair glistened from all the oil that was in the air in the machine room, where he worked. Heyman liked Cioma, and he liked talking with him. Or to be more exact, he liked teaching him, often about matters deep and profound, the kind not usually discussed by workers in munitions factories anywhere, especially in Germany, where factory workers tried not to give anyone reason to suspect they were less than model citizens, questioning nothing and complying with everything.

On their occasional walks or in conversations on park benches (where Heyman and Cioma hid their yellow Stars of David—park benches were off-limits to Jews), Heyman taught Cioma about philosophy, like Friedrich Nietzsche's idea that old, entrenched ways had to make way for the new, the radical, the humane. "That which is falling, deserves to be pushed," Hyman quoted to Cioma, encouraging him to resist the Nazis the best he could. He tried to explain why the world hated Jews, and why this might never end. Heyman traced antisemitism as far back as the patriarch Abraham, who'd rebelled against the idols his father worshipped, idols so fragile that Abraham, as a boy, could smash them with a hammer. Abraham's God, more powerful than all of his father's idols put together, ruled over the sky, the heavens, the universe, and everything beyond that. All life and all beings fell under His domain. Worshipping Him, Heyman told Cioma, was fine. But saying that your god—the Jewish God—was the only God risked making you seem arrogant and smug, and that could make you very unpopular. This, Heyman said, was the price of being chosen, the price that hardly anyone talked about.

One morning after their shift ended, Heyman was waiting for Cioma outside the factory. It was raining. Heyman made room for Cioma under his umbrella and picked up where he'd left off when they were last together: believing in an all-powerful God could make you feel "invincible" at the same time as it made you "vulnerable." Like when the Jews had fought Rome centuries ago. Rome then had the most powerful army in the world. The Jews lost. Ever since, they'd been kicked out of one country after another, nearly wiped out in massacres, slaughters, and pogroms.

This was the winner-as-loser school of theology. Being God's chosen people sounded great, but all the Jews received for the honor was suffering, persecution, and tottering, always it seemed, on the brink of extinction. This, Heyman told Cioma, was "why we fight for our survival."

Survival, in fact, was why Heyman was spending so much time with Cioma, teaching him about history and religion and forging a trust that was rare these days. "Schönhaus," Heyman declared, getting finally to his point after all their meetings and discussions and constant looking over their shoulders, "you went to a college for applied art. You were trained as a graphic designer. I know a woman who's determined to save Jews from being deported. She needs a graphic artist who can forge documents. Do you think you can do it? Would you like to contact her?"

With barely a pause and barely a thought, Cioma said yes. He'd heard about enough Jews who needed saving, who'd hidden in back rooms, cold sheds, or drafty attics, who'd wandered the streets—desperate and alone—looking for their main chance and never finding it. Jews whom no one helped or were betrayed or who died by their own hands or by the Gestapo or the SS. It was time, Cioma knew, that he helped someone. He couldn't save his parents. Maybe he could save someone else.

Heyman gave Cioma the name and address of the woman who wanted to meet him: Edith Wolff. She lived with her parents at Kaiseralle 79. Her father, Theodore Wolff, had been a journalist at what had once been a flourishing liberal newspaper, *Berlin Tageblatt*. The Nazis shut it down in 1939. Walter Heyman, Cioma's "tutor" from Genschow's, had worked at the *Tageblatt* with Theodore Wolff.[3]

Kaiseralle 79 was in Friedenau, a neighborhood in southwest Berlin that had appealed to writers and artists since it was founded in 1871. Rosa Luxemburg had lived a few blocks to the east of Edith's apartment building, Rainer Maria Rilke a few blocks to the west, and Kurt Tucholsky, the best satirist in Germany during the 1920s and 1930s, had lived in the same building as Edith. Friedenau's four town squares, some with fountains and all with benches, encouraged a neighborly friendliness. The kind of people who lived there—poets, journalists, musicians, composers—thrived in their little bohemia, figuring their distance from the rest of the city provided a buffer from some of the Nazis' madness. It didn't.[4]

Cioma visited Edith after a night shift at Genschow's. Edith's mother greeted him coldly, and her father shut the door to his office. Both wanted nothing to do with him. Their fear was palpable. At first, Edith didn't impress Cioma. "She's small and insignificant looking," he thought. "Her hair looks like she cut it herself." Quickly, Edith's "radiant smile" and her confidence won him over. She was small, but there was no denying she was "the kind of person who knows her mind exactly." Edith took Cioma into the kitchen and introduced him to Jizchak Schwersenz, whose glance was "penetrating" and speech was "hurried." Jizchak impressed Cioma, but not as much as Edith had. It was clear she was the one "in control of the situation."[5]

Edith and Jizchak were an odd couple. Jizchak—at twenty-seven years old, eleven years younger than Edith—was balding and taller than Edith by almost a foot. Skinny and intense, he was the model of the Nazis' idea of a stereotypical Jew: wire-rim glasses, a mustache that barely covered his upper lip, and the slim carriage of someone who rarely lifted anything heavier than books. Jizchak's strength was his intellect, not his brawn. Edith was different. With her oval face, hair swept back from her forehead into a short bob, and a smile that rarely left her, Edith was welcoming, friendly. Cioma liked both of them. Especially Edith.

Edith's father was Jewish. Her mother was Christian. Edith—everyone knew her as "Ewo"—had been raised a Protestant. In 1933 Edith converted to Judaism. She was nineteen years old. Her conversion was as much a political act as a moral one: she converted to express her solidarity with Jews. As she began learning Jewish traditions, prayers, liturgies, and values, Judaism nourished her, enriched her, thanks greatly to her good friend Jizchak, who was her teacher as well as the leader of several Jewish youth groups in Berlin. When the Nazis shut them down, Jizchak ran a Jewish school that, somehow, he convinced Nazis was a horticultural academy. The school lasted until Jews were banned from teaching anywhere in Germany. At that point, every Jew over the age of fourteen had to do forced labor—if the Nazis could find them.

They couldn't find Jizchak. He went into hiding in August 1942, reluctantly and unhappily. It was Edith's idea. "Only this way can you save the children," Edith told him. "We'll fight Hitler with every life we save."

Edith and Jizchak knew they had to resist even more after several incidents occurred, all of them soon after the New Year began. Edith's father was soon sent to Auschwitz. Edith never saw him again. On February 27 the Gestapo rounded up almost ten thousand Jews who were working in factories in Berlin. Most were sent to Auschwitz. Edith was safe: an aunt had removed her name from the official registry of the Jewish community. Now she was "just" a Mischling—a half Jew—with a Protestant mother and a Jewish father. And Jizchak, of course, was nowhere to be found. He'd been hiding since August.[6]

The last incident that convinced Edith and Jizchak they had to resist occurred in late February when Albert and Johanna Kleinberger, Edith's neighbors, visited her. They were elegantly dressed, which was odd, and "rather excited," as Edith later wrote. "They had come to say goodbye as if they were going on a trip. They told us that they intended to have a very good meal with music and wine. They had received the 'list'"—a deportation order—"and had acquired what they called 'the remedy' a while ago. We understood immediately that this remedy was poison and their 'trip' was a suicide. The only thing we could do was shake their hands in silence and wish the couple, from our hearts, a good voyage to the world beyond. Three days later, their bodies were found in their apartment."[7]

A few days after the Kleinbergers died by suicide, Edith and Jizchak formed Chug Chaluzi (Pioneer Circle): the only Zionist youth group that was organized in Germany during the war, and the only group that provided food and hiding places for children and teenagers. Chug Chaluzi saved thirty-three youngsters out of its forty, maybe fifty members. It was also the only group whose leader was saved by one of Cioma's forgeries. Without Cioma, Jizchak probably wouldn't have survived. And without Jizchak, those thirty-three youths wouldn't have survived.[8]

Edith found places for the children in Chug Chaluzi to hide, usually in her friends' apartments. Jizchak taught the children with a purpose that was new to him. "What good would it have done for our goals of Zionism and the pioneering life," he asked after the war, "if we had survived without strengthening our Jewish consciousness?" Every subject had a reason for being taught, and every day had a subject, and every future—for there had to be a future—was grounded in knowledge and tradition and in all that could flourish from them. On Sundays, the youngsters in Chug Chaluzi hiked and played sports. On Mondays, they attended cultural events—concerts, operas, or films. Jizchak often acquired tickets by standing all night outside a box office. A clever ploy: anyone passing by would assume he was waiting to be the first in line when the box office opened the next day.

On Tuesdays, Jizchak taught Hebrew and English; on Wednesdays, the history of Palestine and Zionism; on Thursdays, the Bible;

on Fridays, he and the youngsters planned their next week. Saturdays were devoted to reading the play or opera they would see that Monday; discussing politics, Jewish history, and literature; and praying, often for relatives and friends who had vanished. No one in Chug Chaluzi was sure what happened to anyone after they left. Or maybe they didn't want to know what happened.[9]

The Nazis caught some members of Chug Chaluzi. They were deported and killed. Some, like fourteen-year-old Alfred Avraham-Bernstein, were taken in after their parents were sent "away." Accepting Alfred was no problem: Jizchak knew him and liked him. But there was a catch: Alfred wanted Edith and Jizchak to take in his sister. She was nine years old—too young to be expected to lie if she was caught. After long discussions, Edith and Jizchak accepted Lottchen— "A sweet child," Jizchak later wrote, "very quiet, but wise for her age." In case she was caught, Edith taught Lottchen to say that her home had been bombed, her parents had been killed, and she was wandering the streets because she had nowhere to live. Edith was Lottchen's primary caregiver, helped occasionally by one of the older boys in Chug Chaluzi, Heinz Linke. When Edith was arrested in June 1943, Heinz became Lottchen's only caregiver.

In 1944 Jizchak escaped to Switzerland. Edith survived eighteen of Hitler's prisons and "camps" and joined Jizchak in Zurich in 1950. Three years later, they moved to Israel. Little Lottchen also survived the war. In 1955 she married Heinz Linke, who'd taken care of her for the two years that Edith was in a "camp."[10]

All Cioma learned that morning at Edith's apartment was that when Jizchak had been ordered to report for a "transport," Edith had insisted he hide. For that, Jizchak needed fake papers. Fast. Somehow Cioma would turn genuine discharge papers from the German army that Edith had acquired into discharge papers for Jizchak. If Cioma did this well, Jizchak would be the beneficiary of a talent Cioma didn't know he had: he'd never forged anything in his life. Cioma would either save Jizchak's life or end it if he botched things up.

In art school, Cioma had been taught perspective, portraiture, composition, proportion, color theory, and figure drawing—fine and necessary skills for an artist. He hadn't been taught to swap out photos—a new photo for one already on a government document—so anyone looking at it would think it had always been there. If he was caught, Cioma knew he'd be executed, sent to a "camp," or worked until he dropped, then killed. But he liked Edith and Jizchak, and he hated the Nazis, and he had faith that he could do what was new to him and help Jizchak. It was worth the risk, and worth the gamble, and was a way for Cioma to settle his score with the Nazis. He took the job, though he made no promises. "I'll try," he told Edith. "I've never done this, but I reckon I could manage."

"What do you want for it?" Edith asked.

"Nothing," Cioma said, then reconsidered. "Well, maybe one thing. Walter Heyman told me you have a room where people can hide if necessary. I don't need it yet. I might soon. I would be grateful for the address."

Cioma was asking about a small extra bedroom in the apartment of the cleaning lady who worked for Edith's family. Edith gave him the address: Taunussatrasse 29, a seven-minute walk from Edith's apartment.

"The room," Edith said, "is in great demand. If you need it, you'll get it."[11]

13

The Yard Sale
of the Century

B ack home, Cioma got to work. He now had a reason for being
and, specifically, a reason for being in Berlin. And he could put
his art training, brief as it was, along with his innate talent, to good
use. With that came a new way (other than sabotaging machine guns
at work) to resist what the Nazis had done to him and his family and
almost everyone he knew. Quite swiftly, that conversation with Edith
Wolff and Jizchak Schwersenz transformed Cioma. He'd gone from
being a cipher with few, if any ways to resist the Nazis to a twenty-
year-old with drive, determination, and tenacity, eager to join the long
tradition of his people: fighting tyranny, cruelty, malice. Beyond what
Cioma knew was happening to anyone who was sent "east," and beyond
Berliners' willful blindness when they saw Jews on the street with Stars
of David stitched onto their clothing, and beyond the synagogues
and shops that had been destroyed, and the everyday humiliations and
insults—beyond all that, a field of light was opening for Cioma, a blend
of revenge, hope, promise, and possibility.

Cioma's conversation with Edith and Jizchak had given him a
glimpse of a world he'd heard about, a world in which people hid, in

which they were clever and sly and, most of all and most admirably, refused to submit to the Nazis. These people were strong and they were brave. Like Edith and Jizchak. Their strength and courage had emboldened Cioma, and he was ready, on behalf of all those who'd vanished, to forge the military discharge papers for Jizchak.

But first he had to figure out how to do it.

Sitting at his desk in the apartment on Munzstrasse, Cioma sized up the work that lay ahead of him: he had to substitute Jizchak's photo for the one that was on the discharge papers that Edith had given him, and he had to be meticulous: the colors, shape, and other details of the government's official stamp—an eagle with twelve large feathers and twenty-four smaller feathers—which were partly on the photo and partly on the certificate itself, all had to line up precisely. If their alignment was off by a fraction of a millimeter, a sharp-eyed Nazi might spot his carelessness. After aligning Jizchak's photo with the portion of the Nazis' seal that was on the document, Cioma had to attach it to the certificate with the small eyelets that the Nazis had used for the previous photo.

The work was tiring and demanding. Never before did Cioma have to be so scrupulous, and never before had someone's life depended on every stroke of his brush. This was not an exercise in one of his art classes. This was a way to alter life. To preserve life.

Using a magnifying glass, a fine Japanese brush, and watercolor, which he mixed diligently to match the purple the Nazis used, Cioma copied the eagle and the swastika that were on the original photo. Then he found a small blank space on a page from the newspaper, licked it to make it damp, and pressed the paper against the copy he'd made of the stamp that was on the discharge papers. The newspaper retained a mirror image of Cioma's work. Next, he pressed the damp newspaper against the corner of Jizchak's photo that corresponded to the corner of the soldier's photo where the Nazis had stamped their eagle and swastika. Finally, Cioma pried open the eyelets that held the soldier's photo onto the certificate, removed the photo, and replaced it with Jizchak's. Next he squeezed the eyelets shut with the right amount of pressure so they'd retain their original shape.

With Jizchak's photo in place, he was now, for anyone who saw these papers, a soldier who'd been discharged from the army in which he'd never served.

Edith was thrilled when Cioma showed her the discharge papers. They were perfect. "Cioma," she said, "you can have the room at Frau Lange's whenever you want it. And here's another thing: Franz Kaufmann in Halensee is looking for a graphic artist. Here's his address. Go and introduce yourself to him. There's a lot to do."[1]

Cioma wanted to do a lot. But first he went back to his aunt and uncle's apartment. Det was waiting with dinner for him. Det's cooking was always an adventure, and Cioma never knew what to expect when he sat down for a meal. These days, Det was specializing in soups. His mushroom soup garnished with finely chopped parsley was especially tasty. Not so the soup he tried to make from a joint of a wild boar. After he had boiled and seasoned the joint, it was so tough that none of the knives in the apartment could cut through it.

Admitting that his improvisations in the kitchen could go only so far, Det said they should buy a cookbook. Cioma agreed that it was a good idea, but they were short on money. He'd been docked a week's wages at Genschow's after almost getting into a fight with someone who didn't like the fact that he was Jewish. Then Cioma took a good look around the apartment and realized they had "stuff from three well-equipped households in this flat"—his grandmother's, his aunt and uncle's, and whatever furnishings and clothing they'd brought over from his family's apartment on Sophienstrasse. "Let's turn all of this into money," Cioma proposed. They'd sell everything in the apartment, and the deliveryman who'd worked in Cioma's father's mineral water business would deliver the larger or heavier items to whoever bought them. The man still had his horse and wagon. Cioma would split the take with Det.

Det spread the word about the sale to the women in the market where he regularly shopped, proudly reporting to Cioma, "The ladies are keen on buying from us. They've got plenty of money, and most of what we have they can't get anywhere else"—clothing, jewelry, carpets, beds, mattresses, silverware, plates, pots, pans, cupboards, desks, umbrellas, linen, fur coats, a sewing machine, trunks, suitcases: the ordinary clutter of ordinary lives.

Clearing out the apartment went faster than expected. It was like a clearance sale at a well-equipped department store, or a yard sale in a small town where everyone knew everyone else. The women came, they brought their friends, and everyone brought money. In a few days, Cioma and Det went from being paupers to having more money than ever before—ten thousand Reichsmarks. With all that money, Cioma could stop working at Genschow's and go underground. Everyone knew that being a U-boat was risky: if you were caught, you were sent "away." Everyone also knew that *not* being a U-boat was risky: those people were sent "away," too. Cioma had to weigh which alternative would extend his life by a few weeks, or months, or more. He wasn't bargaining with the gods for much. Just for his life.

14

The Reluctant Forger

Cioma decided to keep working at Genschow's for now, making rifle barrels, sabotaging a few of them, staying as industrious as he could while staying true to himself, and trying to look like he cared about his job. He abhorred the tedium and some workers' mutterings that a Jew was among them. Cioma stayed. He had no choice. Genschow's was all that stood between him and a "transport," or deciding he was ready to hide.

Cioma still took walks after work with Walter Heyman, his slightly older friend who'd taught him about Jews' tenacity and history and had sent him to Edith Wolff when she needed someone to fake discharge papers for Jizchak Schwersenz. Heyman was not pleased with Cioma; Edith had told Cioma how to reach Franz Kaufmann, an anti-Nazi Christian who ran a small group that needed phony IDs for the Jews it was helping. Cioma hadn't contacted Kaufmann yet.

"Cioma," Heyman implored, "you're in the fortunate position of being able to help others. The papers you made for Jizchak were perfect. Edith can't get over it. With your talent, she thinks you should rescue more Jews. By working with Kaufmann, you can do that. Go and see him, please. Work with him. Make it clear to him that carefully planning this is as important as having the courage to do it. Otherwise, your life as a forger will be short. Anybody caught with an ID card that you forge will be interrogated by the police about where he got it, or about who swapped the picture or who copied the stamp. Not many people can keep a secret when their fingers are squeezed in a vise—unless they really don't know anything. Then there's nothing for them to give away. That's why nobody must know your real name or your address. That goes for Kaufmann, too."

Cioma had learned that not rushing into situations was the best way to survive. Just living in Berlin was a risk. Every day, more Jews were shipped out; every day, the Gestapo was finding more of the few thousand Jews who were still in the city, somewhere. The hunt was on, and Cioma didn't want to give the Nazis any reason to revoke his exemption from the "transports" that were leaving Berlin every day. But he respected Walter Heyman and he respected Edith Wolff, and if they wanted him to work with Kaufmann, then he owed them the courtesy of learning more about the man.

Heyman's last words about Kaufmann made him more intriguing to Cioma: "He's still the proper German official who hates anything illegal. He's a German, in the best sense of that word. Despite his illegal activities, he's the absolute soul of moral integrity."[1]

That's what Cioma needed to hear. He hadn't heard "soul," "moral," and "integrity" in the same sentence in a long time.

Franz Kaufmann had been helping Jews for over a year. Born a Jew in 1886, he'd converted to Christianity when he was in his early twenties, and received an Iron Cross after being wounded in World War I. Honorably discharged, he earned a law degree and entered government service, mostly administering and auditing finances, rising through the ranks, locally and nationally, and gaining responsibility and respect wherever he went. At first, the Nazis kept him in the government, protected by his marriage to a Christian. In 1936 they fired him, ruling that his conversion hadn't removed his Jewish "stain." With much time on his hands, Kaufmann studied theology at the University of Berlin and joined a Bible discussion group at St. Anne's Church in Dahlem, a neighborhood near his home. Not long after Kaufmann started attending

St. Anne's, its pastor, Martin Niemöller, was arrested for preaching against Hitler; his successor, Helmut Gollwitzer, continued in a slightly safer manner, with sermons focusing less on what the Nazis were doing to Jews than on how they were perverting Christianity: replacing the Bible with *Mein Kampf* and God with the führer. As the pace of Jewish "deportations" quickened, Kaufmann asked his friends in the Bible study group, "Where are our beliefs if we do not use them to relieve the persecuted? Should we live as if nothing has happened?" Kaufmann answered his own question: they'd "hide as many Jews as possible" and "save as many as possible. Every means is right."[2]

Everyone in the group was among the three-tenths of one percent of Germans who were helping the victims of the Nazis; each had their own motives for helping Jews. Kaufmann wanted to remain a good Christian. If he couldn't love the weak and the oppressed, then he was betraying Jesus. Helene Jacobs, the most determined woman in Kaufmann's circle, wanted to restore democracy as well as save Jews. "I'd lost my homeland," she said after the war. "I wanted to defend it." She helped Jews "for the sake of humanity, and because I was a patriot. I was ashamed of what the German people were doing."

Defending Jews let Helene witness decency and goodness when it was least expected. After learning that a Jewish friend had been ordered to board a "transport" the next day, Helene yelled, "Isn't anyone going to murder those Nazi bastards?" Helene's friend heard her outburst not as a rebuke but as a sign of hope, of decency and courage. Yet she still asked, "Should the last good German person I know be filled with hate?" That quieted Helene, as much to protect herself from her own fury as to bestow a gift upon her friend in their final hours together.[3]

Originally, the Kaufmann Circle helped Jews who had converted to Christianity, giving them food or clothing for whatever awaited them at the end of their train ride, and wafers and wine for makeshift communion once they reached that destination. Halfway through 1942, as more Jews were disappearing from Berlin, the Circle resolved to do more. They obtained food stamps for Jews, found hiding places for Jews, made sure Jews had identity cards. Some IDs came from members of St. Anne's who dropped theirs into the collection basket during services. It wasn't a crime to be careless. Everyone "lost" something. Those weren't enough. Kaufmann bought most of the IDs the Circle distributed from gangsters he met in bars or other dives. That upset him. He didn't like hanging out with such lowlifes. The best IDs had photos that vaguely resembled the Jew who'd be using it. Those were hard to find. What Kaufmann most needed was someone who could replace the photo that was on an ID with one of the Jew who'd be using it. He also needed someone whose handwriting, if needed on an ID, carried a flourish of authority. The work had to be impeccable, undetectable, perfect. One small error could endanger the person using it, the person who made it, and the person who arranged all this: Kaufmann. Franz Kaufmann didn't know it yet, but he needed Cioma Schönhaus.[4]

But Cioma wasn't ready for Kaufmann. Not yet. Cioma had faked only one document: the one for Jizchak Schwersenz. Though he'd been praised for it, Cioma wasn't sure he was capable of regularly forging papers and possessed the skills needed to convincingly alter the many kinds of IDs Germany was issuing: passports; military IDs, *kennkartes* (the most official domestic identity card), and *Postausweis* (IDs issued by the post office). All contained photos, signatures, and official stamps. The authenticity of the photo on IDs issued by the post office was confirmed by a postage stamp and two postmarks. Some of these IDs had fingerprints; some didn't. Turning every kind of ID into a piece of paper that would save someone's life was a challenge and a burden, and each required a different set of skills. Before he could work for Kaufmann, Cioma had to know he could fake such a wide range of documents. A heavy burden for a twenty-year-old. A heavy burden for anyone.[5]

The opportunity for Cioma to see if he had the right stuff came on a Sunday afternoon. Invited for coffee at the apartment of a friend, Thesi

Goldschmidt, Cioma found himself the only male among three women. One of them, Marie, was secretary to the military administrator of Warsaw. As they sat around a table enjoying strudel and real coffee that Marie had brought from Warsaw, she confided to everyone: "You should see what they're doing to the Jews in Poland. I'm not allowed to talk about it, but I'll tell you one thing. Make sure you're not sent there."

"We *are* making sure," Thesi said. "Take Cioma here. His parents have been evacuated, he's living in his family's flat and he sold all the furniture that was in it so he can survive. He's about to go underground."

That impressed everyone, especially Tatjana, another of Thesi's friends, who asked Cioma if anything was left in his apartment. Maybe an iron? She needed one. Cioma still had an iron. Tatjana handed Cioma her card and asked him to bring it to her apartment in a few days.

This was a good day for Cioma. He was drinking real coffee, savoring tasty strudel, and he'd made a sale. When he and Det went underground, they'd need every pfennig.

When the women left and Cioma and Thesi were alone, she took him into the kitchen. Cioma was surprised to find a gentleman boiling water for tea. The man exuded a certain authority. Other people should be making tea for him.

Thesi introduced Cioma to Hans Joseph Meyer, the owner of several flour mills in East Prussia. The Nazis had brought Meyer to Berlin to help them figure out the complicated financing he'd arranged for his businesses. Until that was straightened out, Meyer was still the owner, and his mills couldn't be sold to an Aryan. Meyer was taking his time, hoping the Allies would win the war before the Nazis seized his properties. Worthless to the Nazis at that point, he knew he'd promptly be sent "east."[6]

Thesi had already told Meyer that Cioma knew how to copy signatures, fake Nazi stamps, and swap photos on IDs. Meyer needed Cioma. The signature of a Nazi official from Meyer's hometown was on one of the documents he'd brought with him to Berlin. Meyer wanted Cioma to forge the signature on another sheet of official Nazi stationery that Meyer had swiped. On this, he'd already written some figures regarding the value of his properties. He also wanted Cioma to forge a "stamp" on the stationery. Cioma left Thesi's apartment with two sheets of stationery in his pocket: one had a signature, the other would soon have a "signature"—the one faked by Cioma.

Back home, Cioma set up his forging "studio" on the kitchen table, the only table he and Det hadn't sold. A magnifying glass helped Cioma copy the signature of the Nazi official, then copy the Reichsadler, the Nazis' eagle with wings spread out at right angles to each other. The eagle was perched on top of a swastika, the Nazis' totem, their cross, and their benediction. Just as Cioma had done when faking an ID for Jizchak Schwersenz, he spit on newsprint to make it more absorbent, pressed that against the copy he'd made of the eagle, then pressed that against the blank stationery. The eagle, reversed a minute ago, now faced the left, its right direction. By turning a blank sheet of stationery into as official a looking a document as Meyer could have acquired from a Nazi official back home, Cioma proved to himself that what he'd forged for Jizchak Schwersenz wasn't a fluke. He was as good a counterfeiter as anyone in Berlin.

A few days later, Cioma showed Meyer his handiwork. Meyer was amazed. Everything looked real. Everything was fake.

Meyer asked Cioma how much he wanted for his work. Cioma didn't answer. He couldn't answer. He hadn't done this for money. Realizing he'd embarrassed Cioma, Meyer offered to introduce Cioma to someone who would be "very useful" to him: "You'll get more out of knowing him than anything I can pay you." Cioma had no idea who he was talking about.

The next Sunday, at Meyer's apartment, Cioma met Ludwig Lichtwitz—a heavyset man who smiled often and talked faster than he thought. Ludwig was in the same business as Cioma: forging. Except he'd been forging longer than Cioma and had a few things to teach him. He didn't waste any time. Without stopping for pleasantries, Ludwig jumped right in and showed Cioma two military IDs. Both were blank, with no stamps, no photos, no signatures, no names. If Cioma could fill in one of these with all the stamps that were usually on military IDs, Ludwig would give him the other one for himself.

In the meantime, Ludwig invited Cioma to visit his workshop at Waldstrasse 54, in the working-class neighborhood of Moabit. The Embassy of Afghanistan was renting a former grocery store for Ludwig to use as a studio.

"Old friend," thundered Ludwig as if he and Cioma had been pals for years, "we have a lot to discuss. Let's meet in two days. OK?"[7]

Cioma knew everything was about to change, as if enough hadn't already. His father was gone. His mother was gone. His aunt, uncle, and grandmother were gone. Many of Cioma's friends and their relatives were gone. Gone was the coziness of Sophienstrasse—a quiet street in a quiet neighborhood that looked out for its own. Gone was a sense of community, security, and safety. Those, in fact, had vanished a long time ago.

Cioma decided he'd stop working at Genschow's, stop living legally at Munzstrasse 11, and start living underground, maybe a few nights in one place, then a few nights in another; sometimes using his real name, sometimes a fake one, then more fake ones; not sure whom to trust while always aching to trust someone. That was the accord Cioma reached with himself, an accord that was equally exciting and terrifying, and that offered a faint promise of hope: hope for him and hope for anyone he helped.

Cioma got on the subway to meet Franz Kaufmann. After all this time, Cioma was ready for him. He'd forged documents for Jizchak Schwersenz and Hans Joseph Meyer. He was sure that the quality of his work was high, and he could do it consistently. No more procrastinating and no more stalling. Reluctant for weeks, he was reluctant no more.

PART THREE

INTO THE DARK

15

"Better than
Dueling with Sabers"

Cioma biked over to Franz Kaufmann's. The ride wasn't arduous, though Cioma's fears—the fears that just about any Jew had while crossing Berlin in 1942—may have made the thirty-seven-minute bike ride seem like a reconnaissance mission into enemy territory, with Cioma always on the lookout for random ID checks or for someone guessing that he was Jewish and had no right to be on a bike. Jews had been forbidden to own or use bicycles since 1938.

Kaufmann's neighborhood, Halensee, had been founded in 1880 as a cozy outpost of villas and small apartment buildings. At first, its greatest attraction was a fourteen-acre lake and the dense woods surrounding it. Families traveled here from other parts of Berlin to picnic along the shore, relaxing as frogs croaked, children waded in the water, and the heat of the city seemed a planet away. Then came Luna Park, the largest amusement park in Europe. Fifty thousand people came every day for restaurants, gourmet and not-so-gourmet; and carousels, water slides, a life-size replica of an Assyrian palace, fireworks every night; and a sideshow featuring Laplanders, Native Americans, Ceylonese, Eskimos, and bare-breasted women from the South Pacific who

wore only loincloths and garlands of bright flowers and did nothing
all day but smile and play simple games to amuse themselves, proof to
the fairgoers that the rest of the world was full of "simpletons," and no
place could match the "sophistication" of Europe, the most advanced
continent on earth.[1]

The park had been razed now, a victim of the Great Depression.
Nothing was left but nostalgia and memories. One incident that was
hardly mentioned was that Adolf Hitler had visited the park in 1923,
after driving up from Munich to raise funds for the Nazi Party. The party
was then banned in much of Germany, and Hitler, its chairman, could
be arrested any minute. Only his inner circle knew what he looked like.
Hitler wanted to keep it that way and refused to even be photographed.

Taking an afternoon off, Hitler and some of his friends went to
Luna Park, had a few beers, and mostly watched women boxers spar
for a few rounds. Keeping pace with their feints and jabs, Hitler (who'd
never been in a fight in his life) declared that fighting with gloves was
"better than dueling with sabers." (He'd also never been in a duel.) The
day went smoothly until Hitler lunged at a newspaper photographer
who'd snapped some photos of him. George Pahl had seen Hitler once
before and hadn't forgotten his face. As Hitler tried to grab Pahl's
camera, Pahl held it safely behind his back. Somehow, Hitler persuaded
Pahl to hand over the film with Hitler's image on it. Pahl never said
why he did this. Knowing Hitler, threats were involved. Two years into
his political career, Hitler knew how to get his way.[2]

Cioma missed Luna Park, and he missed the fight between Hitler
and Pahl. But he didn't come to Halensee for water rides or to watch
a future dictator snatch a negative from a photographer who was just
doing his job. He'd come to meet Franz Kaufmann, whose small villa
at Kurfürstendamm 125 was set back from the street by a vest-pocket
garden: an oasis in a city that desperately needed one. Cioma rang the
bell then told the woman who opened the door that Edith Wolff had
sent him. "My husband is out," the woman brusquely declared. "Go

away." Cioma didn't. After a slight pause, Kaufmann appeared and greeted Cioma more decently than his wife had. "Come in," Kaufmann said with a smile. "I've been expecting you."

Kaufmann guided Cioma into a study furnished with heavy leather armchairs. Making himself comfortable, Cioma studied the man in front of him. Kaufmann's short cropped hair, large ears, sloping shoulders, and bulbous nose disappointed him. This was not the image of Kaufmann that Cioma had created in his imagination: debonair, inscrutable, just short of swashbuckling—the kind of resolute mien you need when fighting Nazis. Ultimately, Kaufmann's face was an affirmation that someone who looked so ordinary and banal was perfect for the job he'd chosen. With those looks, Kaufmann didn't stand out. That was good. More important was what he stood for.

Kaufmann walked over to a bookcase and came back with a sewing basket full of different colored yarn. Rummaging through it, he pulled out several IDs he'd received from members of his church. He next showed Cioma passport-sized photos of Jews who were scheduled to be "deported" or who were already hiding. By substituting these photos for what was already on various IDs, Kaufmann said, these people would be "safe when they're stopped in the street. If the card fits the owner in terms of sex, age and photo, then the strictest check in the world can't harm a hair on their head."

That was fine with Cioma, though he was having a hard time feeling comfortable with Kaufmann. The man was too direct, too perfunctory—all business and not one minute for getting to know each other. Maybe he was naturally shy and taciturn? Or maybe that's what happens when war consumes the little time we have for our lives and words get in the way of saving people who didn't deserve to die. Cioma didn't know, and from the way things were going, he wasn't going to find it out.

Kaufmann handed Cioma an ID and a small photo. Cioma's job was to swap the photo for what was already on the ID. "Schönhaus,"

Kaufmann said, "make a sample for me. If it's good, I'll give you a lot of work. The need is great. How much will you charge for each pass?"

Kaufmann was accustomed to paying people for their work. Ludwig Lichtwitz, the forger Cioma had recently met in Hans Joseph Meyer's apartment, was receiving one hundred Reichsmarks per forgery. Cioma was different. "At the moment," he told Kaufmann, he wanted "nothing" for faking IDs. "We got a lot of money from selling our household goods," Cioma explained. "We need ration cards. Edith Wolff said I could get one book a month from you."

"That's true," Kaufmann acknowledged. "But you said 'we'?"

"Yes, a friend and I are going underground together."

"Then you can have two ration books a month. When will I have the pass with the new photo in it?"[3]

Cioma promised Kaufmann he'd be back in two days. Then he left, exhilarated that he'd found a circle of like-minded people dedicated to saving Jews and disappointed that the legendary Franz Kaufmann, whom he'd heard so much about, looked so prosaic that if a Gestapo agent bumped into him on the street, he'd pick Kaufmann up, ask if he was okay, and give him a ride home, not suspecting that this dull, plain man was the ringleader of one of the city's most effective cells for helping the people the Nazis hated the most.

Two days later, Cioma returned with the ID he'd made, surprised that five Jews were sitting in Kaufmann's study. All of them, he'd learn in a minute, were getting ready to go underground. Without letting Cioma pause for a second, Kaufmann took Cioma straight into his office and shut the door. They needed privacy. From the folds of a newspaper he was carrying, Cioma pulled out the ID he'd made and handed it to Kaufmann. Cioma's attention to details impressed Kaufmann. "Good idea, that newspaper," he said. "You're right. You've got to use your head."

Kaufmann examined the ID. It was exactly what Edith Wolff had said Cioma would deliver: perfect and foolproof. No one would know it was fake. Relieved and pleased, Kaufmann went back to his study, this time with the ID. Cioma heard one of the Jews thank Kaufmann then leave. When Kaufmann returned, he explained what had just happened: neither Cioma nor the man who'd left had met the other or knew anything about him. In their mutual ignorance, neither could betray the other. These were the layers of security Kaufmann had devised: the forger didn't know whom he forged it for, recipients didn't know who had forged it for them, and Kaufmann—the only person who knew both of them—trusted himself to stay safe and keep his trap shut.

Kaufmann handed Cioma five IDs and five small photos for Cioma to swap with what was already in them. He also gave Cioma his "pay"—two books of ration coupons—one for Cioma, one for Det. Cioma was now on "salary" and on a schedule. Kaufmann told him to return with fake IDs the next Friday at six o'clock in the evening. Kaufmann would then give Cioma five more IDs to counterfeit, and Cioma would return the Friday after that with his handiwork. They would continue like this, week after week.

The meeting went well until Kaufmann addressed the misgivings he sensed Cioma had about this arrangement. Everything was foolproof, Kaufmann stressed quietly: "Schönhaus, it's possible that my villa and what looks like a normal life here is a better way of going about a conspiracy than if I met with my accomplices late at night in a dark place. The Gestapo is not trained in criminology. They think illegal activities only take place under cover of darkness, with participants going around in turned-up collars looking furtive. We do the opposite. I don't fit the Gestapo's preconceived ideas. That's what keeps us safe."[4]

Cioma left, not quite convinced that Kaufmann's way was the best way. He was still afraid that on his next visit, a Gestapo agent might open the door. And yet, Cioma knew he'd be back, with five freshly minted IDs hidden in the folds of a newspaper he'd be carrying.

At last, Cioma was ready to go into hiding. He'd delayed doing so for too long, despite Det urging him not to wait. "One day," Det kept saying, "they'll round up all the Jews at Genschow's without warning. Then it'll be too late." Cioma knew he was right. Yet leaving the world that he knew was almost paralyzing. Once Cioma went into hiding, there would be no going back: the Nazis didn't forgive Jews, especially a Jew who broke as many laws as Cioma was about to break. But he couldn't wait anymore. He'd painstakingly arranged everything he needed to be a U-boat—he had half of the ten thousand Reichsmarks he and Det had earned from clearing out his aunt and uncle's apartment, Franz Kaufmann had promised him coupons for food rations, and a room was waiting for him in the apartment of Mathilde Lange, the cleaning lady who worked for Edith Wolff's family.

There were two more reasons Cioma couldn't wait. He was getting careless. He'd recently lost the official ID the police had issued to him. A few weeks before that, he'd lost another one. He'd reported that loss. If he reported the second one, the police would be suspicious. On top of that, a letter had come from the Jewish Council of Berlin, ordering him to report to the association at 10:00 A.M. on September 30. "If you fail to keep this appointment," the letter threatened, "the severest measures will be taken." This wasn't a cordial invitation to discuss Talmudic hermeneutics with the erudite leaders of the Jewish Community Association. It was an invitation to board a "transport."[5]

The next morning, Cioma slept late. He wasn't going to Genschow's. He was never going to Genschow's. And he certainly wasn't reporting to the Jewish Council. It had taken Cioma a long time to appreciate Det's warning: "One day, it'll be too late." Cioma didn't want to be around when that day came.

Cioma and Det moved into the extra room in Frau Lange's apartment. Lange was a sweetheart: "A dear little old lady with white hair," Cioma said later, who behaved "like a nice old grandmother" toward him and Det. She was even nicer when Cioma handed her the modest rent she'd requested, and thrilled when Det, on their first night in the apartment, made coffee for the three of them—real coffee that Det probably bought on the black market. Cioma then spread out his forging tools on a long table in Frau Lange's dining room and set to work on a new ID for himself. When he finished, he was "Peter Schönhausen."[6]

After all their planning and scheming and hopes, Cioma and Det found that the mattress they had to share was so narrow that, when Cioma lay next to Det, he pulled himself as close as he could to the wall behind him so he wouldn't touch Det. Det was his friend and he didn't want anything to ruin that friendship. Cioma barely slept that night, or any night he attempted to sleep in that room with Det. Luckily, Cioma didn't have to share that dreaded mattress with Det for long.

Just how Cioma found his lovely new roommate came about when he visited Werner Schlesinger just before he went into hiding. Cioma's father had met Schlesinger while imprisoned for selling butter on the black market. The day he was released, Schlesinger visited Cioma and his mother, assuring them that Boris was not only fine but was one of the more respected prisoners, always trying to make life decent for them and help them feel comfortable. Boris sharpened dull razor blades so other prisoners could shave, collected scraps of soap so everyone could wash properly, and shared his daily ration of bread with prisoners who were hungrier than he was. Cioma and his mother nodded when they heard this: that sounded like Boris. He was always putting others before himself.

Schlesinger became the closest Cioma had to a father while his real one was imprisoned. That's why Cioma visited him before he went into hiding: he wanted Schlesinger to know why was about to stop seeing him. People "disappeared" all the time in Berlin; Cioma wanted Schlesinger to know he was disappearing for a good reason. Schlesinger appreciated Cioma's thoughtfulness. He didn't appreciate Cioma's instant fascination with Schlesinger's cousin who was visiting for a few days. Cioma almost gasped when he glimpsed Gerda. Her makeup was "showy," and her figure—or what Cioma could make of it—was "stunning." When she wandered off to another room, Cioma couldn't restrain himself. Gerda, he told Schlesinger, was "fantastic."

Schlesinger didn't waste a second. Don't go near her, he told Cioma. She was no good for him. She was no good for anyone. Only twenty-two years old, she was living with a sergeant, and when he was away with the army, she slept with other men. Many of them. "She'll come to a bad end," Schlesinger predicted. "Don't have anything to do with that girl." Cioma didn't care. Gerda soon came back into the room. In the few seconds they had with each other, she and Cioma agreed to meet the next day at a café on the Kurfürstendamm.[7]

Cioma chose well. Café Kranzler was one of Berlin's more fashionable spots. Located on a ritzy boulevard, it modeled itself after a Parisian café, with small round tables set out on the street. Its customers were either writers, painters, composers, or playwrights, or affluent and respectably bourgeois. By coming here, Cioma was telling Gerda he was worldly and sophisticated and not easily intimidated. Not even by Gerda's beauty.

Gerda looked even prettier than she had at Schlesinger's apartment, and Cioma enjoyed showing her off. It worked. "All the men," Cioma bragged later, "turned around to look at her."

Though Cioma hardly knew Gerda, he blurted out what he couldn't contain any longer: he would not get into bed with Det anymore. He was losing sleep, he was losing his mind, and if anything untoward happened between him and Det on that narrow mattress, he'd never forgive himself. Gerda had a solution: "You can sleep at my place." That was fine with Cioma. He'd wanted to sleep with her since he saw her at Schlesinger's. But, Gerda said, he couldn't join her until her boyfriend returned to the front in a few days. And after that, they'd still have to be careful. Most of Gerda's neighbors knew her, and they knew her boyfriend. If he heard that someone had stayed in the apartment while he was away, he might take the army pistol he always carried and track down Cioma. Maybe Gerda, too.

Cioma didn't care. He needed sleep, and he needed Gerda. Soon, he'd be living for his nights with her, nights of satisfaction and release, for pleasures with this beauty who, for reasons Cioma couldn't fathom, had chosen him from the many men who desired her.

16

"You Shall Be the Emperor of My Soul"

There wasn't much to Gerda's flat. It had one room. On the left side of the room was a double bed; on the right, a washstand with a mirror above it. Between them was a compact cooking nook. The first night Cioma was there, a sweat-stained felt hat, an army cap, an overcoat, and a heavy pullover hung on a coat rack near the door: unwanted reminders that Gerda had a boyfriend in the army, and that soldiers had tempers, pride, and guns, and Cioma might pay a price for whatever he did with Gerda. And that Gerda might pay a price for her pleasures with Cioma.

Gerda made a macaroni dinner for Cioma and herself, then washed, undressed, and lay across the bed—all in one fluid motion. There was a practiced art to her spontaneity: Gerda had done this with other men on other nights. She knew what she wanted, and she knew how to get it, and she knew what poses to strike so she'd be fulfilled before the night was over. But she wasn't blasé about it. That would drain these nights of some of their fun and most of their thrills.

Gerda waited for Cioma to join her. He couldn't. In his entire life, he'd seen only one woman naked—Evchen Hirschfeld, who'd worked at the tailor shop with Cioma's mother and seduced him (briefly and perfunctorily and emotionlessly) one night when everyone else was in bed. Their encounter was so quick Cioma barely knew it had begun, and so disastrous that they barely acknowledged each other afterward. Looking at Gerda's curves and thinking about her youth, Cioma decided she was nothing like Evchen. Gerda's skin was smooth and silky, her breasts firm and full. She was only a year older than Cioma, much closer in age to him than Evchen, who had a decade, maybe more, on him.

Gerda and Evchen differed in another way. Unlike Evchen, Gerda wasn't lying on the bed, waiting to teach Cioma what you do there. Evchen, knowing that her night with Cioma was his first with a woman, had patiently instructed him in undressing her and in every-thing that came after. Gerda, a very different woman on a very different night, had every reason to believe Cioma was experienced and skilled. In the short time she'd known him, he'd never failed to act worldly and wise beyond his years. Gerda didn't know this was the moment Cioma's charade would catch up with him: even he couldn't sustain his act any longer.

Gerda's patience was finally exhausted. "Get undressed and come here," she called out with some aggravation in her voice. Sliding between the covers, Cioma tried to do the little he remembered from those few minutes with Evchen. He tried, and tried again. He knew there was a war on, and Nazis were pounding the streets or knocking down doors looking for U-boats, and that he, like everyone in Berlin, had lost someone they loved or cherished or wished they'd treated better or regretted not apologizing to for their boorish and loutish behavior. There was much, in other words, that diverted Cioma's attention from Gerda, much as he desired her. He was sure they'd have reached their climax by now if it wasn't for everything else that was on his mind. The night he'd dreamed about was turning sour, full of limp embar-rassments that would be best not to tell anyone had ever happened.

"You bore me," Gerda mumbled. "Let's go to sleep."[1]

Slipping on her nightgown, Gerda rolled away from Cioma. For the rest of the night, Cioma lay next to Gerda, eyes wide open, unable to sleep. All he wanted was for the morning to come. In the light of day, he'd decide whether to leave, with his pride possibly still intact.

When dawn came, Gerda was less grumpy, and more generous, more tender, with Cioma. Taking him in her arms, Gerda lightly teased him: "You're a little show-off, aren't you? You're usually not afraid of anything. Why are you so frightened? Come here. I'll show you what we do." And she did.[2]

After that, Cioma was different. He knew what to do, he knew how to do it, and he did it well. His nights, and sometimes his days, with Gerda pleased both of them. Possibly, they pleased Gerda more than Cioma. She'd taught Cioma so well that he was now confident and adept, a fledgling lothario who was taking adventurous initiatives on his own. Gerda liked this new guy. Cioma liked him, too.

Not many women would have been so patient with Cioma, though, to give him his due, when sleeping with Gerda, he may have been spurred on by the satisfaction of cockolding a sergeant in the German army who was off risking his life for Adolf Hitler and his Reich while a Jew was taking his place next to his luscious girlfriend. Cioma's lust for Gerda was fueled by a different kind of lust: revenge against the Nazis. Any Nazi.

Cioma and Gerda settled into a routine. The nights were theirs. The days, he spent in the studio in Moabit where he and Ludwig Lichtwitz forged IDs while Gerda cleaned the apartment, cooked dinner, polished her nails (usually in the nude), and hummed all day long a popular tune that was sweeping Germany: "Du Sollstder Kaiser meiner Seele Sein" ("You Shall Be the Emperor of My Soul")—a celebration of what its composer called the "free country" of a woman's heart, a land where she could dream

a thousand tender thoughts of my love.
This is the land where I live
This is the empire that I will give to you . . .

The Austrian Robert Stolz wrote "You Shall Be the Emperor of My Soul" for his operetta *Der Favorit*, which swept Vienna in 1916. Nine years later, Stolz moved to Berlin, mostly to write music for films. He returned to Vienna in the 1930s, appalled by the Nazis, though he worked often in Berlin—that's where the money was. It was also where the Jews were. Stoltz used his trips to smuggle twenty-one Jews out of Germany in his limousine. His first passengers were a mother and her son and daughter, a five-year-old and a seven-year-old. After sedating her children, their mother laid them down on the back seat and lay next to them before Stoltz covered them with a thick carpet to muffle any sounds they might make. Crossing into Austria was no problem, not with swastikas Stolz's shrewd chauffeur had flying from the front fenders of the limo, and with border guards fawning over Stoltz once they saw the name on his passport. They sang a few bars from his music, asked for his autograph, and waved him through, no questions asked.[3]

Stolz eventually fled to New York City. He stayed for the duration of the war: one more refugee in a world full of them.

Stolz could have been describing Gerda in "You Shall Be the Emperor of My Soul," the song she loved to sing all day in her apartment. The heroine of his song declared her devotion to "the emperor" in her life, the man whose

wishes are orders for me
My soul, which will obey you,
I entrust entirely to you.

Gerda and Cioma had proven themselves to each other: she as a tutor, knowledgeable and patient; he as her student, keen to learn and more keen to perform. Their new test would determine how long they would be lovers. Berlin was not one of the more romantic cities in the world. It never had been—too gray and too stolid—and this year, it didn't even come close. Too many roundups and "transports." Too many lies and betrayals. And too little caring, decency, and honor—collectively, the measures of a person's goodness, and the measure of a nation's glory. Of the many ways that Gerda and Cioma could be pulled apart, the most probable may have been the flagging passions of one of them for the other. That was common, in wartime or in peace. In this case, though, it would have been accompanied by a significant drawback: someone might lose the emperor of her dreams.

One afternoon at a fine restaurant, Gerda and Cioma ate and drank like the gourmands they weren't, ordering large oysters from the Netherlands and a bottle of Gewürztraminer, an excellent white wine from Alsace, a region in eastern France that France and Germany had been fighting over for centuries. Cioma—a big spender in a place where spending was easy—didn't care that the lunch wasn't covered by his food ration coupons. His wallet was jammed with money he'd made from the yard sale in Aunt Sophie and Uncle Meier's apartment. When the waiter brought over the check, Cioma reached for his wallet. It wasn't in his pants pocket, or his jacket pocket, or his briefcase. All Cioma remembered was that he'd last had it when he paid for a tram ticket earlier that day for Gerda and himself. If he was lucky, someone had turned it into the office at the tram station.

Leaving Gerda in the restaurant, Cioma raced to the tram depot. A wallet had been turned in, but the clerk needed proof it was Cioma's. "Look at the ID card that's in the wallet," Cioma politely suggested. "My photo's on it." The clerk looked at the card. Indeed, it had a photo of the breathless young man who was standing in front of him. As the clerk handed Cioma his wallet, Cioma pressed fifty Reichsmarks into his palm as thanks. The clerk protested that was too much. Cioma, a bit giddy after all this, insisted the man keep it. He did.

Cioma returned to the restaurant more slowly than when he'd run to the tram office. He'd have been wise to walk faster. A man in a uniform—a member of the SS—had taken Cioma's place at his table. The SS agent and Gerda were smiling and talking quietly. As Cioma approached the table, the agent stood up, said to Gerda, "Until next Monday evening, eight o'clock," and walked away without a glance at Cioma.[4]

As Cioma sat down, Gerda explained that being friends, in her way, with the Nazi was her idea of an insurance policy, one that would make her and Cioma safer. The agent would protect Gerda, and she would protect Cioma. They'd be untouchable. Cioma walked out of the restaurant, furious that Gerda couldn't see beyond her body's power to pull men in, and at her stupidity—her frustrating, willful, obtuse stupidity—in not knowing that she needed to keep some men away. After nine years of the Nazis running Germany, Gerda had learned nothing. She was as blind, and as dumb, as she was beautiful.

Cioma went back to Frau Lange's and to sharing a narrow mattress with Det. He never saw Gerda again. Life in Berlin was hard enough without Cioma having to recover from his first serious love affair. But he learned an important lesson. Werner Schlesinger was right: Gerda's character was "terrible." There was no doubt she'd "come to a bad end."

Actually, Gerda's life did end badly. She was arrested on June 8, 1943, and killed at Auschwitz two months later. The truth is that Gerda may not have been "Gerda." Most likely, her real name was Ellen Hirschfeld, though while in hiding she usually called herself "Ellen Sheuer" or "Ellen Dimsack." U-boats often changed their names to throw the Nazis off their trail. In this case, Ellen Hirschfeld or "Ellen Scheuer" or "Ellen Dimsack"—or whoever she was on any given day—may have told Cioma she was "Gerda" as a smoke screen:

if the Gestapo caught Cioma, he could only give them a phony name for his pretty girlfriend.[5]

Gradually, Cioma perfected his counterfeiting operation. He wasn't happy with how the eyelets that held photos to his IDs looked after he tightened them with a pair of pliers. Sometimes, they were too loose or their tips didn't quite seal together. Cioma wanted more regularity and consistency. For that, he went to a shoemaker in his old neighborhood—a Communist who hated the Nazis—and bought a small tool, sort of a press, that the shoemaker used to compress small protective sheaths onto the ends of shoelaces. Cioma planned to use the press to tighten the eyelets properly on the IDs he was falsifying.

Cioma wrapped the press in plain brown paper and carried it back to the workshop he and Det shared on the ground floor of an unassuming apartment building at Waldstrasse 54. The building and the neighborhood were good locations for their enterprise. The workshop faced a wider-than-average street with a broad strip of grass down the middle that was lined with benches and trees: a good place for a tired forger to rest after a hard day's work. Cioma and Ludwig had whitewashed the studio's windows so no one could see in, and they made so little noise anyway—by its nature, forging is a silent activity—that hardly anyone paid attention to them. Each apartment on the front of the building had a narrow balcony with a commanding view of the street—a fine perch if you were a snitch for the Gestapo, which most apartment buildings in Berlin had. No one snitched on Cioma or Ludwig. There was no reason to: they were quiet and well-mannered, they minded their own business, and whatever they did in their studio had all the signs of a hush-hush government operation. When a woman asked what they were doing in the former grocery store, they told her, "Military secret, dear lady." She never asked again.[6]

Cioma's refinements on his forging continued. He'd found it was almost impossible to remove the names on the IDs he was working on to give his "customers" completely new identities. Then he discovered Tintentod—"Ink Death"—a liquid ink bleach manufactured by Pelikan, a giant corporation based in Hanover. Tintentod completely changed the quality and the ambition of Cioma's work. He could now erase names and write in new names and, for the first time, work from documents that had been issued to Jews. That relieved him from having to substitute a Jew's photo for an Aryan's. Instead, he'd remove the photo that was on a Jew's ID and bathe the ID in Tintentod to wash away the name that was written there. Cioma then wrote the name by which the ID holder would now be known, attached the original photo to the document, and returned it, through Kaufmann, to the Jew to whom it had been originally issued.[7]

Over the course of his forging career, Cioma faked as many as two hundred IDs. His handwriting ended up on documents that were being used all over Berlin and beyond. So he wouldn't be tracked down if someone using one of his IDs was caught, Cioma subtly changed his handwriting so it bore only a vague resemblance to how he'd written before. As Cioma's skills improved, Franz Kaufmann acquired all kinds of documents for him to doctor: Aryan birth certificates, identity cards issued by the post office or by large companies (AEG, Telefunken, Siemens), food ration cards, driver's licenses. With most of these, Cioma used the same procedure. He'd remove the photo, bathe the document in Tintentod, write a new name on it, and reattach the photo. Modifying each ID was exhausting and nerve-racking; saving lives was hard work. And every Friday at 6:00 P.M., Cioma delivered another eight or ten IDs to Kaufmann, who was so impressed with Cioma's work that he gave him a nickname—the "Escape King." So he was. His IDs let Jews hide within Germany or slip into other countries, usually Switzerland. All these Jews owed their lives to Cioma. Few of them knew that. Kaufmann shielded Cioma's identity so well that, years after the war, the name "Cioma Schönhaus" meant nothing to them.

Without Gerda, Cioma had a lot of free time on his hands, and he had to find some way to fill it. Soon he would, with a puckish sense of humor, a few more romances, fine meals at restaurants frequented by Hitler's closest associates and admirers, and outings on a boat that, in his wildest imaginings, Cioma had never dreamed he'd own. With all that, Cioma came as close to being a Parisian boulevardier as a Jew could be in the Third Reich. Of course, Paris was far away and the lights on its boulevards had dimmed since Germany had occupied that city two years earlier. That didn't matter. The new chapters of Cioma's life would be laced with flamboyant gestures, which had become second nature to him. Soon, they'd be more theatrical and more improbable. Cioma's willingness to take ridiculous, almost absurd risks insinuated that he was either a fool or he was blessed. Or both.

Cioma, the German Nobleman

Coming back late one night to the small room he shared with Cioma, Det panicked as a man entered the apartment building the same time he did. Not knowing who the man was or why he was there, Det didn't go into Mathilde Lange's apartment. That would have been easy. It was on the first floor. If he had, the man might have suspected that Det was staying there, and since neither Det nor Cioma had told the police this was where they were residing, such suspicions were not good. Instead of going into Frau Lange's apartment, Det climbed the stairs to the second floor, hoping the man who'd entered the building the same time he did had an apartment on that level, and he'd leave him alone after that. He didn't. Det climbed to the third floor. The man climbed with him. Then the fourth floor. The man stayed with Det. On the fifth floor, the stranger asked Det where he was going.

"To Frau Lange's," Det answered.

"She doesn't live here. She lives on the first floor."

"I must have made a mistake," Det mumbled, as he turned around and started walking right back where he'd come from. All the time, the man watched Det from above. Once Det was in Frau Lange's apartment, he went straight to the room he shared with Cioma and shook him awake. Det was reluctant to tell Cioma what had happened after they'd done their best not to draw attention to themselves. That included always returning to Frau Lange's late at night when the streets were empty and they could hear if anyone was following them.

Gathering his courage, Det blurted out, "I think I've given away where we're living."

It took some time for Cioma to absorb what Det was saying. He was still half asleep. As he came to, first he tried to make Det feel better—"I doubt it's that bad"—then, as he more clearly realized the trouble they were in, he was more frank: "All the same, we better look for another place." Det said he'd move to a spare room that a friend had offered him a while ago. Cioma was in more of a pinch. He had nothing lined up. All he could think of was getting referrals for a room from a government agency that was a clearinghouse for short-term housing.

The next day, Cioma stood in line at the agency, refining the story he'd been rehearsing all night in his head: his uncle moved to Berlin after his home in Cologne was bombed, Cioma gave the old man the one bed that was in his small apartment, and now he needed to rent a room until he reported to the army in a few days. To Cioma, the story sounded credible. It better. It was all he had.

By now, the woman running the office had heard every kind of story. She'd learned not to judge. She had one job: to move the line as quickly as possible. Without batting an eye when she heard what Cioma had to say, she gave him a list of twenty places where he could rent a room, yelled, "Next!" and the person behind Cioma stepped forward as he walked away, the list of housing possibilities in his hands.

That evening, Cioma visited one of the apartments on the list. The woman who opened the door heard about Cioma's uncle from Cologne, and that Cioma needed a place for only a few days. She liked Cioma. The room was his. But he'd have to tell the police that he was renting it. Do that tomorrow, she told Cioma. It's too late now.

To avoid going to the police the next morning, Cioma told the woman that he'd telephoned home and his mother said orders had come for him to report to the army the next day. She wanted him to spend his last night with her before being sworn in.

Cioma didn't go home. There was no home to go to. Instead, he went to the studio that he shared with Ludwig Lichtwitz. Arriving around eight o'clock in the morning, he worked for about four hours, washed up at a friend's flat, and enjoyed an early dinner at one of the better restaurants in town. Then he checked out another apartment on the list provided by the Accommodations Office, again offering his story about giving his apartment to a dear uncle from Cologne and needing a room for only a day or two. The old man who was renting out the room gave Cioma a form to submit to the police the next day. Cioma spent the night there and never went to the police. The next night, Cioma told his uncle-from-Cologne-I'll-be-gone-in-a-few-days story to a tall blonde who called to her husband, "Horst, come here a minute. Someone wants the room." Horst came: a sliver of a mustache above his upper lip, riding breeches cladding his legs instead of regular pants, boots almost up to his knees, and a swastika armband wrapped around a sleeve. Sizing up Cioma admiringly, Horst told his wife, "If every comrade behaved as sensibly as this young man, we'd have fewer problems. Show him the room." To Cioma, he offered a piece of advice: "You can register tomorrow morning." He never did.

Cioma kept getting a good night's sleep without having to tell the police where he was staying. But he was tired of roaming from room to room, and tired of telling strangers, some of whom he shouldn't trust, about his mythical uncle and the call-up he'd get from the army any day now. It seemed he found a solution to his housing problem when a friend of a friend said she'd take him in. The friend lived with her mother in Grunewald, a forest of 11,350 acres within Berlin's city limits that featured winding paths for long walks and elegant villas clustered around small lakes: a taste of the country in a city that was too urban, too crowded, and too depressed about the war its leader had gotten it into. Cioma had never been in Grunewald, but its quiet and privacy were ideal: he'd get the rest he needed after running around from apartment to apartment, scared that he'd be nabbed any minute. A few weeks here would be like a cure at a posh spa.

Cioma walked a short distance from the S-Bahn station in Grunewald until he was in front of what he called "a dream villa" surrounded by trees, flowers, and a small, closely manicured lawn.

Cioma hadn't been amid such beauty, and such isolation, for almost two years, and he knew it. "I can't imagine a better accommodation for someone who's illegal," he thought with relief.

A young woman greeted Cioma warmly then introduced him to her mother as "the man I want to give a room to"—a Jew, she emphasized, who could be sent to Poland any day. To remind her mother what "Poland" meant, she added, "We heard recently on the BBC what goes on there."

Poland was one thing. Hiding a Jew was another—a potentially fatal act of empathy in a lethally inclined nation, a mistake that Cioma had stoked by telling the young woman that he was Jewish. She was a friend of a good friend of his, and Cioma figured he could confide in her. In fact, he had to: only by confessing that he was Jewish would she know why he needed a room.

Apparently, the stern-faced mother knew nothing about her daughter's plans. And even if she had, she wouldn't have made room for Cioma. "Are you mad?" she exploded at her daughter. "We've got neighbors. You know what the government does to people who hide Jews. We will not do this. Absolutely not." Looking directly at Cioma for the first time since he'd entered her house, she shooed him away like a dog. "Get out of here," she commanded. "Go. Go quickly."

Cioma left, with nothing to do but keep visiting apartments that were on the list he'd gotten from the Accommodations Office. Night after night, he went from place to place, telling anyone who had a room to rent about his uncle from Cologne and how Cioma would be leaving for the army any day now and that he needed a room for only a night or two. Somewhere, he was sure, there was a landlord who wouldn't insist he register with the police. He had to find that person.

Cioma spent most mornings at the workshop he shared with Ludwig. That was the one constant in his life. Hiding was hard enough, and roaming from one place to another every night was exhausting and frightening. Cioma never knew where he'd end up, who he'd end up with, and if he could trust his latest landlord not to report him to the police. In Berlin, paranoia wasn't a diagnosis. It was a way of life.

Cioma rarely left the workshop until he put in four or five hours there, and he rarely went shopping for supplies. If the eyelets that kept photos in place lost their shape when Cioma removed them, he tried to reshape them or substituted small gussets from girdles that women in Kaufmann's circle provided. The gussets were about the same size as eyelets and did the job almost as well. If he had to go out, stationary stores all over Berlin had Tintentod, the solution that Cioma used to magically bleach away the writing that was already on the ID cards he received from Franz Kaufmann. And the Japanese brushes that Cioma preferred to use were still available in just about every shop in town that sold artists' supplies. That was a relief. Their bamboo handle welcomed Cioma's grip, and their bristles, often hair from a horse, deer, or racoon, held their point longer than most other kinds of brushes. That made drawing Nazi seals and eagles less nerve-racking and less tiring. For Cioma, drawing those seals and eagles was inherently tense and demanding. If drawn carelessly or in haste, they risked giving a forgery away. Cioma's forgeries never gave anyone away.

And yet, in this two-man factory for fake IDs that Cioma and Ludwig were running, they were the most indispensable ingredients, more irreplaceable than brushes from Japan or a magic solution that made ink disappear. They had to watch themselves, especially Cioma, who was younger, less experienced, and more likely to get frazzled. That could sap his energy, his focus. Remarkably, Cioma never lost his one-pointedness. He had a job to do, and he wanted to make sure he'd could do it well.

With a lot of time on his hands, especially afternoons and evenings, Cioma almost became a regular at the restaurant in Hotel Esplanade—a vast space with plush carpets, multitiered chandeliers, crystal sconces on the walls, and tablecloths so white they virtually glowed in the dark. It had been built in 1908 as a four-hundred-room premier hotel. Its price tag—twenty-three million Reichsmarks—made Berliners gasp; its seventeen-thousand square-foot, glass-roofed Winter Garden, embellished with yellow Pavonazzo marble, filled with awe anyone who had the money to enter it; and its banquet halls, bordered with reliefs of gilt cherubs, rivaled some of the galleries in nearby art museums.[1]

Kaiser Wilhelm II used to host huge banquets and balls in the Esplanade; Charlie Chaplin and Greta Garbo visited for extended stays; and Albert Einstein attended Sigmund Freud's seventieth birthday party here: the two men were good friends. In 1943, when Cioma began going to the Esplanade, enough affluent Berliners were still around to keep the Esplanade's overpriced restaurant afloat. Freshly showered after a morning spent forging IDs, and wearing a suit and a crisply ironed white shirt, Cioma confidently strolled down the oval walkway outside the Esplanade's oversized front doors, then under its cantilevered awning as a concierge greeted him with the same deference granted any patron. Next Cioma ambled through the Esplanade's hushed corridors to the dining room, where he was ushered to a table. A waiter pulled out a chair for Cioma, handed him a menu, and gave him time to peruse the offerings of the day—always delicious and always many cuts above what was available beyond the cloistered walls of the Esplanade. Cioma knew what money bought, and he knew what his confidence bought. "I pretended to be a German nobleman," he recalled, "and no one questioned that I belonged there."[2]

Cioma ate alone, which meant he had to share a table, with both diners attempting to ignore the other, not sure who they might be sitting across from. In this city of frauds, fascists, and finaglers, everyone was playing an angle. The only time Cioma worried that eating there "maybe wasn't such a good idea" was when he shared a table with the worst slob Cioma ever saw at the Esplanade. The man (who Cioma decided "looked like an intellectual" but didn't act like one) loudly slurped his soup and kept breaking off bits of crisp bread, sprinkling crumbs all over the carpet beneath him. The stranger needed a good course in manners. When he finished his meal and began walking toward the door, Cioma thought, "He's probably an emigrant who doesn't know how to behave properly." Then Cioma heard the head waiter ask his tablemate, "Excuse me, Herr consul general, have you finished dining or will you return?" "Oh," Cioma ruminated, "so that's what a consul general looks like." Cioma scolded himself for judging the man so harshly even while hoping that others weren't judging him: without doubt, Cioma was the biggest fraud, and the only Jew, in the Esplanade that day.[3]

Dining at the Esplanade was great fun, but Cioma still needed a place to live. He'd visited most of the twenty addresses the Accommodations Office had given him. Everyone who had a room wanted him to register his new address with the police.

Then his luck changed. After hearing Cioma's usual story (his uncle, the army, etc.), Frau Schirrmacher (who lived at Kleinstrasse 7) asked if he was registered as a resident of his parents' apartment. Yes, Cioma answered. Then we're fine, she said. If he didn't tell the police he was staying with her, then she wouldn't have to pay taxes on his rent. "If that's what you want," Cioma said, trying to suppress his glee. "I've got nothing against it."

This was what Cioma had needed all along: a woman as wily as he was, and a room almost equally distant from the Esplanade and his forging studio in Moabit. The hotel was eleven minutes one way; the studio, sixteen minutes the other way. And the woman he was renting from didn't seem like the type to pry any secrets from him. She had hers. Cioma had his. Both of them wanted to keep it that way.

Frau Schirrmacher's husband was an army officer. He came home often. One of her other tenants was a leader in Hitler Youth; the other worked in the Foreign Office. As for Frau Schirrmacher, there was a neediness to her, an emptiness that she hoped Cioma would fill. "I always wanted a son like you, and I hope we'll get on well together," she told Cioma while leading up to inviting him to lunch on Sunday. A seasoned liar by now, Cioma gave her what, in the middle of the war, was an entirely believable excuse for not being able to come: ever since his older brother had been killed at the Battle of Stalingrad, Cioma spent every Sunday with his grieving mother. That made complete sense to Frau Schirrmacher, who asked Cioma to convey her best wishes to his mother.

The day after he moved into Frau Schirrmacher's, Cioma finished his daily quota of fake IDs around 10:00 A.M.—early for him. Rather than go to the Esplanade for lunch or return to Kleinstrasse, where he'd have to make pleasant conversation with Frau Schirrmacher, her army husband, or the two Nazis who lived there, Cioma rode the S-Bahn to Pichelsburg, twenty minutes away. It was May 1943. The sky was clear and blue. The forest near the station was green and beckoning. Lying down in a clearing, Cioma was cooled by the ground beneath him, swept away by a repose that was not familiar after all his hiding, running, forging, lying to so many people about so many things. He'd been constricted and constrained for so long that the earth and its dampness and its flora were a revelation, a rediscovery of a world beyond his narrow, straitened, unheralded life. Renewed and refreshed, Cioma looked down the hill toward Lake Stössensee, which wasn't really a lake. Just a large bay off the Havel River, one of a string of waterways that surrounded Berlin. Fifty-eight miles long, the Havel was a major tributary to the Rhine River, a route for small ships heading to the North Sea, and a watery opportunity for Berliners to head out in their leisure boats, if they had one. Many people were boating these days—a release from the war, the deaths, and the toxic apprehensions of living in a perilous police state. As Cioma saw a small flotilla of boats gliding along the water, their white sails billowing and swelling in the wind, he imagined his father telling him to enjoy himself with the money he'd raised by selling everything his family owned. Buy a boat, his father said. Look at those people down there. They're having fun. You should, too. A boat, Boris persisted in Cioma's imagination, would give you something to do when you're not at one of Frau Schirrmacher's Sunday lunches, lunches for which Cioma feared invitations would come so regularly that turning them down would be impolite. If he ever attended one, he'd have to keep all his lies straight—lies about himself, his family, his job, his history, his life. By now, there were too many to remember and too many to recite without contradicting himself.

Cioma didn't want to sit at Frau Schirrmacher's table and regale her with his fibs until she—or maybe the Nazis who lived in her apartment—began to smell something fishy about him. And he didn't want to spend whatever free time he had dodging Herr and Frau Schirrmacher and their two tenants by sitting on a park bench for hours or nursing a beer in a pub. Cioma wanted a boat. He started down the hill to get one.

18

Cioma's Comrade

Rudolf Ladewig was working at the dock the day Cioma came along and said he wanted to buy a boat. Ladewig later told the police that Cioma's "sunny disposition" persuaded him to take the young man out in one of the few boats tied up at his dock that was for sale—a fifteen-foot dinghy. Ladewig didn't know Cioma had been on a boat only once before, and then as a passenger who mostly did what he was told to do. Which meant that whoever was sailing the boat had to tell Cioma to mostly sit down, stay away from the sails, and not touch anything. Passengers new to sailing are best kept away from anything that has to do with sailing. Ladewig also didn't know Cioma decided to buy the boat the instant he saw the brass letters on its stern. The seven letters spelled *Kamerad* (or "*Comrade*" in English). Remembering the Latin saying *Nomen est omen* ("The name is an omen"), Cioma knew he had no choice. Who, in this fourth year of a lousy war, didn't need a comrade?[1]

Unfurling the *Comrade*'s sail, Ladewig steered it toward the open waters of Lake Stössensee. The *Comrade* skimmed along the water, then under a bridge where the Havel River spread out before them. Now and then, a motorboat left them in its wake or the *Comrade* made its own much smaller wake, barely enough to gently sway a canoe or a rowboat, the overlooked proletarian workhorse in boating's rigid class structure. As the *Comrade* picked up speed, Cioma felt a freedom and ease he hadn't in years. He'd been locked up inside himself for so long—on the run, and looking not only over his shoulder but everywhere, all the time—that easing some of the tethers that were holding him in was a rejuvenation, a refurbishing of his soul. It was almost like he was being reintroduced to life, and to himself.

At the dock an hour later, Cioma paid Ladewig 2,500 Reichsmarks for the *Comrade*, and the boat he didn't know how to sail was his. Almost immediately, he decided to show the *Comrade* who was its master and commander, figuring that, since he had watched Ladewig so closely while they were on the water, he now knew the basics of sailing. He didn't. Rowing out of the marina, then past a small lighthouse that marked the entrance to the Havel, Cioma raised the sail, unaware that the wind had picked up since he was out before. The sail was hardly halfway up before the *Comrade* raced away. Cioma had no idea how to stop it. With spray splashing in his face and the *Comrade* flying over the water, Cioma knew he'd been a fool to think, when Ladewig had taken him out, that sailing, in Cioma's words, was "child's play." Panic washed over Cioma as eight words stuck in his throat: "For God's sake, how will all this end?"[2]

The *Comrade* zigzagged from one side of the river to the other. A scary prospect: the Havel was 108 feet wide, twice the width of the Spree River, which flowed through the middle of Berlin and with which Cioma was more familiar. If he was on a more congested river, like the Spree, Cioma could have flagged someone down for help. There was no help here. Cioma pulled the rudder as hard as he could and pointed the *Comrade* toward the shore. Crunching past reeds, then into the riverbank, Cioma lowered the sail, afraid the wind would take him right back where he had come from.

It was too dark to return to Pichelsburg, where Cioma had bought the boat. That was just as well—Cioma might not have known where he fit in. On the eastern shore of Lake Stössensee were a scattering of homes large enough to be called mansions. Some were set back from the water, a nod to the privacy warranted by money and power. In the 1930s and early 1940s, Adolf Hitler frequently visited some of those homes, hideaways of some of his cronies, like Hanns Kerrl, head of the Reich Ministry for Church Affairs, whose flat-roofed, Bauhaus-influenced home he'd essentially stolen from a Jew who owned a large department store in Potsdam. "Stolen" may be a legally imprecise term for what occurred, though, when a high-ranking Nazi offered a Jew a fraction of the worth of his home—when he essentially made an offer the Jew couldn't refuse—"stolen" more accurately described the transaction than "purchased."

The western shore of Lake Stössensee was chockablock with small cabins, some with tile roofs capped by weather vanes with roosters, or with deer antlers nailed above their front doors, bounty from a good day's hunting. It was widely suspected that Jews were hiding in the thick forests that extended almost down to the shoreline, huddling in the woods and the shadows and the hollows.

The lake was Germany in miniature—Nazis on one side: safe, comfortable, secure; Jews on the other side: hiding, hungry, cold. Cioma, who was almost certainly the one Jew sailing on Lake Stössensee that day, had ingeniously figured out the best sanctuary of all: a fifteen-foot dinghy, which left no trail that police could use to track him down, and on which only someone with eagle eyes could spot him. Everyone in Germany needed a sanctuary, and everyone had their version of one: the rich and powerful had underground bunkers that protected them from bombs; Jews had forests and woods if they were in the country, and basements, attics, and sheds if they were in the city. On Cioma's sanctuary—the *Comrade*—he enjoyed nature, and he enjoyed himself, and he didn't risk placing his trust in others: always, these days, a dubious and hazardous proposition. His only problem, and not a small one, was that he didn't know anything about boats and gaining that knowledge would take more time and effort than he'd anticipated. But it would be worth it. If he pulled this off, he'd be the only Jew with a floating sanctuary on Lake Stössensee.

Cioma spent the night on the water, safe along the shore. The next morning, he humbly rowed back to Pichelsburg, the *Comrade*'s sails furled so there'd be no risk of the wind pulling him out to the Havel again. Once was enough. When he got home, he did what he should have done before trying to sail the *Comrade*: he bought a manual on sailing. Studying it late at night, he learned that he'd been too fast to raise the *Comrade*'s sails the first time he was aboard the boat: it would have been better to put some distance between himself and the dock, then raise the sail and point the boat into the wind. Otherwise, the sail would be slack and flap loosely like a flag and the boat wouldn't gain the speed Cioma needed to set the *Comrade*'s course and not be at the mercy of the currents and winds. He also learned that tacking—moving the boat through the wind by zigzagging (with control) from one direction, then another—was useful, but too dangerous and complex for a beginner.[3]

Once Cioma felt reasonably confident on the *Comrade*, he began taking friends out with him, as much for his pleasure as theirs. Usually, they were young women, though not girlfriends. Women liked Cioma for his brio, his dash, his verve: he was great company. Aside from that, friends joined Cioma for the same reason he sailed: it was a release from living in a city where they were hunted like prey and hiding like rats. Hanni Hollerbusch, who'd known Cioma since high school, was one of his favorite guests on the *Comrade*. Spunky and outspoken, she'd been expelled from school after telling the principal that Hitler's claims about Germans being descended from the "Aryans" of India and Tibet were nonsense. Nothing in history, geography, or science backed up Hitler's fantasies. The man's brain was a mush of delusions and hallucinations, few of them sensible, logical, or rational: the debris of a deranged mind. But they got him the attention he craved.

That outburst got Hanni kicked out of school, which was just as well: she was smarter, and more honest, than the principal. With a lot of free time on her hands, Hanni frequently visited Cioma in his family's apartment on Sophienstrasse, cuddling up against the pillows Cioma's mother had embroidered to liven up the couch in their living room, the same pillows that Cioma would use to make himself and his friends comfortable while they were aboard the *Comrade*. Those visits seemed long ago. Now it was Cioma who visited Hanni, sometimes staying in her apartment: a U-boat had to stay on the move.

One day while Cioma and Hanni were aboard the *Comrade*, they passed Nikolassee. Renate Klepper, Cioma's girlfriend from art school, had lived in this neighborhood. She'd been bright and lively, so agile that Hanni remembered "she moved like a dancer," so elegant that Cioma had instantly fallen in love with her. Her stepfather, Jochen, once a high-flying writer, used to be wined and dined at the highest levels of government and in the finest literary salons. Not for long, not with a Jewish wife, Joanna, and Renate, her daughter from a previous marriage, facing "transports" any day. Cioma offered to help the Kleppers hide. No, Jochen explained, they'd be no good at it: "We aren't made for that kind of life. We'd only get caught and be thrown into jail." Then Interior Minister Wilhelm Frick—an old friend of Jochen's—offered to help Renate when Sweden gave her an entry visa. Jumping into action, Frick ordered several security agencies to prepare an exit visa for Renate.[4]

To prod things along, on December 10 Jochen met with Adolf Eichmann, one of the chief architects of the Holocaust. Jochen knew Eichmann from the days when Hitler was touting Klepper's books. Now Jochen, humbled and desperate, sat across from Eichmann, small and bowlegged. Jochen had come to beg, and Eichmann knew it, toying with Jochen, holding out hope for Renate one minute, squashing it the next, all with the practiced malice of an executioner who enjoys nothing more than his job.

With his smooth, well-honed sadism, Eichmann told Klepper that he had "not finally said yes" about Renate's visa and "not finally said no." Offering a sliver of hope, he murmured, "I think the thing will work out" and told Jochen to come back the next day. He'll have his decision then. Klepper returned the next day. Eichmann told him Renate would not get a visa.

A few hours later, the Kleppers turned on a gas valve in their kitchen. They lived on a serene cobblestoned block near where Cioma and Hanni would be sailing a few months later. "Tonight," Jochen wrote in his diary, "we die together. Over us stands the image of the blessed Christ. With this view, we end our lives." Jochen was certain that Renate dying this way was "less cruel than . . . hand[ing] her over to the fate of the deportations. What a world in which parents desire the death of such a beloved child." The bodies of Jochen, Joanna, and Renate were found in the kitchen the next morning.[5]

Aboard the *Comrade* the following spring, Cioma and Hanni sailed so close to where Renate had died that they could almost see her house. They cried. Renate had always cheered them up. They needed cheering now. The happy outing Cioma and Hanni had planned for one of the first warm days of the year had turned into a wake.

This was the saddest of Cioma's outings aboard the *Comrade*. Usually sailing lifted and thrilled him—once he got the hang of it and the amateur was an amateur no more. He'd come a long way. When he'd begun, he had no idea what he was doing. Now, on the rivers and lakes where he sailed, Cioma came close to achieving some sort of balance between the life he had before the war and what was passing for his life now. The *Comrade* allowed him to be buoyant enough to remember the suffering of Renate and her family and not be drawn too much into its undertow of grief and pain. That was the bargain he'd made so he could have a life, or some version of a life: to experience enough of it so he did not shatter while remembering what life used to be, and perhaps what it would be again.

If Cioma had learned anything, it was that if you're going up against the devil, you do it with style, panache, and a jauntiness that keeps him off-balance. The *Comrade* helped Cioma forget about the strain of hiding, about forging documents for people who were as scared as he was, and that his parents were dead, and most of his friends and relatives were dead, and any day now, he might be dead, too. The seagulls and the friendly sailors who waved at Cioma—there were always friendly sailors—were a balm from the city he feared, which used to be the city he loved. Little now connected Berlin to its past, and little suggested it had a future. Still, Cioma was determined to find out what lay ahead. Until then, the *Comrade* let him be what he longed to be: happy, likeable, charming, and, when women were aboard (and when they weren't grieving for the loss of a good friend), flirtatious as hell. Even in Berlin—especially in Berlin—you had to find a way to live life.

19

The Tide Turns

The *Comrade* saved Cioma from having lunch on Sundays with Frau Schirrmacher. That day, he kept reminding her, was reserved for time with his mother, who was still distraught over her "other son's" death on the Russian front. That excuse satisfied Frau Schirrmacher. Someday, it might not. Until then, the *Comrade* was Cioma's haven.

The *Comrade* gave Cioma a break from Frau Schirrmacher and her Nazi husband and Nazi tenants. For other breaks, he stayed with his friend Hanni Hollerbusch though less often than before. She needed her privacy, and she needed her safety: Cioma assumed the police were looking for him. They didn't know his name and they didn't know what he looked like, but they wanted him. All they knew was that someone very talented was forging some of the best identity cards they'd seen. If Cioma was caught, anyone who'd helped him would be in danger. He couldn't do that to Hanni. In Berlin, befriending someone for the right reason could mean death for the wrong reason.

Then, as happened often with Cioma, a woman came to his rescue. Women had always liked him: he was attractive, fun, playful and, since he was an artist, a bohemian. Now there were other reasons to like him. With so many men off at war, Cioma was a rare commodity: he was young, he was a man, and he was available. Plus he had a hard time saying "no" when a woman flirted with him. That was the energy of youth, and that was the recklessness of Cioma. The wrong woman could weaken his defenses, loosen his tongue, lure secrets out of him that he wasn't telling anyone, and shouldn't tell anyone. It was better for Cioma to stay away from women until the war ended. But some instincts couldn't be curbed.

The woman in this case was Tatjana, Cioma's friend who'd sent him to that villa in Grunewald where she was sure he could hide for a while. That didn't work out. To make amends, Tatjana, a Russian immigrant, made Cioma a Russian feast: vodka, caviar, sturgeon, olives, salmon, borscht, blintzes, hard-boiled eggs, chicken fat, and rice. To acquire all this, Tatjana must have had a lot of money and known her way around the black market. Or had great connections. Or all of the above. She and Cioma washed down their dinner with a bottle of French champagne: Moet et Chandon. Excellent then. Excellent now.

Cioma had never been drunk. After the champagne and three vodkas, he was hammered. He talked and talked. So did Tatjana. Then they had sponge cake, which Tatjana liberally soaked with vodka. After that, they went to where they knew they'd end up before the night was over. Tatjana's bedroom saved Cioma another night at Frau Schirrmacher's. It also gave him what he hadn't had for a while: hours alone with a beautiful woman. The next night, he and Tatjana went to the theater to see *Hamlet*, starring two of Berlin's finest actors—Gustaf Gründgens and Käthe Gold. Then back to Tatjana's.[1]

After a few nights with Tatjana, Cioma returned to Kleistrasse 7, mostly because he needed to remain in Frau Schirrmacher's good graces until he found another place to live. If he was away for too long, she'd suspect there was something fishy about him. In the meantime, occasional nights at Tatjana's would serve him well.

Cioma confessed—half truthfully—to Frau Schirrmacher that he'd been away because he was having an affair with a woman who was twenty-four years older than him. His parents, he said, would be furious if they learned about her. If they called and asked about him, would Frau Schirrmacher please say he was a wonderful boarder and spent every night at her place? With a sly smile, Frau Schirrmacher agreed, relieved there was still romance in the world despite the bombings, the blackouts, and the daily news that yet another loved one had been killed at the front. Without romance, there were no tomorrows. Without a tomorrow, why was the war being fought?

Tatjana was a delight, yet Cioma was never satisfied. While walking down one of the city's more fashionable streets, Cioma saw Stella Kubler coming straight toward him. In the art school they'd attended a few years before, Stella was every guy's crush. The woman they couldn't have; the one they wanted. Her beauty was stunning; her smile dazzling. With her blonde hair and blue eyes, she belonged in Hitler Youth, not in a shabby art academy for Jews. She knew it, and she held herself above the lads who desired her, though they wouldn't have known what to do with her. But now Stella was a U-boat, just like Cioma, and he had more to offer than when they were in school. He forged papers and had his own apartment, lots of money, and a sailboat. At the art academy, he'd barely gotten up his nerve to talk with Stella. Now, they were both alone, scared, and on the run. With all he possessed and all he knew about life on the streets and how to avoid the Nazis, he may, for once, have had the advantage over Stella.

Over tea in a café, Cioma put his hand over Stella's. She didn't remove it. He asked if she'd like to see where he was living. She would. They got on a tram to go to Frau Schirrmacher's. Halfway there, Stella warned Cioma it was foolish to do this: U-boats should keep their hiding places secret. They got off at the next stop.

Years later, Cioma told this writer, with his usual bravado, that, by preferring not to go to his apartment, Stella had expressed "her feelings for me": her love, her devotion, everything "that she hadn't been able to articulate before." Maybe. We don't know, and neither did Cioma.

It's just as possible that Stella was simply saying she didn't want to go to bed with him.

Cioma made a fake ID for Stella and saw her once, maybe twice after that. His timing was impeccable. A few months later, the Gestapo arrested Stella and her parents, torturing her until she agreed to work for them as a *griefer* (or "catcher")—one of eighteen Jews in Berlin who found U-boats for the Nazis. It wasn't surprising the Gestapo needed help. With eight hundred agents in a city of 4.5 million residents—one agent for every six thousand Berliners—the Gestapo was overworked and overwhelmed. Jews who found other Jews were paid well, received comfortable quarters and fine food, and were promised that their lives would be spared, unlike the people they were sending to "camps." Stella had another reason to cooperate: the Nazis said they'd kill her parents if she didn't.

Cioma was sympathetic when he learned that Stella was a *griefer*—people were doing almost anything to save themselves. He wasn't sympathetic about her motives. Stella, he said, wasn't "catching" for money, food, or guarantees that she and her parents would be spared. She was "catching" out of vanity. "Apart from her looks," Cioma charged, "Stella had no particular qualities. Probably the mere threat to smash in her beautiful teeth was enough to induce her to cooperate."[2]

Prowling streets, cafés, and tram stops for Jews, Stella approached anyone she suspected was Jewish or who she knew was Jewish, offering them food, shelter, money, friendship. If they took her bait, she led them to where the Gestapo was waiting. Or Gestapo agents might wait for a signal from her, then pounce. That, in fact, is how they had caught Stella. Sitting in Café Ollenmuller on Mittelestrasse in early June 1943, Stella perked up when she spotted Inge Lustig, an old friend, across the room. They smiled and waved at each other. Stella, happy she'd found someone with whom she could let down her guard, waited for Inge to come to her table. She didn't. At a signal from Inge, Gestapo agents swarmed into the café, grabbed Stella, and threw her into their car.

("Catching" didn't save Inge. Eventually useless to the Gestapo—she couldn't meet her quota—she boarded a "transport" like everyone she was turning into the Nazis.)

Sometimes Stella attended the funerals of Christians who had been married to Jews: with the death of their Gentile spouse, the surviving husband or wife—a Jew—was no longer protected from "transports" and "camps." Fortified by the pistol the Gestapo gave her, Stella usually arrested the Jews as they walked home from the funeral; sometimes, impatient to move on to her next job, she nabbed them at the cemetery. Her biggest haul was thirty-six deaf and blind Jews who were hiding in a small factory that was only a few blocks from where the Schönhauses had lived on Sophienstrasse. Stella's kindest act as a *griefer*—her only kind act—involved Cioma. Her first assignment from the Gestapo was to find the forger they knew as "Peter Petrov"—one of Cioma's phony names. Handwriting on the ID Cioma had made for Stella was similar to the writing on a document the police had recently found that they linked to "Petrov." On top of that, a prisoner who they had in jail and had a passing acquaintance with Cioma, told them that "Gunther Rogoff," another of Cioma's aliases, had a workshop somewhere in Moabit.

Stella pretended to look all over Moabit for Cioma—killing time in cafés, standing on street corners, lurking in alleys. But finding Cioma's studio wasn't easy: neither Stella nor the Gestapo knew its address, and Moabit spread out over three square miles, a large swath for one person to stake out. After two weeks, Stella told the Gestapo that "Petrov" or "Rogoff" or "Cioma," or whoever he was—Cioma's multiple names were hard to keep up with—was too slippery for her. Find other Jews, the Gestapo ordered. She did. Jews tried to kill Stella by poisoning her coffee in a café. She didn't touch it. They tried to lure her to an apartment where Jews were supposedly hiding. She didn't go. They sent her notes, warning they'd kill her if she kept turning in Jews. She persisted. They tried to pay a Jewish dentist to poison her while he worked on her mouth. Forget the money, he said: smuggle me out of Germany. The resistance couldn't do that. Stella's cavities were filled, safely.

Over the next two years, Stella turned in several hundred Jews. Her parents were killed anyway. She survived the war, served ten years in an East German prison for collaborating with the Nazis, then moved to West Berlin, where she was tried and convicted again. Her prison time in "the east" served as her prison time in the west. Stella never stopped denying all the horrible things people were saying about her, insisting that she'd only appeared to cooperate with the Nazis, and she did that once: when she pretended to look for Cioma. Almost everyone assumed she was lying or that she was lying to herself. Such self-deception, Primo Levi wrote, was common among survivors of traumas like the Holocaust, people who were so shattered by the truth of their lives that they fabricated "a convenient reality" for themselves, one "less painful than the real one." By repeating this reality to themselves and to others, noted Levi, who survived almost a year in Auschwitz, "the distinction between true and false progressively loses its contours" and they "fully believe" the story they concocted about themselves. Stella told her story, and she told it well. When she couldn't sustain it any more, she died by suicide in 1994, unable to escape the gloom and guilt that had enveloped her for decades.[3]

By now, Cioma was a connoisseur of hiding. He walked the streets with confidence, looked people in the eye, ate well, dressed well, and was careful about whom he talked to and what he told them. He had friends he trusted and who cared about him. He had girlfriends. More than before he went into hiding. The documents he was forging were saving lives, and the police and the Gestapo had no idea who was making them or how he'd gotten so good. They admired his skill, and they fiercely wanted to catch him. Cioma's job was to make sure they didn't.

Then Cioma got even more careless than he had been. He'd already lost two IDs the police had issued to him. That was bad. Now things got worse.

Cioma, with mother (left) and grandmother, approximately 1926.

Gruss aus
Berlin
21.8.02.
Je vous
prie de
votre
Revanche.

Avec
salutation
cordiale.
Paul Grabé

Hackescher Market, Berlin. The Schönhauses' lower–middle class apartment was a few blocks behind
the market's thriving prosperity.

N HERALD

LATE CITY EDITIO

BOSTON AND VICINITY—Greater
warmer today and tomorrow.
High water, 2:14 A. M.; 1:35 P. M.
report on page 2

1933—TWENTY-FOUR PAGES   • • • •   TWO CENTS

s Lashing
s on Common

HITLER PLEDGED TO RULE SANELY AS GERMAN HEAD

DALADIER FORMS FRENCH CABINET ON LINES OF OLD

Socialists Stay Aloof—Uneasy Over Hitler Advent

PAUL-BONCOUR IN NEW MINISTRY

Also Chautemps and Other Radical Leaders—Grave Times Seen

Germany's New Pilot

ADOLF HITLER
"Now, let's eat."

NAZI LEADER JOINED BY CHIEF OF NATIONALIST

Coalition Lacks Reichstag Majority, but Relies On Centre

PROMISES TO GOVERN CONSTITUTIONALLY

Will Seek Foreign Good Will—To Steer Clear Of Anti-Semitism

CLARENCE W. ROWLEY

RK ADMITS

Front page of the Syracuse, NY *Herald* the day after Hitler became chancellor. Sanity was not on his mind.

Book burning, Berlin, May 1933. Not far from where the Schönhauses lived.

> History has taught you nothing if you think you can kill ideas. Tyrants have tried to do that often before, and the ideas have risen up in their might and destroyed them.

From the US came Helen Keller's admonition against the book burnings. A socialist, her books were also burned.

Gestapo headquarters, Berlin. Cioma and his mother reported here, May 1942. Cioma's mother deemed the Gestapo agent who ordered them to report to a "transport" "quite decent."

Cioma's parents were murdered several weeks after they boarded their "transport." Decades later, Cioma and his sons had these *stolpersteine*—memorials to the Nazis' victims—installed outside the Schönhauses' apartment building on Sophienstrasse.

Cioma was rarely without a girlfriend. TOP RIGHT: Lotte Windmüller, killed at Auschwitz. CENTER LEFT: Dorothee Fliess,
smuggled out of Germany with her family by anti-Nazi members
of Germany's intelligence agency. RIGHT: Renate Klepper and
her family, all committed suicide when the Nazis wouldn't give
Renate an exit visa.

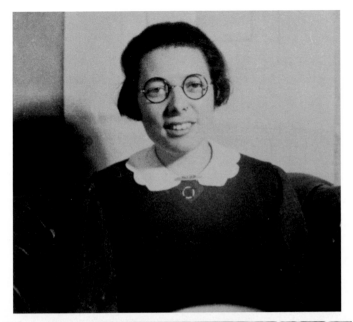

Edith Wolff, top, persuaded Cioma to make a fake ID for Jizchak Schwersenz, second from right immediately above. Wolff and Schwersenz organized the only Jewish youth group formed in Germany during the war. By saving Schwersenz, Cioma saved most of the kids in the group.

Spandau *Blick von der Heerstraßenbrücke*

Cioma filled his leisure time by dining at the Hotel Esplanade and sailing his boat, the *Comrade*, on Lake Stössensee.

Franz Ferdinand Vogel, the reverend in the church opposite the Schönhauses' apartment building, delivered many sermons against Hitler. When the Nazis banned him from the church, congregants sang hymns to him on Sundays as he stood on the balcony of his apartment on the church grounds. The balcony is in the upper left of this photo.

Franz Kaufmann. Organized an anti-Nazi group for which Cioma made fake IDs.

Helene Jacobs. Key member of Kaufmann's group. Cioma hid in her apartment during the summer of 1943.

Looks mattered in Europe during the war. Stella Kubler, blonde, blue-eyed, and Jewish, passed as an "Aryan" until she was caught. The Nazis then recruited her to catch Jews who were hiding. Meanwhile . . .

. . . Cioma, who also didn't "look" Jewish, raised doubts when he reached Switzerland that he deserved refugee status.

The only forgery by Cioma that exists. "Issued" to
Heinz Geutzlaff, aka Kurt Hirschfeldt, who survived
the war.

Tintentod. Liquid ink bleach Cioma used to erase names
on IDs. He filled in the space with the fake name of its new
recipient.

The small pouch Cioma carried while biking to Switzerland. Inside were his fake ID and maps for his journey.

Cioma spent the first night of his bicycling escape in Wittenberg, a hotbed of antisemitism. Above, a Nazi rally next to the town square. Right, a sculpture on a church in Wittenberg depicting a rabbi pulling a Talmud from the ass of a pig. (The sculpture is still there.)

In Stuttgart, Rev. Kurt
Müller hosted Cioma for a
few days.

Theologian Karl Barth (left) and his assistant,
Charlotte von Kirschbaum, convinced the Swiss
government to give Cioma haven, then helped
him with finances, education, and housing.

Cioma (far left) at a refugee camp soon after arriving in Switzerland.

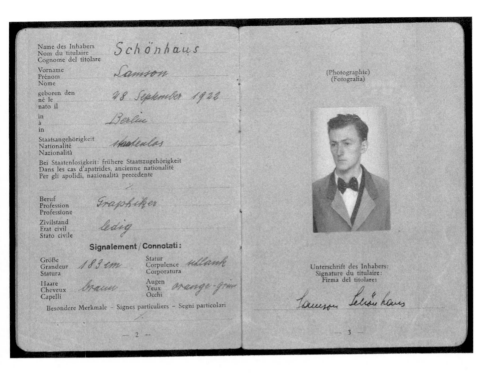

Refugee IDs Switzerland issued to Cioma, 1944 and 1949. The master forger forged no more.

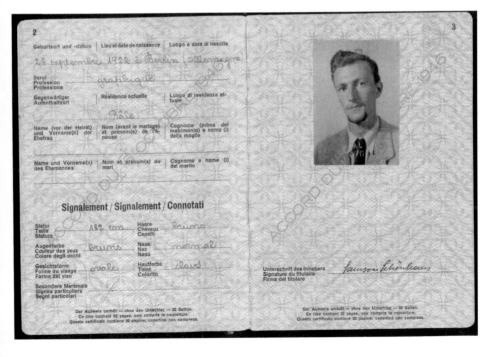

Cioma and his wife, Rosmarie-Susanne, early 1950s. They met in art school and were "very much in love" until they weren't. They divorced in 1956.

Cioma in 2006 with the map from his 1943 biking trip spread out before him.

Cioma taking his five-year-old son, Michael, for a bike ride, 1955. This is the only known photo of Cioma on a bicycle.

One day, Franz Kaufmann was in a particularly thoughtful mood and began ruminating to Cioma about what they'd gotten themselves into. "Basically," Kaufmann mused, "our activities are criminal. But under a criminal regime, this is the only appropriate way to behave. Schönhaus, you're young, you're adventurous and you have a positive attitude toward life. That's why you're successful. I'm a former civil servant. I've had to rethink a lot of things." The rethinking had remade Kaufmann. He'd turned from a dutiful bureaucrat into someone who questioned authority, faith, and laws, and what it meant to be a German and a Christian. He'd served the state as a lawyer. Now he was doing his best to shift the devilish path of the government he hated.

"Anyway," Kaufmann said to Cioma, a little abruptly, "back to the business at hand." The business was simple and they'd done it before, though this time Kaufmann gave Cioma twenty-one documents to fake. Cioma would return them to Kaufmann by the end of the week, each with a new photo and a new name. Cioma took the documents to his workshop in Moabit. It was a chilly day, and Cioma was looking forward to spending it in the studio, where a small woodburning stove would keep him warm. As usual, Cioma carried the documents inside the folds of a newspaper—the *Thurgauer Zeitung*, the only Swiss paper sold in Germany during the war. When he got to the studio, he threw the paper on a table and rummaged around for some of the tools he'd need for forging. Meanwhile, Ludwig Lichtwitz began heating up the stove, placing kindling on top of paper he'd already lit with a match. When Cioma had gathered all the tools he needed for that day's forging, he looked around for the newspaper he'd brought. He couldn't find it. Maybe Ludwig had seen it?

"Sure," Ludwig said. "I saw it. It's no big deal! It was yesterday's paper."

"Well, yeah," Cioma said, "but inside it were twenty-one IDs I got from Kaufmann."

"Oh, my God," Ludwig almost shouted. "I just lit the stove with it."

Somehow, Cioma had to explain this to Franz Kaufmann. Racing to Kaufmann's neighborhood, which was about five miles away, Cioma was terrified. He had every reason to be. Kaufmann had trusted Cioma and he had believed in Cioma. No more. Kaufmann was so furious that he barely believed Cioma's story about Ludwig burning the documents in the stove. "You're telling me your friend burned the passes by mistake?" Kaufmann asked incredulously, his voice rising, his temper bursting. Maybe Ludwig and Cioma were keeping the IDs for themselves, to sell on the black market when the time was right and keep the profits for themselves? Each document would sell for about three thousand Reichsmarks, a tidy sum for two Jews who were on the run.[4]

Kaufmann couldn't yell at Cioma anymore. He needed him, and he knew it. Cioma was one of the best forgers in the city. With barely a word, Kaufmann handed Cioma five IDs to falsify, sixteen fewer than he'd given him the day before. His trust in Cioma had frayed; his need for fake IDs hadn't. It was better for Cioma to counterfeit fewer IDs this week than leave all the people who relied on him in the lurch. And better for Kaufmann that Cioma proceed slowly. Giving him another twenty-one IDs was too dangerous. Soon, Kaufmann hoped, the young man would straighten himself out. Ludwig, too.

20

"Don't Show Your Face in Public"

With the Nazis persecuting more Jews every day, there was a greater need for fake IDs for those who were hiding, or those who were about to, and more pressure on Cioma and Franz Kaufmann to mend their rift. Cioma had to give Kaufmann reason to trust him again; Kaufmann had to smother his chagrin and disappointment. Focusing on saving lives, and no more than that, was essential. Which perhaps was why, for Cioma's next assignment, Kaufmann told him to meet his "most important female assistant" at 10:00 A.M. at the U-Bahn station at Breitenbachplatz. A young woman standing in front of a large map of Berlin would know that Cioma had been sent by Kaufmann if he asked for directions to a nearby street. The purpose of their meeting would be apparent when Cioma met her. It was Helene Jacobs, who was essentially Kaufmann's second in charge. Cioma had never heard of her.

When the Breitenbachplatz station opened in 1913 in southwest Berlin, it was one of the more elegant of the U-Bahn's forty-six stations. It still was. Daylight flooded the tracks from clerestories in the ceiling. Niches in the walls featured round bronze plaques of animals, plants, and scientific instruments—tributes to the Kaiser Wilhelm Society, one of Germany's premier scientific institutes, only a few blocks away.

The ceiling along the entire length of the station was lit with highly polished brass lamps, each fit for a throne room.[1]

Cioma hadn't come to admire the station, impressive as it was. He was here for this mystery woman. He easily found her, though she wasn't what he expected. Cioma found Helene Jacobs's complexion "poor," her clothes "completely unfashionable," and her hair (which fell over the right side of her forehead in one long wave, almost as if she were trying to hide behind it), "straggly." In short, Helene was unremarkable: her looks didn't warrant more than a single glance. That was fine for the game she was playing. If you were helping Jews in Berlin in 1943, it was better to look like a nobody. Drawing attention to yourself could backfire. Beauty and glamour were burdens, beacons to the authorities to look in your direction. Helene's blandness was her equivalent of a magician's misdirection. Any Gestapo agents or police looking for anti-Nazis would never give her a second look. Helene Jacobs was a splendid foil for Hitler's enforcers.

Still, Helene intrigued Cioma, with her confidence, sense of purpose, and "wide, intelligent" eyes that fully took in whomever she was talking with. In this case, she was taking in Cioma. After he asked for directions to a nearby street as Kaufmann had instructed him to do, Helene drew eight documents from her purse. Attached to each was a photo of the person who would be using it. Cioma's assignment was the usual: erase the name that was on each document, write in a new name, and swap a new photo for the old one. He had to do it overnight and deliver the "revised" documents to Helene's apartment, at Bonner Strasse 2, the next day. Cioma had never worked so fast before, with so little sleep, and so much adrenaline, and so much pressure to prove himself after Ludwig had accidentally burned twenty-one ID cards in the stove back in their workshop.

Helene's apartment, not far from the U-Bahn station where Cioma had met her the day before, was located in a five-story building with a yellow stucco exterior—middle-class housing in a middle-class neighborhood: buildings and residents as bland as Helene. Cioma climbed the stairs to Helene's snug, dark, modestly furnished apartment. After Helene welcomed Cioma, she introduced him to Kurt Müller, whose vise-like grip surprised Cioma when they shook hands. Müller was from Stuttgart. As a lawyer during the first half of the 1930s, he'd defended women, the poor, and anyone who was politically persecuted. Then Gestapo agents placed him in "protective custody" in prison for five months: his good deeds had annoyed them for too long. When he got out, Müller resigned from the bar, studied theology, and became a pastor for an anti-Nazi church in Stuttgart. It was safer—slightly—to fight Hitler from a pulpit than a courtroom. In 1942 he began hiding Jews who lived in Stuttgart, going so far as to help a few cross into Switzerland. All of them needed fake IDs. For that, Müller relied on Franz Kaufmann and Helene Jacobs, and Kaufmann and Helene relied on Cioma. In time, they fell into a pattern: Müller brought Helene photos of Jews who needed IDs, Cioma swapped these for photos that were on the IDs he received from Kaufmann or Helene and painted Nazi seals over them, and Müller took them back to Stuttgart, four hundred miles to the south.[2]

On his first visit to Helene's, Cioma handed Müller the IDs he'd falsified overnight. Müller walked over to a window, examined them in the bright light, pronounced them "excellent," and said he'd be back for more: Jews in Stuttgart needed IDs. Then Müller put on his hat and left for the train station. He had a feeling that Cioma and Helene could use some time to get to know each other better.

Cioma was pleased that Müller liked his handiwork, relieved he and Kaufmann had patched things up, and delighted that he'd settled on a new fake name—Peter Petrov—which rolled off the tongue smoothly and was backed up by the best ID since he'd begun forging: a "passport" from the Russische Vertrauensstelle (the Bureau for Russian Refugees), the agency the Nazis created to deal with Russians who were living in Germany. Each passport confirmed the bearer was "sufficiently" Aryan, detailed when and why they'd left Russia, and specified their marital status and other details, specific and mundane. It also had a photo of the bearer and his or her fingerprints. This was the next best thing to a "real" German passport. A friend who worked in the bureau had stolen it for Cioma. By hand, Cioma filled in the details, wrote "Peter Petrov" on the appropriate line, and attached his photo to the document. His friend, who was practiced in this fine art, took Cioma's fingerprints and added them to the "passport." His friend, Mr. Jankowski, also put a receipt in the bureau's files, acknowledging that a passport had been issued to "Peter Petrov."

Cioma was now as Russian as anyone could be in the Third Reich: as duly registered with the authorities as he could be. If anyone in the government inquired about "Petrov," the Russische Vertrauensstelle would rummage through its files, find "Petrov's" dossier—planted there by Cioma's friend—and report that his record was clean, with no investigations, accusations, or incriminations. On the street, Cioma wouldn't have to worry that a policeman or a Gestapo agent would look at his papers, mutter "fake" or "phony," and haul him in. If all went well, Cioma would never have to make a forgery for himself again. Or so he thought. These things never work out the way they should.

One day, after returning to his workshop from Helene's apartment, Cioma puttered about, gathering supplies and tools for a good day's work. Then he reached into a pocket. His wallet and his papers—his "Peter Petrov" papers—were gone. He checked all his other pockets. They were empty. Maybe he'd dropped his wallet and papers on the tram after he bought his ticket or on the street. He didn't know, and there was no way to find out. Most of his money was in his wallet; without that, it'd be hard to eat in a restaurant or take a tram or subway. And without his "Petrov" passport, he couldn't prove who he was even if who he claimed to be—"Petrov"—didn't exist. More damaging was that the "passport" didn't have "Peter Petrov's" photo in it. It couldn't. There was no "Peter Petrov." It had Cioma's photo. And his wallet had a card that a library near his workshop had issued to "Petrov." Cioma had gotten it to flesh out "Petrov" and make him more of a real person, with real habits and real interests. Look, Cioma could tell anyone who stopped him: that's my photo and those are my fingerprints. And look: I read books. Call the Russische Vertrauensstelle or the library if you don't believe me. With the "passport" lost, Cioma had no proof that he was a person who didn't exist.

Cioma had lost his wallet and papers before. That was when he was having dinner with his girlfriend, Gerda, in a restaurant. He'd found them in a lost and found at a tram station fairly quickly. More recently, he'd lost two official IDs that the police had issued to him. But Cioma's latest loss occurred just as he was sure he'd invented the perfect alias for himself and acquired the perfect papers. Now his "official" passport with his photo and his wallet with his library card were somewhere in Berlin. The longer Cioma couldn't find them, the greater the odds the Nazis would.

Cioma called the library where he'd taken out a card. Maybe he'd dropped his wallet and passport there. A librarian told Cioma they'd found the wallet and passport and asked him to stop by to pick them up. But Cioma trusted hardly anyone these days, especially a stranger who was asking him to retrieve documents that may have already gotten him into trouble. Cioma also suspected that the librarian's split-second answer about finding his papers meant the police had already been asking about "Peter Petrov." If so, they were taking their search for him seriously, and it was best if Cioma stayed away.

The first person Cioma thought about getting advice from was Werner Schlesinger, one of Cioma's father's best friends, who'd been keeping a close eye on Cioma since Boris had been jailed for selling butter on the black market. Cioma knew that Schlesinger often went to a restaurant in Steglitz, roughly a half-hour subway ride from Cioma's workshop. Guessing that the police had narrowed their search for him to the neighborhood around his workshop—they probably figured that the library was convenient to wherever "Peter Petrov" lived or worked—Cioma pulled a hat down over his face so no one would recognize him and headed to the subway.

In Steglitz, it wasn't hard for Cioma to find the restaurant where Schlesinger hung out. It was right at the corner of a major, asymmetrical intersection: Schlossstrasse was so wide it was almost a boulevard while Markelstrasse was so narrow cars could barely squeeze through its single lane. An oddity of city planning.

Inside the restaurant, Cioma passed a bar on his right then pushed through double doors into a larger room. About fifty customers were sitting at small marble tables. Schlesinger's wife, Ruth, and a few friends of hers were sitting just behind the double doors. Cioma sat down, ordered a beer, lit a cigarette, and didn't say much. He preferred to wait until Ruth's husband arrived. For now, it was better to be quiet and silently follow the conversation with a neutral nod or a thin smile. If Cioma had any chance of surviving his new crisis—these days, there was always a crisis with Cioma—he had to parse every gesture, every syllable. The wrong shrug or grimace could give him away.

Cioma didn't have to wait long for Werner Schlesinger. As Schlesinger walked briskly into the dining room, his wife dashed toward him, scolding, "Why do you always come late when you know how much it worries me?" Werner winked at her. To Cioma, he whispered, "Police."[3]

Cioma had to leave. Fast. Edging his way toward the double doors that led to the next room, the one with the bar, and beyond that to the street, Cioma made out two shadowy figures behind him. Cioma moved faster now, through the barroom, then out the door to the street and down the steps to the sidewalk, where he tried to stroll along like everyone else: just another guy who'd enjoyed a good meal and maybe a few drinks while having a night on the town. Walking this nonchalantly would have been impossible if he hadn't learned, after months as a U-boat, how to look confident and not show his fear. But once Cioma rounded the corner at Markelstrasse, he broke into a run and sprinted for almost a mile until he reached Südwestkorso. Walking for the next mile and a half, he turned left onto Hohenzollerndamm. A half mile later, he turned left onto Auguste-Viktoria-Strasse, then a left into Paulsborner Strasse. His friend Tatjana lived at Paulsborner Strasse 92.[4]

Both Tatjana and her visitor—Mr. Jankowski, Tanja's friend who'd stolen the "passport" from the Russische Vertrauensstelle that Cioma had doctored for himself—were surprised to see Cioma. Earlier that day, Jankowski said, a detective named Wulkow had turned the Russische Vertrauensstelle upside down, convinced that the "passport" they'd found with "Peter Petrov's" name in it belonged to a Russian spy. They needed every clue that would help them find "Petrov." Wulkow announced to everyone in the Russische Vertrauensstelle that posters with photos of "Petrov"—Cioma's photo—were going up all over Germany. Photos would also be in every police station and in the next edition of the *National Police Gazette*. Jankowski's advice to Cioma: "Don't show your face in public."[5]

The next day, Cioma visited Franz Kaufmann. It didn't go well. Cioma losing his wallet, his "passport," and his library card confirmed Kaufmann's concerns about his best forger's carelessness. The first time Cioma lost anything was inexcusable; now it was unforgiveable. Cioma was a liability, a danger to everything Kaufmann had created and everyone who worked with him.

Kaufmann called an old friend, Johannes Popitz, to find out how much trouble Cioma was in. Popitz—Hitler's finance minister since 1933—had been resisting the führer since Kristallnacht in 1938, the night, all over Germany, synagogues were torched, business and homes ransacked, and Jews either killed or sent to "camps." That one night convinced Popitz that Hitler was the ruin of Germany. Popitz was no liberal, and he wasn't fond of Jews. He would have been happy with a "respectable" Germany run by a central government whose powers were absolute. Popitz never defined "respectable."[6]

Half an hour after Kaufmann called him, Popitz called him back. He'd talked with the police. Everything Cioma had heard from Jankowski was true: the police were sure "Petrov" was a Russian spy, a manhunt for him was underway all over Germany, and "Petrov's" photo—Cioma's photo—was on its way to every police station and would be in the next issue of the *Police Gazette*.[7]

Cioma needed a new place to hide. Kaufmann made a few phone calls. No one wanted him: a Jew who was wanted as much as Cioma was too dangerous to take in. Kaufmann's last call was to Helene Jacobs. Though her apartment, she said, "was by no means safe from Gestapo raids," she'd take in Cioma: "We need him for our work."[8]

Cioma first stopped by his workshop for supplies—watercolors, brushes, and his eyelet puncher. Everything he needed to make more IDs, especially for himself. He didn't have one now. Then he boarded a double-decker bus and climbed to the top deck. Ordinarily, the ride from the workshop to Helene's took half an hour. For Cioma, today's ride dragged on. Time had stopped for him. Life had almost stopped. After a few stops, he became aware of a bald man sitting three rows behind him. The man now moved up two rows and sat right behind Cioma. Leaning forward, he instructed Cioma in a low voice, "Take it easy, my lad. Calm down."

"What do you want?" Cioma asked.

"Stay calm," the man repeated. "Take it easy."

If this man—whoever he was—wanted Cioma to be calm, he'd be calm. Cioma's only consolation was the black tie that was in his pocket. If he was arrested, he'd hang himself with it before the torture started.

Ludwig, Cioma's friend with whom he shared his workshop, had come along to visit friends who lived just off the bus route. As Ludwig stood up to get off the bus at Olivaer Platz, the man sitting behind

Cioma looked from him to Ludwig, then back again. He didn't know who to stay with. Finally, he went down the stairs close behind Ludwig. Cioma relaxed then realized the bald man might be sitting on the lower level of the bus, waiting for Cioma when he left the bus. There was only one way to get out of this trap: Cioma would jump off the bus and run. Cioma was a fast runner. The bald man would never catch him.

As the bus slowed down to make a turn, Cioma stood near the top of the stairs on the double-decker, placed his hands on the railing of the stairs, lifted his legs, and slid toward the street—silently. If the bald man was sitting on the first floor of the bus, Cioma didn't want to give him a reason to turn around. At the bottom of the stairs, Cioma jumped off the bus and ran as fast as he could. After a few blocks, he ducked into the lobby of an apartment building and looked out. He didn't see anyone. Cioma waited a few minutes to catch his breath then started walking toward Bonner Strasse 2—Helene's building. She'd turn out to be the most welcoming, and the most giving, of the many people Cioma had stayed with since he started living on his own.

Thus began Cioma's summer of 1943. He never returned to Frau Schirrmacher's. He never went sailing on the *Comrade* again. For three months, he would live with a woman who was seventeen years older than he was (Cioma was twenty; Helene was thirty-seven), and who treated Cioma to wine, tasty dinners, homemade strudel, and to herself. She was more worldly and better read than Cioma, and they discussed history, literature, religion, and, of course, politics. It wasn't a bad life for a young Jew who was hiding, and, in more ways than one, it was a good education.[9]

PART FOUR

THE EXODUS

21

"Simple Is What You Are, Schönhaus"

Throughout June, July, and August, Cioma and Helene had long discussions about their dream world, in which everyone followed Leo Tolstoy's teachings about pacifism, loved their neighbors and loved God, and pursued perfection not by blindly obeying orders from the church or the government, but by following their heart. Some people thought Tolstoy was a wild-eyed anarchist. Others admired his search for pure freedom, and a return to how God made us, wanted us, shaped us: original man and original woman, natural and pristine. In Helene and Cioma's dream world—Tolstoy's dream world—there'd be no antisemitism and no hate. Distinctions between religions would vanish, and humanity would be one. In that same spirit of oneness, Helene assured Cioma about remaining in her apartment, "You don't need to worry anymore. Nobody will come for you here. Stay here until the war is over. You brought your tools with you. We'll share the work: I'll collect the passes from Kaufmann, you work on them, and I'll distribute them."[1]

And so they did, this son of proletarian Jews and this Lutheran who'd been attending St. Anne's Church in Dahlem since 1934, a red brick-and-stone church with arched windows, an oval domed transept over the altar, and a belfry topped by an eight-foot-tall cross. In 1940 she joined Franz Kaufmann's Bible study group at St. Anne's.

St. Anne's was one of the centers of Nazi resistance in Berlin. Its pastor, Martin Niemöller, often began services by puckishly announcing, "All right, now that the gentlemen of the Gestapo have joined us, let us pray in God's name." Niemöller knew he was being watched, and the Gestapo knew it was there to do the watching. Only one of them knew that God was watching both of them.

At 6:00 P.M. almost every day, Helene joined other congregants in St. Anne's as they recited the names of pastors and friends who'd been arrested or the names of those the Nazis had banned from speaking in the church because their opposition to Hitler was too overt, too blunt. In late 1941, Helene and others in Kaufmann's group began sending food and clothing to Jews who'd converted to Christianity and been "transported" to "the east." The members of Kaufmann's group hoped that their small packages would bring the prisoners some measure of comfort or, at minimum, an assurance that they had not been forgotten. In truth, the Nazis made sure that the packages from St. Anne's hardly saved anyone and, often, didn't reach those for whom they were intended. From the Nazis' perspective, the packages had one purpose: to kindle hope, not in their prisoners, but in the people who sent them. That hope might convince the members of St. Anne's that these really were camps, and that the "transports" were ordinary trains that took ordinary people to ordinary places, and that the stories people were hearing about chimneys spewing black ash all over the countryside were nasty exaggerations from the führer's enemies, of whom there were many.

When asked once why she was sending food and clothing to people she'd never met, and probably never would, Helene answered with a firmness not expected from someone who was so thin she barely cast a shadow: "These people are human," Helene answered evenly and decisively. "They're hungry, and they're cold, and they're desperate. They are no different from you or from me." With that, whoever had questioned Helene was silent, as much for incurring her wrath as for facing their own indifference, passivity, or fear, or whatever was keeping them from doing what this deceptively inconsequential-looking woman was doing. Helene's calling—her courage—brightened her mien until you knew, if you were half awake, that there was nothing banal about her at all—not her looks, not what Cioma called her "scraggly hair," and definitely not her conscience.[2]

On April 1, 1942, Helene had attended Elyse Kayser's final communion. In a day or two, she'd board a "transport." Kaysey "could not have been given a better final word," Helene thought about the reading that day from the prophet Zephaniah: "I will deal with all that afflict you. I will save the lame and gather the scattered. I will make those who were disgraced throughout the earth receive praise and fame."

The communion, Helene reflected, "united more firmly" the members of St. Anne's who were about to be deported and those who loved them and were staying behind.[3]

Four days later, it was Easter, and thousands of Berliners strolled in front of the Kaiser Wilhelm Memorial Church, whose sanctuary seated more than two thousand congregants and whose widely admired spire towered 371 feet over the Kurfürstendamm, the city's most fashionable boulevard. Easter was the day, and this was the place, to parade in your finery, pleased with your tweed jacket, Tyrolean hat, and coat trimmed with fur and beads. A little girl with a long blonde braid held her mother's arm, certain she would always be safe, secure, and loved, and that everyone she knew would be the same. Her little world inoculated her from the thrumming and the pain beyond it. Best for her if it stayed that way.

No one promenading on the Kurfürstendamm, surely not this child, could know that, ninety-six hours earlier, Helene Jacobs's friend

Elyse Kayser had been "transported" to the Warsaw Ghetto. Or that a few weeks later she would die of pneumonia, and that others from St. Anne's who had been deported with her would try to give her a proper burial, though proper burials for Jews were rare and improbable in Warsaw. The bodies of the dead were usually thrown onto carts and dumped into mass graves.

Helene Jacobs certainly didn't know this. But in her heart she wept for what she was sure was Elyse's fate. She could not let this happen to anyone again.

That July, Helene hid her first Jew in her apartment: Clarisse Blumenthal. Fifty-four years old, Blumenthal had been injured while working in a factory. It was no secret that injured Jews were sent to concentration camps. When Helene and Franz Kaufmann heard about Blumenthal's injury, Kaufmann provided her with coupons for food and a fake ID, and Helene gave her a room in her apartment. Blumenthal stayed there for three weeks then moved to a town in Lower Saxony where she got a job in a spa, its lawns dotted with pergolas, chairs, and benches for sitting, reading, and lighthearted conversations that avoided talking about the war: people came here to relax, not to dwell on unpleasantries. Blumenthal hid in plain sight until the end of the war, a quiet victory for Helene Jacobs and a quiet affirmation of the power of the teachings of the apostle Paul, whom Helene revered. "Love," Paul said, "is the fulfillment of the law." Helene loved.

22

Hiding, Loving, Fleeing

T rusted visitors came to Helene Jacobs's apartment while Cioma stayed there. One was Ludwig Lichtwitz, Cioma's friend who'd been on the double-decker bus the night they were harassed by the bald man they were sure was a policeman. Cioma was relieved to hear the man hadn't followed Ludwig that night. "He stayed on the bus," Ludwig assured Cioma. "He was probably waiting for 'Peter Petrov'"— the "Russian spy" whom officers all over Germany had been ordered to find.[1]

Cioma couldn't go outside, so his friends made sure he wasn't bored. Helene and Franz Kaufmann brought him IDs and passports and stamps to forge, and Ludwig and Cioma played chess or listened to the BBC with the volume so low they could barely hear it. Listening to foreign broadcasts had been a crime since the war began: a ridiculous law that made the majority of Germans criminals. All over the country, people were pressing their ears to their radio's speaker or bundling themselves and their radio in a blanket to muffle the sound. As many as three quarters of German adults regularly listened to the BBC. The SS wasn't oblivious to the radio hijinks going on all around them. Everywhere, men and women stopped gardening, or pushing their babies in perambulators, or gossiping with their neighbors and went inside five minutes before the BBC's news came on the air. The BBC came first.[2]

Cioma would have liked to scramble inside to hear the latest news from England. That would mean he wasn't confined to Helene's apartment. But confined he was, and here he stayed until conditions beyond his control changed in a manner favorable to him, and to millions of others.

Though his movement was restricted, Cioma experienced a freedom he hadn't for years, a liberation of his mind and an emancipation of his heart. With Helene, he could explore ideas that had barely engaged him before, ideas that challenged, inspired, and lent hope. All of them stirred his mind, which had lain fallow for too long. Also, with Helene, Cioma could explore certain pleasures with a new and deeper intensity: until now, his adventures of the flesh had been brief and sporadic—a few nights with one woman or another, then weeks, maybe months with no one. Now he could enjoy Helene for what would turn out to be an entire summer. As if this weren't enough, Cioma and Helene had the time and the imagination to weave, in their fantasies, a future—a good future—that might be salvaged from the destruction Hitler had wrought. Their hope, and their faith, that this would be reality carried them through the day.

Not being on the run—apartment to apartment, night after night; and apartment to forgery studio, day after day—had its benefits. This new stability nourished Cioma. Stronger, calmer, more open, he entered a new world, a new community, inhabited by good and reliable people: Helene, Kaufmann, Ludwig and, occasionally, Kurt Müller from Stuttgart. The Nazis had destroyed Cioma's old world—the one his parents and friends had cultivated on Sophienstrasse. Cioma knew that, and he knew there was no turning back. In Helene's small apartment on Bonner Strasse, Cioma built a new world with a brave woman and with the few equally brave people who stopped by to provide news of the outside world or distract him with chess or the latest broadcasts from the BBC or with gossip and jokes. For months, Cioma had lacked this consistent warmth of human fellowship—companionship he craved, companionship he needed. Now that he knew it still existed, he was assured, to some degree, that the world after the war would be populated by good friends and devoted lovers, all yearning, like Cioma, for community, decency and dignity. Minus those, they might as well not have survived this bloody war.

Life for Cioma became predictable. He falsified IDs, played board games, listened to the radio, cooked dinner, and made love with Helene, though, sometimes, air raids interrupted. Like the time an air raid warden knocked on Helene's door, asking why she wasn't in the air raid shelter in her building's basement.

"Oh, come on," Helene said. "The British always miss."

"Don't argue," the warden scolded. "Just follow orders."

Helene did. Cioma couldn't leave her apartment. Even if he had, he would have been kicked out of the air raid shelter: it was only for building residents, and Cioma hadn't informed the police he was living there. And if someone recognized him as a Jew, he'd be kicked out of the shelter anyway. Since 1941, Jews hadn't been allowed in shelters. The best they could do was huddle in the hallways of buildings where they lived or worked.[3]

At one point, Cioma asked Ludwig to bring back all the rope that was in his locker near the dock where he kept the *Comrade*. A few hours later, Ludwig returned, lugging several dozen feet of rope—long, short, all of it useful. He and Cioma tied it all together and knotted one end to a radiator in Helene's apartment. If a bomb hit Helene's building, Cioma would lower himself to the street.

Life at Bonner Strass was the reverse of the constant running around that Cioma had been doing: biking or riding on trams or subways from one end of Berlin to the other, looking for safe houses and safe people, praying that no one would follow him to Kaufmann's to pick up more IDs to counterfeit, or to the workshop where he forged them, or on a double-decker bus where he had to slide from the top level to the street to escape from a bald man who may, or may not, be a policeman who may, or may not, be looking for him. There was a balcony at Helene's where Cioma got some sun, and there was good food, and Cioma looked forward to visits from Ludwig and from Franz Kaufmann, who brought Cioma more documents to falsify, once as many as thirty-seven. But Kaufmann was a worrier, and he worried that Cioma wouldn't stay inside. Cioma's restlessness, his innate cockiness, could get them all in trouble. "You've got to keep your head down, Schönhaus," Kaufmann told Cioma. "Your 'wanted' poster is everywhere. Don't move an inch outside until it's all over."

Helene agreed. "You can rely on me to make sure Schönhaus stays here," she assured Kaufmann.

Kaufmann had complete faith in Helene, in her courage, in her contempt for the Nazis, in her devotion to truth and justice. But he'd overlooked an aspect of Helene that surprised him. Delivering more IDs for Cioma one day, Kaufmann took a good look at Helene, then at Cioma, then back to Helene. His gaze finally settled on Cioma.

"Schönhaus, Schönhaus," Kaufmann playfully scolded. "What have you done to our little Helene? I wouldn't have recognized her. Look at that perfect complexion, those flowing locks, those radiant eyes. It's obvious the prince has kissed a frog and turned it into a princess."[4]

Kaufmann's words were clumsy. No woman likes to be called a "frog," even after they've been transformed into a princess. Kaufmann might have been too stunned to bother with delicacies and sensitivities, and maybe they didn't matter anyway. He was enjoying himself. Whatever was going on between Cioma and Helene—and Kaufmann knew what it was—was probably inevitable when two people share close quarters, particularly during a war and when they're lonely, desperate, and needy. What Kaufmann thought didn't matter. Cioma and Helene's romantic entanglement would make an indelible impression on their minds and on their hearts. Years later, they'd look back on it with fondness, and with the pain that is rarely absent from love affairs that end in sorrow and disappointment. Rare is the love that's been withdrawn that can be drawn again. In time, Cioma and Helene would accept that. For now, they had each other, and now was all that mattered.

Most of the time, it was Cioma who made dinner. Often, they had wine with it. They usually made love. They were a couple, settling into habit and routine, but not into monotony. Monotony was boring, and, during a war, nothing was boring. The only routines they fell into—dinner, getting IDs, faking IDs, delivering IDs, making love, and long talks about things that mattered—helped relax them both. This was the ploy of smart, canny people. It was also how you held the world at bay.

Late in the afternoon of August 17, Ernest Hallerman, a member of Franz Kaufmann's cell, called Helene, asking her, rather insistently, if they could meet as soon as possible. He needed her to pass on a message to someone else in their group. Helene had already arranged to meet a couple at the Feuerbachstrasse S-Bahn station. She told Hallerman to meet her there.

It took Helene twenty minutes to walk to the train station. The couple was waiting outside for her with photos that Cioma could use when counterfeiting IDs for them. Stay here, she told them. Helene went through the station's doors and found Hallerman. She didn't know that a Gestapo agent was watching her, and another agent was watching Hallerman. She was arrested before she exchanged five words with Hallerman.[5]

From the balcony outside Helene's apartment, Cioma had watched her walk toward the S-Bahn station. As afternoon darkened to evening, Cioma made dessert for the two of them—pancakes with plums—and poured champagne: a glass for him, a glass for Helene. Still, Helene didn't return. Ten, eleven, twelve o'clock came—"the longest hours of my life," Cioma later said. So long, and Cioma was so worried that he "almost went mad." Around one o'clock in the morning, he forced himself to "remain calm and rational." If Helene had been arrested, Cioma knew the Gestapo would soon arrive. Everyone knew how the Gestapo operated. Its agents did everything by the book. The only surprise when dealing with them was how faithful they were to everything civilization was not.[6]

Cioma began running around Helene's apartment, stuffing into a briefcase anything that might connect her to him. The police may have had the wrong name for Cioma—"Peter Petrov"—but not the wrong photo: he was the young man looking slightly to his left in the photo of "Petrov" that had been printed in the special edition of the German police bulletin and was on WANTED posters everywhere. The young man with dark hair swept back from his forehead and a sharp aquiline nose and a white dress shirt whose collar hugged his black tie. The young man wearing a dark suit jacket and an equally dark expression on his face, an expression too dark and too serious for someone barely out of his teens. That young man was unmistakably Cioma Schönhaus, and that young man knew he had to make himself scarce, for his sake and for Helene's, and for the sake of everyone in Franz Kaufmann's circle. Everyone was at risk if Cioma didn't leave Helene's apartment. Fast.

Around 5:00 A.M., Cioma boarded a bus for his workshop in Moabit. He felt reasonably safe: most policemen weren't up before dawn. Along the way, Cioma's satisfaction that he was one step ahead of the Gestapo evaporated. He realized he'd forgotten the eyelet puncher he used for forging IDs and a briefcase full of cash intended for a Gestapo agent who said he'd save Jews from the ovens: one thousand Reichsmarks for each of them.

At the workshop, Ludwig tried to talk Cioma out of going back to Helene's apartment. If the police caught him there, Helene would be in even more trouble than she was already.

"Don't worry," Cioma said. "Before I go to the flat, I'll phone from the phone booth on the corner near her. If no one picks up, I'll know it's safe to go in. It's simple."

"If you ask me," Ludwig fumed, "simple is what *you* are, Schönhaus."

Cioma got on a bus toward Helene's apartment, jumped off at Süd-westkorso, and walked half a mile to a phone booth so close to where he'd been staying that he could see if the lights were turned on when he called. He dialed Helene's number: Wagner 31 35. The phone rang ten times. No one answered and no one turned the lights on. Cioma climbed the stairs to Helene's floor, let himself into her apartment, and left the door slightly ajar so he could hear if anyone was coming. Throwing the money and the eyelet puncher into his rucksack, he ran down the stairs to the street.

On the bus back to his workshop, Cioma saw a sign for a barber. Cioma got off at the next stop, walked back to the shop, and told the barber, "A military cut, please. By this time tomorrow, I'll be in the army."

"At least you've got something worth cutting," the barber said with a laugh. "It's a long time since you saw a barber."

With his new haircut, Cioma could pass as a soldier. But he had a new problem: what did he do now? The Gestapo and the police were getting closer to him every day. They had his photo. And they'd arrested Helene. Soon they might arrest Kaufmann, or maybe Ludwig, or anyone else who knew anything about Cioma: where he lived, where he ate, where he sailed, where he worked; whom he met with and who brought him IDs to falsify or took them to Kaufmann when he was done with them. Cioma might change his routines and his patterns, but some facets of his personality were so subtle, so below his level of consciousness—how he carried himself, walked, talked, or used his arms or hands—that he wasn't aware of them. What he didn't know about himself, the police or the Gestapo might.

Cioma had to figure out where to go next and how to get there. Maybe his boat, the *Comrade*, was his answer. If he was lucky, he might sail 80 miles northward on the Havel River until it flowed into another river, the Elbe, and then another 250 miles to Cuxhaven, where the

Elbe flowed into the North Sea. The North Sea could take Cioma to England or Scotland if he didn't get lost first. He'd never been on such a large, dangerous body of water: the North Sea was 600 miles long and 360 miles wide and spanned 220,000 square miles. To cross it, sailors had to know what they were doing. Cioma didn't. He was on his way toward becoming a decent sailor, but he was still a beginner. And even if he kept his bearings while on the North Sea, the *Comrade* wouldn't have a chance. Waves crested to nineteen feet, and currents moved in different directions—surface water in one direction, deeper water in another. If the waves or currents didn't sink Cioma, German patrol boats would. They were everywhere.

Cioma turned his attention in the other direction, away from the Havel and the Elbe and the North Sea and toward Switzerland, six hundred miles south of Berlin. It wasn't surprising that Switzerland appealed to him. It had been beckoning to him for some time. His friend Dorothee Fliess and her family had emigrated there, part of a scheme by anti-Nazis in the Abwehr, Germany's intelligence agency, who'd convinced Heinrich Himmler that the Jews they were smuggling out of Germany would go to the United States to spy for Hitler. Himmler fell for the ridiculous scheme, and Dorothee and her family spent the rest of their lives in Switzerland. And on one of Cioma's visits to Thesi Goldschmidt, a good friend of his in Berlin, her mother had offered to show him something "that will interest you." Spreading out a map of southern Germany, Mrs. Goldschmidt continued as if they were two ordinary Germans enjoying tea and biscuits in the middle of the afternoon, calmly planning their next vacation. Looking keenly at the map, Mrs. Goldschmidt proposed, "Now, let's find a border crossing for you. Would you like to do that?"

Cioma would.

After his conversation with Mrs. Goldschmidt, Switzerland stayed on Cioma's mind, night and day. He tacked up a large map of Germany on the wall next to the kitchen table in his aunt and uncle's apartment, studying it over dinner and marking with different colored pins various points where he might enter this country he'd never been to, a country he was sure would save him.

Around the same time, Cioma dreamed he was on a horse, racing through falling snow that was so thick he could barely make out a troika that was ahead of him. Pulling alongside the sleigh, Cioma recognized its one passenger: Napoleon Bonaparte. The emperor pulled out a pistol and shot at Cioma. Upon hearing the gun's report, Cioma's horse bolted ahead. At a fork in the road, a sign labeled SWITZERLAND pointed toward the left. Cioma pulled the reins in that direction. As he approached the border, Cioma realized he'd better cross it on foot and leave his horse behind: the horse didn't have papers to enter Switzerland. At that point, Cioma woke up.[7]

23

"The Lifeboat Is Full"

Ernest Hallerman, the member of Franz Kaufmann's group who turned in Helene Jacobs, also turned in Kaufmann two days later. Terrified he'd be executed now that he'd been arrested, Hallerman gave the police one name after another. He was sentenced to eight years in prison.

Kaufmann, who was born a Jew, may have thought he'd converted to Protestantism. Not according to the Nazis. To them, "conversion" was another trick of the Jews: a sneaky way to make people think they'd stopped being Jewish. But the Nazis couldn't be outsmarted. "Once a Jew," they said, "always a Jew," and this Kaufmann they had on their hands was as typical a Jew as it got: he'd tried to fool them by "converting," then he'd manipulated a weak, vulnerable woman—Helene Jacobs—to do his bidding. Helene was good at what she did; Kaufmann was better: he got people to work for him. And he was as tricky as all the other Jews in Germany, and in the world. His people were known for deceit, deviousness, and chicanery, and he wasn't disappointing them. And poor Helene had been taken in by more than Kaufmann. Helene's own faith, the Nazis wrote in their charges against her, had instilled in her a "religiously based sense of sympathy" for the weak and the helpless, and Christianity, to which Helene was devoted, suffered from a "lack of understanding of the question of race." Hardly anything was more important to the Nazis than race. They were infuriated that Christianity got it all wrong. Poor Helene. To the Nazis, she was pathetic, duped by everyone, and everything, she trusted.[1]

When the Nazis arrested Kaufmann, he was carrying his small notebook full of the addresses, phone numbers, and names—real names and cover names—of everyone in his group, and in a few other anti-Nazi groups, and of Jews whom Kaufmann was hiding. This was the Nazis' Rosetta stone, their key to catching some of the people they'd been hunting for months. Helene, whom the Nazis held in such contempt, was the one who'd warned Kaufmann not to carry the book around with him, and not to write down all his secrets in one place.

"You rely on me to make sure Schönhaus is safe," she'd told Kaufmann rather heatedly. "But what about your notebook if you're arrested? You would endanger everybody who's placed his trust in you."

"You're right," Kaufmann assured Helene. "I'll make sure my notebook is safe when I hear from Minister Popitz that they've got something on me and I'm a wanted man. For the moment, thank God, that is not the case."

But Kaufmann never heard from Popitz, the finance minister who'd warned him that Cioma's photo was going up all over Germany after he'd lost his "Peter Petrov" ID. Helene was right: when Kaufmann lost his notebook, he endangered everyone who'd placed their trust in him. The Nazis' interrogations didn't help either. By the time they rounded up everyone who was in Kaufmann's notebook, and everyone he told them about while he was tortured, they had arrested more than fifty people. Some went to labor camps, where a few were worked to their deaths; a handful received jail sentences for as long as eight years.[2]

Most exciting to the Nazis was learning more about the forger they knew as "Gunter Rogoff" or "Peter Petrov." The day after he was arrested, Kaufmann told the Gestapo that "Rogoff/Petrov" was actually Cioma Schönhaus, "a very likeable young man who I know would much

rather have been using his skills as a graphic artist than for forgery."
Schönhaus's studio, he confessed, was in Moabit. He didn't know the
address. One address he did know was where Cioma had rented a
room—Kleinstrasse 7. [3]

The Gestapo moved fast, first sending Stella Kubler, their glamorous
griefer, to prowl around Moabit, hoping she'd nab Cioma for them. She
was the Gestapo's best asset when it came to finding Cioma. She'd
met him in art school, had run into him on the street a few months
prior, and was the only person the Nazis had on their hands who knew
what Cioma looked like. Proof that they knew each other was that the
handwriting in her ID matched the handwriting in "Rogoff's" ID,
the one he'd lost in the library along with his wallet and money. Stella
complied. Freshly tortured and newly threatened with the murder of
her parents if she didn't help find Cioma, she set out for Moabit, afraid
of what might happen if she didn't.

Gestapo agents also visited Frau Schirrmacher, who'd rented a
room to Cioma at Kleinstrasse 7. Schirrmacher told them Cioma had
moved out the morning of June 16, more than two months before,
leaving behind a few books on sailing and nothing else. There was
one more thing, Frau Schirrmacher added: Cioma had bought a
sailboat in May and he usually sailed it on Lake Stössensee. A search
of docks and boatyards along the lake led Gestapo agents to Rudolf
Ladewig, who worked in one of the boatyards and remembered a
"young man" whom he'd sold a boat to in May. He'd given his name
as "Peter Schönhausen"—Cioma went by so many names—and his
address as Kleistrasse 7—Frau Schirrmacher's address. Ladewig
recalled that "Schönhausen" sailed frequently, often "accompanied by
several young ladies." His visits to the boatyard "stopped abruptly"
around the middle of June—the same time Cioma moved out of Frau
Schirrmacher's. [4]

The Gestapo was closing in on Cioma, though it had no idea where
he was. They only knew where Cioma had been. And Cioma, who was

hiding in his workshop in Moabit, didn't know what the Gestapo knew. He only knew that whatever they knew about him couldn't be good. Not after both Helene and Kaufmann had been arrested.

In January 1944 Helene Jacobs was sentenced to two and a half years in prison—a lax sentence by Nazi standards, perhaps because the judges pitied her: she'd been duped by Kaufmann *and* by Christianity. They were also flummoxed that someone as plain as Helene—so forgettable—could have done what prosecutors claimed she did. For the judges, for any good Nazi, bravery and valor sprang from striking, almost heroic good looks: a Teutonic, statuesque physique if you were a male; a wide pelvis (good for childbearing) if you were female; blonde hair and blue eyes for men and women. Aryan beauty was the beauty of the future. Not someone like Helene. What the judges didn't know was that Helene's lack of Aryan beauty was her secret weapon.

The judges were less kind toward Franz Kaufmann. They had no pity for him. His conversion had been a fraud: his blood was Jewish blood, no matter how many tricks he tried to pull. And since no laws protected Jews, and since being Jewish was crime enough, Kaufmann was sent to Sachsenhausen on February 17, 1944. He was killed the same day.[5]

Switzerland was Cioma's only hope. It was small—only sixteen thousand square miles—and landlocked, and surrounded by Nazis to its north (Germany), fascists to its south (Italy), and German-occupied countries to its west and east (France and Austria). Yet for Cioma, Switzerland was magical and mythical: a European Shangri-la with yodelers and Saint Bernards, and the creamiest of chocolates, and mountains that provided climbers challenges they'd brag about the rest of their lives.

Switzerland had been living off this image for a long time. Sometimes it worked. Sometimes it didn't. Mark Twain visited Switzerland in 1891 and was not impressed. With its mile-high summits "thinking their solemn thoughts with their heads in the drifting clouds," Switzerland was a visual feast. But the sounds of Switzerland gave Twain a headache. Cuckoo clocks were "silly and aggravating," and yodelers—hucksters in lederhosen—preyed on innocent tourists. Hiking in the mountains one day, Twain gave a yodeler a franc out of "gladness and gratitude" for his high-altitude concert. Soon, Twain came upon another yodeler. He gave him half a franc. Yodelers then began appearing every ten minutes. The first one received eight cents, the second six cents, the third four cents, the fourth a penny. By the time he was done, Twain was paying yodelers not to yodel.[6]

Yodelers aside, Switzerland made for an ideal refuge. It was peaceful. The Swiss hadn't fought a war since 1515, when a humiliating defeat by the French convinced them to never enter into another conflict. And it was salubrious—a place where goat's milk and clear mountain air cured anything, a message dear to every reader of a beloved children's book. According to *Heidi*, cities spawned disease and sickness, and mountains were the holy fount of good health and good cheer. When Heidi first returned to the Alps from Frankfurt, where she'd been sent to work, she was weak and pale. Clara, her friend from Frankfurt who visited Heidi, was confined to a wheelchair. Almost overnight, Heidi was hale and full of energy and Clara needed her wheelchair no more—proof of the purity of the Alps and of the evils of life in the big city.[7]

Cioma was sure that healthy, peaceful, neutral Switzerland would save him. First he had to get there. Then he had to get in. There was a good chance Cioma couldn't do either.

Mostly, Switzerland was accepting political refugees from Germany. Anyone persecuted for their race or religion was sent back. It was also following international law that required it to take in army deserters. In this case, the German army. Accepting German soldiers who said they'd had it with Adolf Hitler while rejecting the Nazis' victims—Jews, Roma, homosexuals, the physically and mentally disabled, Poles, and many others—troubled many Swiss. That didn't bother Heinrich Rothmund, the head of Switzerland's federal police. Rothmund's job was to enforce his country's laws, which were keeping Jews out of Switzerland. His best virtue—if it could be called a virtue—was that he was frank about his contempt for Jews. Nothing was more honorable than an honest bigot. Switzerland, Rothmund boasted, hadn't resisted "excessive foreign influence and *Verjudung* just to have immigrants forced on us today." *Verjudung* meant "Jewification."[8]

Rothmund didn't mention that only nineteen thousand Jews lived in Switzerland—one half of one percent of its entire population, or that Switzerland had been discouraging Jews for years, banning kashrut, Jewish ritual slaughter, in 1893, then a few years later stamping Jews' applications for citizenship with a Star of David. Switzerland didn't have to tell Jews they weren't welcome. Jews knew it.[9]

With German Jews forced to leave behind almost all their money, Swiss officials worried that Jews allowed into the country wouldn't be able to support themselves and they'd strain its economy. The Swiss government's additional problem was that it couldn't distinguish between German Jews and German Gentiles. To put it more crassly, being unable to sort out who had money and who didn't. If this continued, Switzerland might have to accept everyone. Or no one.

To help out, Germany offered to print a red *J*, two centimeters high, on the first page of Jews' passports. The *J* pleased the Swiss, even after learning about Hitler's exterminations. Swiss diplomats who were stationed all over Europe were reporting to their home office about the killings they'd seen or heard about, and in late 1942 a Swiss businessman told officials in Bern that he'd learned, on his latest trip to Berlin, that Germany would soon "gas all male Jews between the ages of 16 and 60."[10]

None of that moved the Swiss. Many police officers or soldiers stationed along the border followed orders, or made up their own. One soldier dragged a pregnant woman back into Germany, though Swiss law allowed pregnant women into the country. Several soldiers forced five Jews to crawl to the next border crossing while

Germans were shooting at them. A fifteen-year-old girl was sent back to Germany after Swiss soldiers sexually abused her: their superiors decided she had seduced them. She was killed in Auschwitz. When a Dutch military attaché protested to Swiss officials about their country's brutality toward refugees, he was told the same methods were being used elsewhere. "Yes," the attaché agreed, "by the Gestapo."

Even as a newspaper in Zurich lamented that "the Jewish question has become a Jewish slaughter," Swiss officials kept inventing reasons to keep Jews out. More Jews, they said, meant more antisemitism, and that would make life worse for the few Jews already living in Switzerland. The most common excuse was that Switzerland was running out of room. "The lifeboat is full" went the standard inanity for not saving human beings. Ridiculous, retorted a Swiss politician. "Our lifeboat isn't overflowing. As long as it isn't, we will continue to fill it. Any other action would be sinful."[11]

In truth, Switzerland wasn't running out of room. It was running out of compassion, even while it was complying with German demands, like enforcing blackouts everywhere in the country at ten o'clock every night. The blackouts frustrated British pilots, who needed landmarks while flying to Germany on their latest bombing runs, bombs that might end Jews' misery. But now couldn't.[12]

Though we can't say exactly what Cioma heard about Switzerland, some news did drift in. Germany wasn't hermetically sealed off from the rest of the world. There were the bodies of escaped forced laborers or prisoners of war that washed up every day on the Swiss side of Lake Constance, the spacious body of water between Germany and Switzerland. Or about dogs ripping Jews apart on the German side of the border after Swiss officers sent them back. Or about the Jewish couple that committed suicide in the train station in Singen, a German city along the Swiss border. Realizing they couldn't travel any farther, they ended their lives with some degree of dignity: better ending it in a train station than in Auschwitz, or Buchenwald, or Bergen-Belsen, without pride, honor, and dignity.[13]

By the end of the war, Switzerland would send as many as 27,000 Jews back to Germany. Offsetting that were the 51,000 refugees it took in from all over Europe, including 2,592 Germans. Of those, 1,404 were Jews. Clearly, Switzerland's lifeboat wasn't full. Not even close. The Swiss historian Georg Kreis has said that "the *wrong* people were trying to board the boat"—guards from "camps" and members of the SS, deserters from the German army, German citizens with money and an eye on their main chance to get out of Germany. The "wrong people" were ruining the chances of those who were truly desperate. The Swiss "lifeboat" was still afloat, despite all the alarms about it sinking any day now.[14]

Ludwig Lichtwitz, who shared his workshop in Moabit with Cioma, thought Cioma was the "wrong" kind of person, though not "wrong" in the way that Georg Kreis used the word. When Cioma told Ludwig about his latest idea—he'd bike to Switzerland—Ludwig laughed about Cioma entrusting his life to two wheels that weren't exceptionally sturdy, and to a route that Cioma would improvise along the way, and to a fake ID that would be closely examined, as he biked along, by the SS or the Gestapo or by more ordinary Germans—hotel clerks, policemen in small villages, garden-variety snitches—whose loyalty to Hitler was unshakeable.

"So, now," Ludwig chuckled, "we're heading for Switzerland, are we? Couldn't think of anything easier, I suppose? How are you going to pull it off? If you ask me, Schönhaus, it would be easier to put a bullet in your head right away. You can borrow my revolver if you like."[15]

Cioma didn't like.

Cioma didn't appreciate that all his friends thought that biking six hundred miles to Switzerland was ridiculous. Just because no one had ever done it didn't mean that no one could.

On the other hand, Cioma, like everyone he knew, had heard stories about people who'd tried to get to Switzerland. Most involved hiking through the woods between Germany and Switzerland or taking a boat across some of the lakes or streams that lay between the two countries. Maybe, Cioma insisted, none of these stories had happy endings because none of them involved a bike.

Cioma knew at least one person who didn't get into Switzerland—a woman who wasn't happy with the ID he'd made for her. She demanded he change the occupation on her new ID from chambermaid to something more lofty.

"Anyone can see I'm not a chambermaid," she complained, too full of herself for her own good. "I'm the wife of a managing director. The occupation must be changed."

Cioma refused: forged handwriting—even his—could sometimes be detected. CHAMBERMAID was on the ID to which he'd pinned her photo. CHAMBERMAID would remain.

Two weeks later, soldiers stopped her in a forest near the border. Examining her ID, one soldier said, "What do we have here? Oh, a chambermaid, that's all. I tell you what," he told his comrades, "why don't we let the old dear go?" And they did. She thanked Cioma when she got back to Berlin. "Being a chambermaid," she told him, "saved my life."[16]

Hans, another friend of Cioma's, agreed with Ludwig that biking to Switzerland was absurd. In fact, just trying to get there any way you could think of—hiking, sailing, boating, swimming—was absurd. "Schönhaus," Hans explained patiently, "almost everybody who tries to go to Switzerland gets caught, even before they're anywhere near the border. Why take this risk? You can keep living in your workshop with Ludwig and you'd have nothing to fear"—the Nazis would never find him there. If Cioma had to get to Switzerland, Hans said, there were better ways than Cioma's stupid idea about biking. "This is bound to go wrong," Hans insisted. He urged Cioma to consider another way to get there. Hans was already looking into one of those better ways for

Cioma: A train conductor Hans slightly knew who worked on the railways' southern routes had offered, for one thousand Reichsmarks, to move Cioma from the passenger section of a train to the luggage car as it got close to the border. According to the conductor, the rest of the train remained in Germany while the luggage car was allowed to roll into Switzerland.

Cioma asked Hans if he'd confirmed what the conductor told him. "He seems pretty reliable," Hans replied, somewhat defensively. "You're being very cautious about my plan, Schönhaus, but you don't mind risking a bike ride to Switzerland."

Cioma disagreed: "Going to Switzerland my way puts my fate in my own hands." Going to Switzerland Hans's way put his fate in the hands of someone he didn't even know. To prove his point, Cioma called German Railways, pretending he was a diplomat who would soon travel from Germany to Switzerland. Claiming he'd have many suitcases with him, Cioma asked if the luggage car would continue into Switzerland. No, Cioma was told. All luggage cars remain in Germany. He'd have to hire a taxi to get his luggage across the border.[17]

Cioma would have been arrested if he'd accepted the conductor's offer. Maybe shot. That didn't change Hans's opinion about Cioma's plan: biking to Switzerland was still one of the dumbest things Hans had ever heard. It was one of the dumbest things all of Cioma's friends had heard. Germany was a garrison, an armory, a fortress. Roadblocks were everywhere. ID checks sprang up in a flash: on a corner, a sidewalk, or a highway; in the middle of an intersection; in a store, a restroom, a phone booth. The Nazis were paranoid about security. Cioma would be lucky if he got a few miles out of Berlin. He'd be lucky if he got out of the city.

With Switzerland bending so easily to German pressure, and with Cioma's friends trying to talk him out of what they saw as a suicide mission, then why was Cioma so dead set on going to this fantasyland whose mountaintops disappeared in the clouds and citizens yodeled all day and politicians warned that their "lifeboat" was about to capsize? The answer was simple: he had no other place to go. He also had no reason to stay in Germany. Helene and Kaufmann—his two main contacts in the cell for which he was faking IDs—had been arrested. Without them, he had no way to obtain IDs to counterfeit, or to distribute them once they were ready. And Cioma was no dunce. He knew that hardly anyone held up under the Nazis' torture and soon Helene and Kaufmann would spill some of their secrets about him. (He didn't know that Kaufmann already had and that Helene never would.)

And why on a bike, a flimsy contraption if ever there was one?

That answer was also simple: Most of the people who tried to get into Switzerland hiked, rode a train, swam, or sailed. No one biked. Cioma's originality, his creativity, his irrepressibility might take the Nazis by surprise, and nothing was more to Cioma's advantage than throwing the Nazis off-balance. They loved order, and precision, and knowing that one thing would follow another, that there was a logic that followed from one event to another. Biking to Switzerland would follow nothing that had come before it.

Cioma loved his friends more now that he felt the full force of their concern about his biking idea, even if everyone called it dumb. He didn't care. This was his plan, and he would get out of Germany his way. Its novelty might just make it work. There was just one problem. He needed a bike.

24

The Great Balancing

The bicycle Cioma's cousin had given him before emigrating to the United States was falling apart. For several years, Cioma had used it and abused it, riding it in good weather and bad, from one end of Berlin to the other and sometimes beyond. The bike was safer than public transportation: the police and the Gestapo often checked passengers' papers on buses, trams, trains, or the subway. They stopped cyclists less often. On his bike, Cioma could set his own speed and route, pacing, and timing. He could travel early in the day, late at night, up alleys, and down boulevards; weave in and out of traffic when he suspected someone was after him; or just as easily race straight ahead when he was in a hurry: just another cyclist in a city of many cyclists. There was almost an innocence to a bike, an unruptured memory that tied it to childhood or to a teenager's adventure with some friends just as the sun was setting in the early days of summer. Cioma understood that, and he appreciated it. He also understood that Cousin Morris's bike had become a liability. With bad tires, bad brakes, and a battered frame, it would never get him to Switzerland. By now, it was barely a bike. In Cioma's words, it was "scrap metal."[1]

Cioma turned to Hans Marotke, the cobbler who, a few months ago, had sold him the eyelet puncher he used when forging IDs. Along with repairing shoes, Hans occasionally sold used bikes. Maybe he had one for Cioma.

Hans's shop was in Mitte, roughly five blocks from where Cioma's family had lived on Sophienstrasse. Cioma hadn't been there for months, so filled was the neighborhood with sad memories. He went anyway. He had no choice.

"So, we want to buy a bike, do we?" Hans asked with a hint of a twinkle in his eye when Cioma explained why he'd come. "Bikes don't exist anymore. Not new. Not used. They're all gone."

"What," asked Cioma, persistent as ever, "if I pay two or three thousand marks for one?"

Hans perked up. "Hang on, did I hear right? You can pay three thousand marks? Come back tomorrow. I'll have one for you."[2]

Hans hadn't lied to Cioma. Bikes barely existed in the "real" world, the world of Nazis and bureaucrats, and wartime shortages for just about everything. No doubt the three thousand Reichsmarks Cioma offered Hans was outrageous—the average German was earning only about forty Reichsmarks a week. But neither Cioma nor his circumstances were average, and his offer reflected the inflated prices for everything. In Hans's world—a world parallel to the Nazis'—bikes did exist, at a price: bikes that had all their parts and would hold together for more than two blocks. Cioma had come to the right place. More black-market deals went on every day in Mitte, where Hans had his shop, than in any other neighborhood in Berlin.[3]

In some ways, this ambiguity about bikes—black market, regular market; high prices, competitive prices—reflected Germany's original ambivalence about bicycles. When bikes first caught on, mostly as a fad in the 1870s, the upper class embraced them as a "sport" like any other, say hunting or sailing. This class in particular was drawn to bikes because it could afford them—most were imported, usually from England—and they had the time to master these cumbersome vehicles: with their oversized front wheels, early bicycles tended to tilt, fall, or tumble. Rich folk had room on their estates for all that tumbling and falling. As mass manufacturing lowered the price of bikes, and as wheels of equal size, front and rear, made them easier to ride, they caught on among the middle and lower classes. For them, bikes were transportation, not sport: a way to zip around neighborhoods, cities, towns, villages. They were also a way to assert control. Everyone could now be their own motor, their own driver of their own horseless carriage. Without the expense of a horse.

Individual control was poison to Nazis. The only Germans who controlled anything were the Nazi upper crust. Everyone else served the state, and the state served Adolf Hitler. To them, bicycles were nuisances. They got in the way of progress, and they gave autonomy to people who the Nazis felt shouldn't have any.

Bikes these days weren't just a means to get from one place to another. In the wrong hands, they were weapons—vehicles of sabotage. Not long after taking power, the Nazis abolished the bicycle associations that were all over Germany. One of the first to go was a Socialist club—the Arbeiter-Radfahrerbund Solidarity, otherwise known as the Solidarity Workers-Cyclists Association. Its three hundred thousand members in five thousand chapters made it the largest workers' sports club in the country. When the club went, so, too, did the bicycle factory near Frankfurt that it owned. The Nazis didn't like that Communists, Socialists, and other ne'er-do-wells could use some of the twenty thousand affordable bikes the factory produced every year to sneak up on the police or Gestapo, shoot or stab them, then bike away, quietly, invisibly; or use them to deliver messages or easily evade checkpoints. All this made the innocent bicycle as close to a stealth weapon as the Nazis encountered.[4]

All that was why the German government wanted to keep someone like Cioma Schönhaus away from a bicycle. He didn't care. He was desperate. The day after Cioma visited Hans Marotke, the shoemaker had a bike for him. Cioma's family had known Hans for years—first as the cobbler who repaired their shoes, then as the trader who acquired a bike for Cioma's Cousin Morris, and next an eyelet puncher for Cioma. Hans knew the Schönhauses were Jewish, and he knew he was taking a huge risk by selling them anything, especially that eyelet puncher and even more so those bikes. For years, Jews had been prohibited from owning or using bikes, and they had to turn theirs in if they already had them. If Hans had been caught, he'd have been fined, imprisoned, or both. But he had no choice. As a Communist, he hated Hitler. As a longtime admirer of the Schönhauses, he was fond of Cioma.

The bicycle Cioma bought was ideal for the ride that lay ahead of him. It had a luggage rack, a chrome headlamp, with a dynamo powered by the rotation of the front wheel and tires—balloon tires—that were some of the most advanced of the day. A step up from the hard rubber of other tires, balloon tires floated on a wide cushion of air: they were twice as wide as other tires. Many cyclists favored balloon tires for their softer, gentler ride, especially since they transmitted substantially fewer vibrations on cobbled roads than the usual tire. That was good: Cioma would be riding over many cobbled streets and roads. All that cushioning would keep him comfortable and save his energy. He'd need it.[5]

For the rest of his life, Cioma would most remember two things about his bike: how those balloon tires coddled him, and how the seat—"so comfortable," he'd recall decades later—cradled him with its padding and caressed him with its leather. After being on the run from the Nazis for so long, Cioma deserved to be spoiled a little. The seat spoiled him a lot. Still, for all the comforts and accessories his bike offered—more than he had a right to expect in the middle of a war—there was one drawback, given the terrain and the distance that Cioma would be traveling: the bike had only one gear. He'd have preferred several: there'd be hills and low mountains on his trip, plenty of them. On the other hand, considering the handful of bikes that anyone was selling, even on the black market, and Cioma's rush to get out of Berlin, he couldn't be picky. He took what he got, and he was lucky he got anything.[6]

Now that he had a bike, Cioma needed to know how to get to wherever he was going; he hadn't settled on where he'd cross into Switzerland or how he'd get there. For that, he went to a shop that sold maps. It was on Gendarmenmarkt, a large square in central Berlin that for years had been dominated by a statue of Friedrich Schiller. The Nazis put the statue in storage: Schiller may have been one of Germany's greatest writers, but his devotion to freedom was too much of a rebuke to Hitler, such a rebuke that seven words from Schiller's tragedy *Fiesco* could have been Cioma's mantra for the ride ahead of him: "To save all, we must risk all." Cioma's bike ride would risk all.

In the shop, Cioma watched how other customers requested the maps they wanted: each of the three large maps of Germany that were hanging on the wall was divided into grids, and each grid had a number. The number designated the map a customer wanted. Customers called out the number to a clerk who was on a ladder that was leaning against the wall. The clerk pulled the map they'd requested from one of the drawers that were built into the wall, holler, "Got it, got it, got," then reach down and hand it to the customer. When it was Cioma's turn, he shouted out the numbers of all the maps that showed Germany's border with Switzerland. Surprised that no one warned him that they weren't for civilians—the maps were literally guides to escaping from Hitler's hell—Cioma next asked for maps of all the roads between Berlin and Switzerland. With each request, the man on the ladder hollered, "Got it, got it, got it" and handed a map to Cioma. Cioma paid for the maps, tied them to the luggage rack of his new bike, and happily pedaled away, thinking of his adventure that would begin in a few days.

Cioma's friends may have worried, with reason, if he'd ever get to Switzerland, but they overlooked the fact that a bicycle was perfect for

Cioma. It fit his character, his personality, his happy-go-lucky ways. It fit everything about him. Cioma chose a bike to get him to Switzerland for the same reason he'd been pulled toward a sailboat. He intuitively knew that a bicycle and a small sailboat, like the *Comrade*, were among the simplest of conveyances. His life was already complex; he didn't need more complexity to gum it up. After living by his wits for so long, he was accustomed to relying exclusively on himself. Aboard the boat, he'd had himself; on the bike, he would also have himself. He'd become so self-reliant, so turned in on himself, that he assumed he'd always be his own source of strength. There was no other place for him to turn. Cioma had learned this early on. Hashomer Hatzair, the youth group his mother had signed him up for when he was a teenager, had insisted on "absolute truth," on not caving in to "despair or pessimism," on refusing to "allow elements of weakness to enter one's life." All were consistent with who Cioma had become. All good members of Hashomer Hatzair, Cioma knew, were committed to community and to life, to being ready, "at every instant," to "oppose the forces of oppression." Cioma was one of oppression's most determined, and wiliest, of opponents.[7]

There were other reasons why a bicycle was Cioma's natural vehicle of choice. It would bestow upon him what few vehicles could: a respect for grace, for balance, for rhythm, for breath and, in the end, a deeper respect for himself. On a bike, breath and wheels become one, wheels and road become one. An intimacy develops that Cioma wouldn't have experienced if he'd looked at the German countryside through the window of a train, had a seat on a train been available to Cioma. The bond between Cioma and his bicycle would resemble that between true friends. Cioma's sailboat had been his friend. His new bike would be one also. You don't trust strangers with the journey of your life.

For years, Cioma had ridden around Berlin on his cousin's bike. He'd been too rushed to enjoy the more common pleasures of cycling: setting your own pace, thriving in a type of solitude, closely observing minor sights and pleasant distractions—a stone, a stick, a penny, a lovely young woman in a doorway, a letter to a beloved that had fallen out of a lovestruck suitor's pocket. Trained to be an artist, to savor the visual world around him, pedaling to Switzerland would offer Cioma ample opportunity to be aware, and alert, and appreciate what was near him, and what was within him. By the end of his adventure, he might see as he never had before: see the world better and see himself better. But first, he had to begin. And that required a form of courage that was new to Cioma: the courage to say goodbye to the few people in Berlin he still knew. Police raids, Gestapo arrests, and "transports" to "camps" had thinned the ranks of Cioma's family and friends. By itself, that made saying goodbye difficult and painful. Goodbyes were no longer polite, reflexive social gestures, expected upon parting from others for a mere day or two, say at the end of a workday, or a dinner with family, or a date that you wished would never end. In Berlin, too many goodbyes were final, and too many goodbyes had never been said that should have been. Cioma wanted to make sure he said his before he left for Switzerland. He was aware of the void of goodbyes he wished he'd said, and of the silences that were left in their place.

25

Pigs to Avoid

Cioma had a bicycle and he had maps. Now he needed camouflage. Without Franz Kaufmann to provide an ID that Cioma could modify for his trip, Bolette Burkhardt, a pastor at the Sophien Church, gave Cioma an army ID that a congregant had donated to their cause. It worked perfectly. After Cioma forged eighteen "official" stamps in it, a friend—Claus Schiff, a draftsman—wrote "Hans Brück," Cioma's new "name," on its inside pages. It was better for Claus to write in the ID than for Cioma to do it. That way, if Cioma was stopped while biking, the handwriting in his ID couldn't be traced to him. He'd never mastered disguising his own handwriting.

In a secondhand shop on Kleine Hamburger Strasse, Cioma bought the kind of rucksack and shorts and shirts Hitler Youth used on their hikes and marches. Farther down Kleine Hamburger Strasse, Cioma found a bookshop that carried *From the Kaiserhof to the Chancellery* by Joseph Goebbels, Hitler's propaganda minister. Carrying Goebbels's book in his rucksack would convince any policeman that this cyclist with a ready smile and a reedy build was a good Nazi: a zealot for the führer, for the Fatherland, for the war. Hitler's *Mein Kampf* was the Nazis' Bible; *From the Kaiserhof to the Chancellery* was commentary from the apostle closest to Hitler. Anyone who found Goebbels's book in Cioma's rucksack would have a hard time suspecting that photos of this innocent-looking young man had been posted in every police station in Germany.

In his bike's hollow handlebars, Cioma hid four rolled-up sheets of stationery he'd stolen from the armaments factory where he'd worked. On each sheet, he'd forged a one-week leave of absence from the factory. Each had the name "Hans Brück," each identified "Brück" as a "technical draftsman," and each had a different week's date on it, starting in early September through early October, when Cioma expected to arrive in Switzerland. A cork kept the papers from falling out, and a thin, almost invisible thread attached to the cork let Cioma pull it out when he needed his "leave of absence" papers for the next week.

Tatjana, Cioma's former girlfriend, was sure Cioma would lose his ID just as he'd lost some of his other IDs. To make sure that didn't happen, Tatjana sewed him a small pouch. He kept his ID here, along with two of his new maps (if he folded them tightly enough), and details on two people who might be useful later: the address of Cioma's cousin who lived in New Jersey, in case he needed a sponsor in the United States or someone who could vouch that Cioma was who he said he was, and the name and phone number of a famous theologian who lived in Basel. Friends told Cioma to contact the theologian if the Swiss police gave him any trouble. Tatjana sewed a thin strap to the pouch so he could wear it around his neck while cycling. The pouch itself was a clever piece of camouflage. Made from bright red fabric festooned with a flowery pattern, Cioma said it made him look like "an overprotected mummy's boy rather than a notorious forger trying to escape over the border."[1]

It was apparent Cioma had thought carefully about what he needed not just to get to Switzerland (maps, a book by Goebbels, a Hitler Youth rucksack and uniform, a new ID, and a new name) but what he needed to stay in Switzerland (contact information of people who could vouch for him or fend off bumptious Swiss officials). This bike ride was no improvisation that Cioma impulsively pulled together at the last minute. Its clear-eyed planning was the only way it could work—the summation of months of hiding in Berlin, during which Cioma had come to grips with all the ways—large and small—that Hitler's police, the Gestapo, and the SS could be frustrated and, in Cioma's own small way, defeated.

The maps, of course, were essential. They were the only way Cioma could know which roads to take or avoid, and how to bike in northern Germany versus the southern part of the country. Each region had its advantages, and each lacked some. The north was fairly flat, its roads rough and rutted and "cobbled" with stones that were centuries old in some places. Moderately steep hills were in the south, followed by rugged, more challenging terrain, but the roads were better paved than in the north. And no matter where he was, north or south, the new four-lane superhighways—Hitler's pride: the autobahns—would have helped Cioma if he could have biked on them. Bicycles were banned from these roads of the future.[2]

Now that Cioma had everything he needed, he was ready to set out. Since he'd first decided to bike to Switzerland, his plans had changed slightly, or friends had wanted him to change them. Early on, Ludwig Lichtwitz, sure that Cioma's plan was doomed, had offered Cioma his revolver: blowing his brains out was the same as cycling through the middle of Nazi Germany. Another friend now offered Cioma his pistol. His idea was that Cioma could bike close to the border, shoot anyone who tried to stop him, then run to Switzerland. Cioma didn't like that. He imagined a border guard or policeman lying on the ground, bleeding to death with photos in his wallet of his wife and children, who'd never see him again. Cioma struggled: "I would be that man's murderer." He told his friend to keep his revolver: "I can get across the border without that."[3]

Another idea was no less dangerous: Cioma would swim across Lake Constance, the large lake between Germany and Switzerland, at its narrowest point. That might be possible. Cioma was a strong swimmer, though the bodies that washed ashore of those who'd tried to make the swim were enough to persuade him not to try.

Cioma preferred a plan in which no one got killed, no one got shot, and no one drowned. He considered a friend's plan to bike as far as Feldkirch (five hundred miles to the south in Austria), then hop on a coal train bound for Switzerland. Cioma's friend had gone so far as to scout around Feldkirch to see if his idea made any sense. It did. Every day, trains were lined up at the station in Feldkirch, waiting for all their cars to be filled with coal. From a wooded slope next to the tracks, Cioma would be able to see when the last car was being coupled to the train. As it slowly passed in front of him, he'd slide down the hill, and jump on a freight car. The train, according to Cioma's friend, wasn't checked at the Swiss border.

Cioma set his sights on Feldkirch while keeping swimming across Lake Constance as a backup plan. There were only two catches: He'd never jumped onto a freight train. That was dangerous. He could be killed. And he'd never seen Lake Constance. He knew it was big. He didn't know how big. Swimming Lake Constance could also be dangerous. He'd have to fight strong currents and chilly temperatures, and pray that a sharp-eyed German solider didn't shoot him from the northern shore.

Either way—swimming or riding a train—this was Cioma's moment. Through ten years of Hitler's tyrrany, he'd clung to half-remembered shards of what it meant to be human, to take risks for others and for himself. And now, on two wheels of a bicycle that was new to him, on roads he'd never traveled, through villages he'd never seen, he'd balance his way back into life, toward a future that was real and had promise and potential. Cioma had no doubt that a good future awaited him. The optimist in him was his North Star. It was what drove him forward.

September 3, 1943, was one of the first nights the British bombed Berlin in earnest. The Royal Air Force dispatched 320 planes to Berlin.

Two hundred and ninety-eight returned. After trying to sleep in their workshop that night, Cioma and Ludwig ran from one doorway to another, looking for anything that would shield them from the death raining down from above. Hearing the hiss of an incendiary bomb that had landed in the apartment building where they were taking shelter, Cioma poured sand on it, then dumped water on top of the sand. He'd heard this was how you defuse an incendiary bomb. The hissing stopped. As the all-clear siren wailed, an air-raid warden invited Cioma and Ludwig to join him on the roof of his building. Everywhere they looked, there were flames, death, ruin—people without homes, buildings without shape, mangled pipes, charred bricks, and rising plumes of dust and smoke. Back on the street, Cioma heard a man tell his wife to let everything that was in their apartment burn: "Never go into that building again. A beam will fall on your head." An old man wandered around—dazed and numb, stumbling over scorched and blackened bricks: the remains of where he'd lived until an hour earlier. He looked uncomprehendingly at Cioma, as if to ask why people the man didn't know were trying to kill him from the skies.[4]

Cioma was right on schedule: he'd always planned to leave in early September. With all the bombs falling now, he was relieved he was getting out of Berlin just in time. Throughout the previous year, there'd been nine air raids on Berlin. Allied planes had been too busy destroying U-boat ports in Germany and France to divert planes to Berlin. Aside from that, the Allies didn't have too many planes that could fly the 1,200-mile round trip from England to Berlin. They did now. Soon, Lancasters, Halifaxes, Stirlings, Mosquitos, and B-17s were incinerating Berlin almost every night: 440 planes one night, 677 another, 891 a third. As the Allies began bombing in earnest, Sir Arthur Travers Harris, commander in chief of Bomber Command for the Royal Air Force, mocked the Germans for their "childish delusion that they were going to bomb everyone else, and nobody was going to bomb them." Apparently, the German High Command had never considered the brutal reciprocity of war. "In Rotterdam, London, Warsaw and half a hundred other places," said Harris, referring to the Nazis' targets earlier in the war, the Germans had "put their rather naïve theory into operation. They sowed the wind, and now they are going to reap the whirlwind." That reaping was more than the Nazis had bargained for, and it was exactly what Cioma was about to avoid. [5]

If Cioma had stayed in Berlin, the stench of corpses would have become as familiar to him as the wailing of mothers who'd lost their children, wives who'd lost their husbands, and husbands who'd lost their comrades. He'd have seen apartment buildings, churches, trams, bridges, squares, statues, and monuments blasted into ruin, the detritus of order, civilization, and sanity. Like everyone, Cioma was tired. Unlike everyone, he had a bike, a plan, and a date for his escape to begin. It couldn't have come any sooner.

The morning after the bombings, Cioma washed the soot from that night's fires from his face, checked the air in his bike's tires, and strapped his backpack to the luggage rack. It was warm. Seventy-six degrees Fahrenheit. Perfect biking weather. Ludwig mumbled, "Something for your new start in Switzerland." Pressing a one hundred franc Swiss banknote into Cioma's palm, Ludwig walked away before Cioma could thank him. [6]

Cioma carried his bicycle over fire hoses, burnt furniture, and freshly shattered glass. Ten blocks later, he entered a neighborhood where there'd been no bombing, no fires, no panic, and no ruin. Climbing onto the seat of his bike—the seat whose comfort he'd remember for decades—Cioma began pedaling away from the life he'd never expected to live.

Except for a few squirrels, the streets were empty. From a bridge in Pichelsberg, Cioma looked down on the *Comrade*, his beloved boat, moored snugly in a marina beneath him. Cioma never saw it again.

Cioma kept biking, elated he'd crossed Berlin's city limits. "Nobody stopped me!" he wrote to a friend after the war. "And we always thought

the police surrounded Berlin and didn't let anyone pass." The previous night's bombing may have been to his advantage: the police
may have been too distracted with its aftermath to pay attention to
a lone cyclist.

Next came Potsdam, where gilded carriages had clattered over
cobblestones a century and a half before, carrying royalty and philoso-
phers (such as Voltaire) to Frederick the Great's summer palace, a folly
dedicated to ego, fortune, and Frederick's need to get away from the
intrigue and conspiracies that were always roiling his court in Berlin.
Sometimes he dined with friends in a secret dining room where servants couldn't overhear the conversation. Or he'd luxuriate amid ornate
rococo furnishings, massive silver balustrades, and busts of writers and
composers, many obscure and most soon forgotten.[7]

Cioma had no time for kings, no matter how great they'd been. He
was just getting started, learning the feel of his bicycle, shedding the
dreads and apprehensions that had become his habit. He needed to
lighten himself, the best he could, of his past so he could concentrate
on this moment, and this bike, and this journey. Eleven miles south of
Potsdam, Cioma stopped for pea soup—his first food of the day—at
an inn in Beelitz, a small town famous for burning alive its entire
Jewish population in 1243. The Jews, local Christians claimed, had
desecrated communion wafers. Since for many Christians, consecrated
wafers are literally the body of Christ, the Jews had defiled the Son
of God. In Cioma's lifetime, the town was mostly known for growing
white asparagus. What had happened to those Jews in the thirteenth
century was the stuff of history, and largely forgotten. Germany was
doing more than enough right now to its Jews to more than compensate
for its lapse of historical memory.

Cioma could have stayed at the inn in Beelitz. But thrilled that,
at last, he was out of Berlin, he kept pedaling, past fields, forests, and
nature preserves, past a village where Martin Luther had preached
three centuries earlier under a lime tree because he'd been banned from

the town's church, and past another village where prisoners from several nearby "camps" were making weapons in a munitions plant. Three hours after he left Beelitz, Cioma reached Wittenberg, juddering to a stop in front of a hotel that, over the years, had attracted impressive clientele: Friedrich Schiller stayed here in 1804, Napoleon I twice—in 1806 and 1813, and Maxim Gorky a century later. Cioma never passed up a good recommendation.

At the front desk, Cioma presented his papers with his new "name"—"Hans Brück." Ordinarily, the desk clerk wouldn't have cared if Cioma's ID read "Fritz Schmidt"—the German equivalent of "John Doe" or "John Smith." Germany may have been a police state, and it may have been wartime. But most hotels were happy just to get another customer for the night. Travelers were scarce these days. Yet something about Cioma made the receptionist ask for his ID, claiming that she was required by law to send all IDs to the authorities so they could confirm their authenticity. "Thank God," Cioma realized years later, "I didn't act sheepish. I told her no one is allowed to part with his army ID. I volunteered to take it to the police myself the next morning. I stayed away from the police station the next day."[8]

Cioma's hotel room overlooked Wittenberg's main square. He was happy, he was tired, and he was sleepy. And he was proud. He'd biked almost eighty miles on his first day out of Berlin—roughly the same distance a professional cyclist covers in a day, and more than a respectable distance for someone who, until now, had mostly biked around Berlin. Cioma had chosen well: Wittenberg, his first haven after hiding for almost a year in Berlin, was a jewel box of a town with pastel-colored homes and shops lining its two major streets, many clustered around an ancient, well-preserved market square, and sunlight so bright and clear it was almost celestial. The heavenly skies were not out of place: Wittenberg was where the Protestant Reformation had begun in the 1500s when Martin Luther protested the Catholic Church permitting the rich to buy indulgences—"forgiveness" for their sins. The poor repented by praying, fasting, helping the weak and the ill. The wealthy bought their way into heaven. Luther argued that, by filling its treasury this way, the Vatican was encouraging the rich to sin even more, knowing they could always bribe their way out of trouble. But what was especially unsettling, given what had driven Cioma to gamble on a bike ride, was that Wittenberg had a long history of antisemitism, and was one of the earliest strongholds of Nazism in Germany. In effect: not a great place for Cioma to spend the night.

Wittenberg was a city of many myths. The myth that you could buy a good afterlife for yourself, the myth of miracles that were proudly displayed in a local church—straw from Jesus' cradle and a bottle of breast milk from the Virgin Mary—and the myth that anyone saw when they passed the sculpture on an outside wall of Luther's church, which showed Jewish children suckling on a pig's teats as a rabbi reached into its rear end for the Talmud. The sculpture had been on the church for two hundred years before Luther arrived in Wittenberg in 1512. Taking a good look at the pig, Luther proclaimed that the wisdom of the Talmud, one of Judaism's holiest books, was no greater than what you'd find up a pig's ass. Already, Luther's Reformation needed reforming.[9]

Centuries later, the good people of Wittenberg were among the first Germans to rally around Hitler. As early as 1921, a large swastika was flying across the street from Wittenberg's train station and signs were hanging in shop doors: JEWS ARE NOT ALLOWED. Nazis held large rallies in Wittenberg's town square and, in 1933, the year Hitler was appointed chancellor of Germany, they gained a majority on the city council, and the town's anti-Nazi mayor was thrown into prison. He was found dead in his apartment soon after he was released. The cause was never determined. This was not a town for anyone who was friendly to Jews.[10]

If Cioma had ventured beyond his hotel room, he'd have come face-to-face with Nazism that may have been stronger and more virulent than what he'd seen in Berlin: most Berliners never liked Hitler. And he never liked Berlin. For him, it was just a place to hang his hat, govern from, and have tantrums from. By staying in his room, Cioma didn't have a chance to learn how the Nazis had transformed Wittenberg. It was now a major manufacturing center, with factories churning out arms, dynamite, and warplanes, and more than seventeen thousand forced laborers (mostly Jews) living in barracks. Most of the town's minuscule Jewish population—about seventy people—had already been sent to Auschwitz, Theresienstadt, or Sobibor. Only a few escaped the Nazis' dragnet: one managed to get to Shanghai, another to Palestine. Only two weeks before Cioma arrived in Wittenberg, a sixty-five-year-old Jewish woman had committed suicide, worn down by humiliations and degradations.[11]

Cioma was smart: a hotel room was the best place for a Jew to be in Wittenberg. As long as no one knew he was a Jew.

With hundreds of miles remaining on his trip, Cioma couldn't be distracted by Nazi crimes, or by a sculpture of a pig on the walls of one of Wittenberg's most famous churches, or by sorrow over Jews who'd been sent to "camps" or died by suicide. If he wanted to get to Switzerland, he had to focus on biking and on roads and on remembering he was "Hans Brück," not Cioma Schönhaus. He'd have time later to dwell on what he'd seen.

Eighty miles in one day—the distance Cioma had traveled from Berlin to Wittenberg—would be his personal best for his entire trip. This, his first day of biking, was the easiest leg of his adventure. The roads had been flat, and no one had suspected Cioma wasn't who he claimed to be. Ahead lay hills: some steep, some long, some challenging, some no more than drawn-out slopes. Also ahead were ardent, enthusiastic Nazis. Hitler's most passionate supporters had always been in the south. That was important to keep in mind, though they weren't a match for Cioma's ability to make up stories about himself and about his life. Getting out of Germany, he'd learn, required clever improvisations as much as pedaling his bicycle another mile down the road. His imagination was fertile, and he'd use it completely unabashedly.

26

"I'm Crossing My Fingers for You, Schönhaus"

Cioma's second day on the road was similar to his first. Seventy-one degrees Fahrenheit. Clear. Dry. No rain. Perfect biking weather for Cioma to ride his perfect bike. South of Wittenberg, Cioma crossed a bridge that took him over the silvery, graceful Elbe River. The Elbe curved around Wittenberg on its seven-hundred-mile journey from Czechoslovakia to the North Sea in northern Germany, connecting cultures and regions, providing livelihoods for millions of people who lived near its basin, and giving anyone with a canoe or a small sailboat opportunities for lazy outings on weekends—paddling about, drifting along, racing other boats for the sheer hell of it. For Cioma, it was just another river to put behind him.

Cioma had barely gotten started when a policeman on a bicycle waved at him from the other side of the road. Cioma figured this was the first of what would be many police checks, each nerve-racking, each a test of his ability to put up a good front and an obliging smile. The slightest jitteriness could reveal him for what he was.

The officer who'd waved at Cioma was only being helpful. "Can't you see?" he called out. "I'm using a bicycle lane that's clearly marked, and you're not."

"I thought you only had to keep to the right," Cioma yelled back.

"Not when there's a lane devoted to bicycles," the officer explained before biking away toward the next intersection.[1]

Cioma understood that riding in bike lanes was a reasonable request. They made life safer for everyone. Still, he was amused at what the policeman could have yelled at him had he known that the young man on the other side of the road was one of the most wanted individuals in Germany.

Continuing (in a bike lane this time), Cioma ducked when his head almost hit some apples that were dangling over the bike path. Feeling frisky after his brush with the law, Cioma picked an apple from one of the trees in the orchard next to the bike lane and lay down in the grass. Biting into it, Cioma savored the first fresh fruit he'd had in months. No one was around to stop him: many of the men who'd lived around here had either been killed in the war or were still fighting. Cioma enjoyed his apple so much that he threw a few into his rucksack and biked down the road to the town of Bad Düben. In a stationery store, he bought a box large enough for four apples and mailed them as a thank-you gift to Ludwig, who was back in Berlin. Cioma had much to thank him for. There was the hundred-franc note Ludwig handed Cioma the last time he saw him and the ration coupons he'd given Cioma for meals in restaurants and cafés while he was biking. Ludwig had promised to send Cioma more coupons if the first batch didn't last through the middle of September. Cioma had no idea if he'd be in Switzerland by then. If not, those coupons would come in handy. Those four apples he was sending Ludwig barely expressed Cioma's gratitude. He was deeply thankful for having such a good friend.

A few hours later, Cioma reached Halle, a large city with culture (George Frideric Handel was born here), education (several universities had campuses here), and the site of decisive military battles over the centuries (Swedes versus Saxons during the Thirty Years' War; French versus Prussians two centuries later). Cioma walked into a hotel, rather full of himself. Rather than wait for the receptionist to hand him a registration form, he asked for one, his way of saying he had nothing to hide.

Cioma took a shower, put on a clean shirt, and went downstairs for dinner. The dining room was full. A sea of brown uniforms stretched out in front of him: Adolf Hitler's finest and bravest who, in a year or two, would be among his deadest. These days, the war wasn't going Hitler's way.

As Cioma walked into the dining room, three soldiers made room for him at their table. "Have a seat," one of them said, pulling a chair out for Cioma. "Enjoy hotel food while you can," the soldier teased. "Army food is disgusting. You'll find that out. You're young. You're strong. You'll be drafted soon. Have fun." Cioma explained that working for a munitions company had deferred him from the army. That didn't matter. "Sooner or later," the solider insisted, "they'll pull you in."

"I don't think so," Cioma confided. "I've got lung trouble, you see." Nothing life-threatening, Cioma assured his new friend, but bad enough that he was not good material for the army.

One of the soldiers at Cioma's table was envious. "I could do with something like that," he sighed, thinking about Cioma's deferment, lung troubles, or both. To the soldier, Cioma seemed to have a charmed life. Cioma squirmed. He wasn't used to anyone being jealous of him. Hiding and falsifying IDs and having your photo posted all over Germany were nothing to be jealous about. Cioma was relieved when someone called out, "Eat up, mates. Food's getting cold," and they could talk about something other than Cioma's phony medical problems.[2]

The next morning, Cioma read in the paper that a Jew had been arrested trying to get to Switzerland. He'd slept in cornfields during the day and traveled at night. Children had turned him in. Cioma tried not to think about the Jew. Dwelling on other people's mistakes would only slow him down and make him second-guess his decisions.

After breakfast, Cioma began biking again, past towns where Hegel, and Goethe, and Humboldt all wrote—all geniuses, all gone, and all struggling to make sense of the universe and history and humanity—sense that Cioma could use now. And past towns where industrialists made fortunes, and factory workers scratched out a living, and forced laborers from "camps" made no living. For a while, Cioma biked along the Saale River as it wound its way north toward the Elbe. Though not as wide as the Elbe, the Saale made up for that by being more interesting, with exceptionally fertile soil along its banks in the south, rapid currents farther north, and a string of castles, most of which had seen better days, on the heights overlooking most of its 250 miles. The castles were too high to draw Cioma's attention. He had to keep his eye on the road. But the Saale was right at eye level, and it was cool, and it was tempting, and Cioma decided to go skinny-dipping. That wasn't rare in Germany, especially before the war, when nudists lined river banks all over the country, reveling in the Nazis' cult of the body. Cioma wasn't tall, blond, or blue-eyed, and it wasn't very smart for him (or any male Jew) to go skinny-dipping these days, when being circumcised was the equivalent of a death sentence. Luckily, he was safe. The only people who saw Cioma were two farm girls on the other side of the river who were tying together stalks of grain for market. Even if they did see him, these girls were too far from Cioma to clearly see his genitals.

With his clothes back on, Cioma rolled along. Wherever he went, there was one constant sight: steeples. This was a nation of churches and of steeples, no matter what size the town. Steeples loomed over the treetops and gleamed in the sun, testimonies to the ubiquity of misguided worshippers who had declared war on people like Cioma. Sometimes, the sheer beauty of what Cioma passed helped him forget why he was biking, like fields that were a bright green after their poppies and grain had been harvested, and subtle perfumes that filled the air from fruits, trees, and flowers—smells that Cioma had never smelled before, smells he would never forget.

Cioma was appreciating his bicycle more now. It was bringing him closer to the world, and its colors, shapes, and contours. Any bike would, of course. Bicycles' ultimate beauty lay in their lack of pretension, in their elegant and splendid marriage of form and function, working in tandem, each furthering the other. It's been said that bicycle riders tend to be dreamers. Cioma was a dreamer. He'd dreamed of saving his parents. That hadn't worked. He'd dreamed of saving others by forging IDs. That had worked, for a while. And now he was in the middle of his greatest dream: saving himself. That had brought him to this bike, and this road, and these towns and sights, and toward casting off the ballast of his sorrows. Wherever this took him, Cioma knew it had to be better than what he'd left behind in Berlin.

One night, Cioma stayed at the Hotel Bamberger Reiter: *Bamberger* for its location—the city of Bamberg—*Reiter* (rider) for a famous statue of a man on horseback that was in the local cathedral. Cioma was too tired to visit the cathedral, but he wasn't too tired for dinner in the hotel's dining room. He was never too tired for a good meal. Though full, the dining room was quiet. Everyone was listening to Hitler delivering a speech on the radio, his first broadcast in six months. Bitter, angry, petulant, Hitler denounced the "traitors" in Italy who'd surrendered to the Allies two days before, praised Benito Mussolini—"the greatest son of Italy since the downfall of the Roman Empire"—who'd been arrested, and promised that Germany would win "the laurels of victory, the prize of life. . . . Every emergency only strengthens our resolution."[3]

This was standard Hitler—blustering, threatening, bragging. Yet there was something off about the speech. It was a recording. Not live, and Hitler loved live audiences. It only lasted sixteen minutes; he ordinarily droned on for one or two hours. And Hitler sounded flat and pallid, so washed out that, to an analyst for Reuters, "He was just a German hurrying through a speech to reassure the nation that the breakaway of a third of the Axis did not mean much to German security."[4]

The patrons in the hotel's dining room were numbly attentive. If they showed any displeasure, the police or the Gestapo might show up in the middle of the night. Cioma also put up a good front. Dressed like he was a member of Hitler Youth, he sat dutifully throughout the speech, his gaze fixed on the radio's speaker, out of which spilled the words of the man Cioma most despised.

Over the next few days, Cioma biked through a string of small towns and stayed in a variety of hotels and inns, keeping his head down and saying as little as possible. Cioma came to Stuttgart—so large it had four train stations, twenty-one hotels, three hospices, and five pensions, and so devoted to culture it had seven theaters, six concert halls, and ten museums. Cioma could have pretended he was back in Berlin. He didn't. He didn't want to be in Berlin.[5]

Cioma purchased apple cake as a present for the one person he knew who lived in Stuttgart: Kurt Müller, the pastor Cioma had met in Helene Jacobs's apartment who had taken some of Cioma's fake IDs back to Stuttgart for Jews who were hiding. Müller's optimism had impressed Cioma. There were still good Germans, he'd told Cioma. "That's why you'll enjoy your trip though this beautiful country, Cioma. And why, in spite of everything, you'll feel at home."

As soon as Müller opened his door and saw Cioma, he cried: tears of joy. Müller had been sure that everyone in Franz Kaufmann's cell had been arrested, maybe killed. He'd heard nothing from any of them, and he knew the consequences of resisting.

Over coffee with the Müllers, Cioma had his most relaxing conversation since leaving Berlin. He didn't have to lie that bad lungs were keeping him out of the army as he had with soldiers in a hotel in Halle, or worry that someone might see he'd been circumcised as he had while swimming naked in the Saale River, or be scared that a sharp-eyed policeman would discover that this charming young man who was riding a bicycle had the best fake ID he'd ever seen. With the Müllers, Cioma could be himself, the self he'd almost forgotten how to be.

The Müllers were surprised that no one other than hotel clerks had asked to see Cioma's ID since he'd left Berlin. Like everyone else, they thought Germany was being run as efficiently as the Nazis claimed, and they were amused that Cioma almost resented he'd never been stopped. "I was looking forward to putting my ID to the test," he explained.

When Cioma handed Müller the ID he'd faked for himself, the pastor blurted out, "Good heavens," astounded by how closely it matched the colors, eagle, and lightning bolts of genuine IDs that were issued by the Nazis, and by the pages and pages of "stamps," all drawn by Cioma and all indistinguishable from the real thing.

Taking Cioma by his arm, Müller said they were going to a suburb near Stuttgart. Müller wanted to show Cioma's ID to a friend of his—a pastor who lived in Degerloch. After a short train ride, Müller and Cioma found Hans Vorster and his wife sitting in the garden behind their house. Müller showed Vorster Cioma's ID. Vorster wasn't impressed.

"So what? It's an ID. What's special about it?"

"Goodness, Vorster," Müller said. "It came to Schönhaus blank. He filled it in himself. He completed all the stamps."

Now Vorster knew what he was holding. "My word!" he exclaimed. "Show me that again! And you're a Jew? Living illegally? What now?"

"Now," Cioma said, "now I go to Switzerland."

Cioma enchanted Vorster. He insisted that Cioma spend the night with him and his wife, who was already preparing a special dinner to celebrate their unexpected guest, and his unexpected news and his unexpected feat. That night, the four of them sat on chairs in the garden, enjoying bread, ham, eggs, wine, and the sort of conviviality that was rare four years into the war. Before retiring for the night, Vorster told Cioma: "I'm crossing my fingers for you, Schönhaus, and hoping you make it. We'll miss you. Who could have foreseen this pleasant gathering?"

The next morning, Vorster wasn't hoping that Cioma would get to Switzerland. He hoped Cioma would stay with him and his wife. "With your passbook," Vorster said, "nothing can happen to you here. You'll be safe. But crossing into Switzerland is one of the worst crimes. If they pick you up, things will be bad for you. Stay with us until the war is over."

Cioma had to remind Vorster that he was "a wanted man twice over"—as "Gunther Rogoff," the forger, and as "Peter Petrov," the Russian spy. Worse was that the Nazis had a photo of him, the photo that had been in "Petrov's" passport. Cioma would only endanger the Vorsters if he stayed with them. "The war," Cioma elaborated, "could go on for a long time. France is still occupied, the Wehrmacht is still deep into Russia and the Nazis never run short of personnel for hunting people down." Vorster understood, reluctantly.

Cioma went back to Stuttgart for his bicycle and to say farewell to the Müllers. As he climbed onto the bike, Müller reminded Cioma about what he already knew: "Most people who try to get into Switzerland haven't a chance." Cioma wasn't most people. So Müller blessed Cioma—"May God watch over you and keep you"—and asked for a favor: "When you get to Basel, give my regards to Karl Barth," the anti-Nazi theologian with whom Müller had studied in Switzerland. "He believes in me," Müller said, "and that gives me courage."[6]

And Müller believed in Cioma. That gave *him* courage.

27

"I Only Want
to Warn You"

The towns Cioma passed through got smaller (their population rarely got above 2,500), and their architecture rarely varied (more churches, more basilicas, more monasteries, though two of them had been turned into "insane asylums" over a century before). Drinking and agricultural habits were largely stable, town to town: many towns grew hops for beer then sold the beer made from those hops in local taverns. Also stable were the stories passed down, generation to generation. This was the eastern edge of the Black Forest, the large mountain range often associated with stories by the Brothers Grimm. The brothers' better-known stories, like "Little Red Riding Hood" and "Snow White," celebrated virtue, innocence, youth, and courage. Children all over the world loved them. It was the brothers' stories that weren't widely celebrated that Hitler would have read to his children at bedtime, if he had children. Stories like "The Girl Who Was Killed by Jews" (whose plot is pretty self-evident) or "The Jews' Stone," in which Jews kill children, then use their blood in ghoulish rituals. Cioma wasn't biking through the Black Forest to kill anyone. He just wanted to get through it as quickly as possible.

Cioma could have been in one of the Brothers Grimm's fairy tales. He biked past neat little thatched cottages, and women wearing old-fashioned black velvet jackets embroidered with flowers to brighten them up, trees with almost magically oversized nuts and fruits, and markets selling delicious gingerbread cookies. For meals, he bought vegetables and sandwiches made with black bread stuffed with dried figs, butter, and Limburger cheese. The food was good. That wasn't his problem: it was the mountains. Berlin, where Cioma had started out, was 115 feet above sea level. Some of the mountains in the section of the Black Forest where Cioma was biking were higher than 2,000 feet. He was thankful he didn't have to cope with the mountains farther west of him: some of them topped 5,000 feet. But even the lesser mountains were daunting. Soon, though, Cioma would be on their downside and could pretty much coast the rest of the way, downhill toward Lake Constance, where the roads pleasantly dipped and rose as they paralleled their way along the lake.

The days were bright and sunny; the women Cioma passed were often pretty; and the villages were quaint, each, it seemed, with its own pastor who officiated in a small, cozy church with a low steeple. If Cioma was making anyone happy as he pedaled along, it was the loyal Nazis he passed in some of these villages, proud that this strong, healthy paragon of Hitler Youth was biking through their little town in the middle of nowhere, a testament to the genius of their beloved führer, an undeniable guarantee that their master race would endure, and survive and rule for the thousand years that Hitler had prophesied, and perhaps longer.

Then Cioma approached Lindau, a town along Lake Constance famous for its commanding views of the snowy mountains on the Swiss side of the lake. Just outside Landau what Cioma had feared for weeks finally happened: a solider flagged him down. Carrying a rifle and standing in the middle of the road, the soldier's helmet was tipped slightly back from his forehead. A shock of red hair peeked out. The boy must have been no older than Cioma, and just as nervous as he was.

"Halt," the solider ordered. "Where are you going?"

"Feldkirch."

The soldier asked for Cioma's ID. Cioma pulled his ID from the pouch that was dangling around his neck, the one that Tatjana had sewn for him in Berlin. The soldier examined the stamps in Cioma's ID (all forged by Cioma) and compared the photo in it to the cyclist before him. Handing the ID back to Cioma, the soldier waved him along with a friendly, "Carry on!" With that, the tension that had been building for weeks within Cioma dissipated. The Nazis weren't supermen as they claimed. They weren't even superboys if they had to rely on this juvenile to guard their roads. Cioma had tried not to be cocky since he'd left Berlin. That was wise. Now he had to suppress his glee that the Nazis just might not be as tough as they pretended.[1]

Biking along Lake Constance was a breeze. When the road wasn't flat, it rolled so gently that it almost massaged Cioma. As the lake spread out before Cioma, he realized it was more a small sea than a lake: forty miles long and nine miles wide, its surface area topped two hundred square miles. If Cioma had the *Comrade* with him, he might have sailed to Switzerland. But dwelling on what might have been wouldn't get him anywhere, certainly not across the lake. He'd never sailed on such an open body of water anyway, and the eastern end of the lake—where Cioma was biking—was famous for its foehn winds, hot, dry gusts that swooped down from the Alps and changed the stability of a boat's sail without warning or mercy. In any case, Cioma didn't have the *Comrade* with him. If all was well, it was where he'd left it: moored to a dock on Lake Stössensee in Berlin, hundreds of miles to the north.[2]

Once Cioma passed the eastern end of the lake, he headed south toward the Austrian town of Feldkirch, planning to do exactly what his friend Claus Schiff had recommended after he'd scouted out Feldkirch's train yard: Cioma would hide in the woods next to the yard, watch the last car be coupled to the train, slide down a short slope, and jump on a freight car as it slowly trudged away toward Switzerland. For now, that seemed like the easiest, and the safest, way to get out of Germany.[3]

In Feldkirch, Cioma checked into the Hotel Zum Löwen, had dinner, slept in what he called a "room that looked like a large cell in a well-appointed convent," and walked to the train yard the next day. Everything was exactly as Claus had described it. Cioma planted himself on the slope overlooking the train yard, ready to slide down to a train when it passed him. But he had no idea how long everything would take: loading a coal car took time, coupling it to the rest of the train took time, moving another car in place so it could also be loaded with coal took time. Waiting for the entire train to be ready to roll would tax the patience of anyone, and Cioma had run out of patience. He figured it'd take a few hours for all the cars to be loaded and coupled, then moved out of out of the train yard. Noon came. The middle of the afternoon came. The train was getting longer. It wasn't moving. More cars were in line for coal. To kill time, Cioma whittled on a long stick he'd found. That didn't help. Everything he'd done since leaving Berlin had been building toward this moment, and the moment wasn't cooperating. The longer Cioma remained in Germany, the greater the chance someone would recognize him from his photo in the *National Police Gazette* and in police stations all over the country. Or he'd be stopped again, this time by someone smarter than the young soldier who'd flagged Cioma over near Lindau, someone who would figure out that his ID was fake. A dazzling work of forgery, but still fake. Every minute Cioma sat on the hillside overlooking the train yard was one minute closer to never getting out of the prison his country had become.[4]

By late afternoon, Cioma realized the train wouldn't leave the yard for a few more hours. That gave him time to enjoy dinner at the hotel, then return to the train yard, ready to spring toward the train once it started moving.

Cioma shared a table in the hotel's dining room with a young secretary who worked in the lodge. It was her day off, and Cioma found her attractive. When she flashed her blue eyes at him, Cioma reached for her hand, thinking, "You've got a hotel room, and this might be the last chance you'll ever have to feel the warmth of a young woman." Cioma knew women, and he knew himself, and he rarely missed an opportunity to be with one, especially if that opportunity was sitting right in front of him.

Air-raid sirens punctured Cioma's reveries. Everyone in the dining room raced to an outdoor terrace and looked up. B-17s were bombing Feldkirch. Cioma grabbed the secretary's hand, and they ran toward an air-raid shelter. A shout from her drew Cioma up short: "My handbag! I left it on my chair!" Cioma ran to the dining room, grabbed her bag, and raced back to the woman. She rewarded him with a kiss.

As the all-clear signal sounded, Cioma scolded himself. He'd come to Feldkirch for one thing: to hop aboard a train to Switzerland. "Don't be stupid," he told himself. "If you want to go to Switzerland, get on that train. The air raid was a warning for you to go back to the train yard."[5]

Cioma did just that, exactly as the last car was being coupled to the train. Sliding down the slope, Cioma waited for the train to pass so he could jump aboard. But he hadn't reckoned that an electric loco-motive would be pulling the train, and that electric engines accelerate faster than steam engines. By the time the train passed Cioma, it was moving so fast he couldn't jump onto it safely. Back at the hotel, Cioma realized he'd have to hop aboard the train when it was closer to the station, before it had a chance to pick up speed.

Cioma had almost reached the train yard the next morning when a stranger stood in his way. He'd seen Cioma there the night before. Soldiers saw him, too, the stranger said, and they'd searched for him, either while Cioma was having dinner at the hotel, holding hands with the pretty secretary, or after he'd gone back to the hotel later that night, peeved that the train had been too fast for him to board. The stranger wasn't offering Cioma advice about what to do. "I only want to warn you," he politely said as they parted.[6]

Cioma gave up on hopping aboard a train. He couldn't do that if soldiers were looking for him. Retrieving his bike from the hotel, he pedaled north toward Lake Constance—where he'd come from. His new plan—his plans were always changing—was to bike along the lake's northern shore to its western corner. When he got there, he'd either swim across the lake at night—in its western reaches, it narrowed to half a mile—or he'd find a stretch of the border that was hardly patrolled and cross there. On foot. Feldkirch had been a disaster. Swimming or walking to Switzerland were now Cioma's only choices.

No More Hopeless Plans

B iking along the lake was a joy. Cioma passed fields of vegetables and fruit trees, and vineyards that yielded award-winning grapes. Islands occasionally appeared on his left. One of them, Mainau, was entirely owned by a family that devoted most of the island to exotic flowers and an orangery, the only one in the region. Another was Lindau where, only a few years before, most of Germany's zeppelins had been built, including the 804-foot-long *Hindenburg*, the largest airship ever flown. As Cioma raced along, beauty and history were blurry companions, guides to what had once made his nation excel in art, and science, and life.

The scenery, the road, the sun, the ease (and fun) of cycling put Cioma in such a good mood that he sang a song from Bertolt Brecht's *Threepenny Opera*—"The Song of the Futility of All Human Endeavor."

> *Make a hopeless plan,*
> *To show how bright you are.*
> *Then think up another one,*
> *That gets you just as far.*

Cioma was fed up with making hopeless plans. He hadn't been able to hop aboard a coal train in Feldkirch; for all he knew, he might not be able to get into Switzerland at the western end of Lake Constance. All of his plans had taken him "just as far," as Brecht wrote for *The Threepenny Opera*, and no further. He needed a new plan. One that could take him into Switzerland without swimming and without praying a soldier was looking the other way as he crossed the woods separating Germany and Switzerland. His problem was that he was all out of plans.

Other lines from *The Threepenny Opera* would have helped Cioma more than that song about futility—more upbeat, more hopeful lyrics like *one must live well to know what living is. The wickedness of the world is so great, you have to keep running so your legs won't be stolen from under you.* Cioma's legs had served him well, pushing the pedals on his bike for weeks. But he needed to live well, as Brecht said. For that, he needed a new plan, a better plan, and he had to conjure it up fast.

Over lunch—appetizer: cauliflower soup; entrée: trout—in a hotel overlooking Lake Constance, Cioma devised a plan. It was more fantastical than any of his previous ideas, but it was a plan, and he needed one. And it had promise. The western end of Lake Constance flowed into the Rhine, which separated Switzerland and Germany. Cioma would knock on the door of someone he chose at random who lived in Öhningen, a town along the Rhine. He'd say he was on vacation from Berlin and his boss—in his fantasy, Herr Faber, an executive at AEG, a giant firm that made electrical equipment—was sure that the kind family that lived here would be delighted to host Cioma for a few days. Cioma would say Faber was a "good friend" of whoever he was talking to. That would at least make that person pause for a moment, and search their memory for a "Faber" sometime in their past.

"Young man," the good citizen of Öhningen would tell Cioma, "I don't know any Herr Faber at AEG, but all the same I think I know what you want. Come in. Have soup with us. After dark, I'll show you the way over the border. You're not the first to turn up here."

Cioma asked his waiter for a phone book. Flipping through it, Cioma randomly settled on his "host" in Öhningen: Ferdinand Schmidt. The phone book listed Schmidt's address on Stuttgart Court.

Cioma now knew his destination for what he hoped would be his final hours in Germany. He didn't think any more about swimming across Lake Constance, and he knew he'd never hop aboard a freight train anywhere in Germany or Austria. His new friend, Herr Schmidt, would take care of everything—if he didn't turn Cioma over to the police first.

Cioma checked into a hotel with a splendid view of Lake Constance. He slept well. There was no way he couldn't, not after another long day of biking. And not after settling (in his imagination) how he'd get into Switzerland, courtesy of Ferdinand Schmidt. Then there was a loud bang on his door. It was four o'clock in the morning. Cioma opened the door. A policeman demanded to see Cioma's papers. Cioma handed over his ID. Glancing at it, the officer muttered, "All in order! Heil, Hitler" and walked away. Cioma went back to sleep. On what he believed was his final night in Germany, his forgery had saved his life. He slept until ten o'clock the next morning.[1]

That afternoon—a Sunday—Cioma biked to Öhningen. Friends in Berlin had warned him that the police here kept their eyes out for anyone trying to get into Switzerland. That made sense. With Switzerland right next door, and a steady stream of Jews, anti-Nazis, and army deserters flowing through their out-of-the-way village, Öhningen's constables were busier than the police in many larger towns in Germany.

As far as he knew, Cioma was the only Jew around. That was no distinction: since Berlin, he'd been the only Jew around wherever he went. What distinguished Öhningen, though, was that the Nazis hadn't forgotten about this tiny town that was about as far from Berlin as you could get and still be in Germany. A handful of Jews had been here since the seventeenth century: three in 1666, seven in 1743, fourteen in 1779. Öhningen's Jewish population peaked in 1825 at 224,

39 percent of the town's 570 residents. Slowly, most moved away, attracted by opportunities in larger cities. By 1933, twenty Jews remained. That didn't discourage the Nazis. The number of Jews didn't matter; their presence, no matter how small, did. As synagogues and stores owned by Jews were burning all over Germany on the night of November 9–10, 1938—Kristallnacht—little Öhningen was no exception. The SS desecrated tombstones in the local Jewish cemetery, torched the town's 113-year-old synagogue, and beat up three Jews before sending them to Dachau. In 1940 the few Jews left in Öhningen were sent to a "camp" in Gurs, France. The next year, Öhningen's census read: "Juden—Kleine" (This translates, quite succinctly, as "Jews—none"). [2]

None. That left Cioma, as usual, by himself. Aside from enjoying the company of Kurt Müller and Hans Vorster in Stuttgart, Cioma had been alone since leaving Berlin. The solitude didn't bother him. The fate of the Jews who'd been emptied out of Germany did. It was now his turn to empty himself out of this country. For that, he needed no one's help. Like the good boy he'd been raised to be, he stopped at a florist in Öhningen. Well-bred Germans, he knew, bring flowers to their hosts. He bought a bouquet. Flowers were also a good cover if a policeman asked where he was going. "I'm visiting the Schmidts," he'd say. "This is for Frau Schmidt." The flowers implied everything except that he was a Jew trying to escape to Switzerland. He was just a polite young German—a member of Hitler Youth, it would seem, to anyone giving him a once-over—bringing a small present to the family that was kind enough to host him for a few days.

Cioma attached the flowers to his handlebars and biked on. He passed an SS man, rifle on his shoulder, chatting with a young woman. They waved at him. He smiled. Cioma asked an old man for directions to Stuttgart Court, where the Schmidts lived. "First left," Cioma was told. "Then straight. About ten minutes by bike."

Cioma biked up a steep hill from the village, turned left onto a narrow dirt road, then straight through ruts and small craters as the

road narrowed and curved slightly. He saw a Swiss flag flying in a field
off to one side. His heart pounded: he was tempted to bike toward the
flag. Then he caught himself. The Nazis, he remembered, had rigged
their side of the border with trip wires and patrolled it regularly with
guards and dogs. He'd never reach that flag.

The Schmidts' home was at the top of a small incline. Cioma rang
the bell. There was no answer. Maybe no one was home. He walked
to a small cottage about twenty feet from the main house and called
out, "Hello! Anyone here?" A soldier opened the door.

"I'm here to see the Schmidts," Cioma explained, sticking to his
story, "but nobody's answering the door."

"They're there," the soldier said. "Try again. It's all a big house."
But first, the soldier invited Cioma into the cottage so he could write
down details from Cioma's ID. "We've got to write everything down,"
he explained. "It's a bunch of red tape."

Cioma walked into the parlor. Three other soldiers were there,
their rifles in a rack by a corner. As the first soldier wrote down details
from Cioma's ID, a fifth soldier, carrying a helmet and rifle, came
in from his patrol. Pointing toward Cioma, one of the soldiers joked
to the newcomer, "Here you go, Paul. Another one for you. Take him
in." Everyone laughed. Cioma played along with their game, slapping
Paul on the back and saying, "Yes, Paul, you've got to take me in now."
Everyone laughed some more, and Cioma was sent on his way: "Go
visit the Schmidts. They're definitely there."

Cioma rang the bell. This time, the door opened. The man staring
out at Cioma had a ruddy face and wore a hat with a small feather
flaring out of one side and leggings that extended from his ankles to
his knees. Herr Schmidt, seemingly prosperous and perhaps pompous,
was about to go hunting.

After Cioma told Schmidt the story he'd prepared, Schmidt yelled
to his wife, asking if they knew a Faber in Berlin—Cioma's "boss"
at AEG whom Cioma claimed had told him to visit the Schmidts

in Öhningen. Frau Schmidt came out, took one look at Cioma, warned him the soldiers next door might suspect he was there to cross the border, then warmed slightly and suggested he try another Schmidt—Dr. Schmidt—who lived in Öhningen: "They have friends in Berlin. It must be them you want."

Cioma biked away. About two hundred feet down the hill from the Schmidts' house, he looked to his right. The Swiss flag he'd seen before was fluttering on the other side of a small stream. After weeks of biking and close calls and wondering if he'd always be stuck in Germany, Cioma knew this was his chance—damn the trip wires, damn the patrols, and damn the soldiers who'd shoot him on the spot. Looking over his shoulder, he saw that the soldiers and the Schmidts were back inside. He turned his bike off the dirt road and coasted down a steep meadow. At the bottom, he pushed his bike into the woods. Even if the soldiers came out of their cottage, the steepness of the hill would prevent them from seeing what Cioma was up to. Kneeling next to his bike, Cioma pulled on the thread that was attached to the cork he'd stuffed in the handlebars weeks ago to keep his "leave of absence" papers from falling out. The thread was also attached to the Swiss bank note—one hundred francs—that Ludwig Lichtwitz had given Cioma the morning he left Berlin. Cioma took the note and left the papers in the handlebars. He wouldn't need them again.

Cioma said the Sh'ma Yisrael under his breath—the traditional Jewish prayer that affirms the oneness and the mercy and protection of God—and jumped into the stream. It was only about twenty inches deep. Cioma walked downstream for several hundred yards then scrambled onto the opposite bank of the stream. He was waterlogged, he was cold, and he felt great. The waters were jubilation itself. Cioma was in Switzerland.

It was October 3. In the month since Cioma had left Berlin, he'd biked almost 600 miles: 497 miles from Berlin to Lindau along Lake

Constance, thirty from Lindau to Feldkirch, sixty-five from Feldkirch
to Öhningen. On average, he'd biked twenty-two miles a day. About
the only breaks he'd taken were to swim in the Saale, pick some
apples in an orchard near Daube, and visit the two pastors in Stuttgart. He'd taken those respites the first week or so he was biking.
That was before the enormity of the task he'd set out for himself
really sank in—its dangers, risks, challenges, complications. Though
Cioma had taken every measure to pass as a loyal German—his ID
was foolproof, he dressed like he was in Hitler Youth, he had a military haircut, his rucksack held a copy of Joseph Goebbels's *From the
Kaiserhof to the Chancellery*—all that and still the cumulative tension
of biking through the middle of Germany had slowly seeped into
Cioma's mind, muscles, and soul. There was the unrelenting dread
that he was being watched, that someone knew he was not who he
said he was, that he didn't belong on these roads or on his bike but
in one of those "camps" from which no one returned. The strain of
not being able to confide in anyone (other than the two ministers in
Stuttgart) was isolating. The apprehension that anyone who looked
at him askance would call the police was exhausting. The gnawing
anxiety of deciding on the spot which roads to take, which towns
not to ride through, and which inns and hotels offered a modicum of
comfort and safety, that, too, was draining. All this was an affront
to Cioma's lifelong cheerfulness. It was hard to be happy-go-lucky
when your world could collapse any minute.

Yet the bike ride was a pure and audacious expression of Cioma's
nature. Since 1933, he'd refused to let the glumness of the Third Reich
swallow him, to draw him into its shade and its gloom. His bicycle,
his boat, his forging, the lives he saved, his many girlfriends were his
proclamations of defiance, his stubborn announcements that he would
be neither extinguished nor smothered. Beneath Cioma's bright, alert
face; his charming, sunny disposition; and his impeccable forgeries lay
an optimistic discipline, a certainty that he had a future and a purpose,

that many tomorrows would follow the difficult one of today, and of the yesterdays that had preceded them. Cioma's exquisite attachment to his future assured that he had one.

Some friends had thought Cioma wouldn't make it out of Berlin. He did. Some thought he'd be stopped at a gauntlet of checkpoints. He wasn't. There was no gauntlet. And no one thought that he'd have something else to celebrate in addition to escaping from Germany. On September 28, five days before he entered Switzerland, Cioma turned twenty-one years old. Cioma's friends were sure he'd be dead before he reached Switzerland, and before his birthday. In his twenty-one years on earth, Cioma had suffered, learned, lost, and loved. Wiser and bolder than most twenty-one-year-olds, had Cioma turned northward from Switzerland and surveyed the Germany that lay in that direction, he would have been incredulous at what his nation had become, and equally incredulous at what he had done. As his mother told him, "The Nazis will never stop the sun from shining." She was right.

On September 30, 1943, the Ordnungspolizei, the German Criminal Police, issued their second "special bulletin" about Cioma, modified with new details (some wrong, some right) from their "interrogations" of Franz Kaufmann and of members of his cell or other cells:

> *Since September 14, 1943, the Jew, Samson Schönhaus, born 28 Sept 1922, is on the run from Berlin after forging passports. It is said that he left Berlin on a bike in the direction of Lake Constance. He has forged army and postal ID cards on him, under the name Peter Schönhaus.*
>
> *Description: 1.8m, blond, parted hair, short knickerbockers, dark jacket.*
>
> *Border check points have been notified.*
>
> *Peter Schönhaus is to be arrested.*[3]

The police got Cioma's birthdate, destination on his bike, forging activities, and attire right. They got his ID wrong: he was carrying an army ID—fake, of course. He didn't have a postal ID. They referred to him as "Samson," Cioma's real first name, though no one had called him that since he was a little boy. He'd left Berlin on September 4, not September 14. The most glaring error was that Cioma was traveling under the name "Peter Schönhaus." He hadn't used "Peter" since buying a sailboat the previous spring, and for his entire bike ride, he'd been calling himself "Hans Brück."

Finally, the timing of the bulletin could not have helped the police find Cioma. It was sent out on September 30. Three days later—October 3—Cioma crossed the stream into Switzerland. Only with extraordinary good fortune could the police have arrested Cioma in the seventy-two hours between issuing their bulletin about "Peter Schönhaus" and Cioma wading through that exhilarating, liberating stream. Fortune shone on Cioma Schönhaus. It had for a long time.

"I Know You. I Know You Very Well"

Cioma found himself on the edge of a small village—Stein am Rhein. Men and women walked by. Some looked at him, still in his Hitler Youth browns. Some preferred not to: all kinds of people were washing up on their shore these days. No one knew who this wet, raggedy young man was. He'd popped out of nowhere. Was he a disgruntled Nazi? A Gestapo agent who'd seen the light of day? A soldier seeking asylum? A Jew seeking refuge? Ducking behind a pile of wood, Cioma removed his shoes, then his socks so he could wring them dry. Suddenly, a small voice piped up, "Daddy, someone's shoes are over there." A little boy was pointing at the shoes Cioma had placed on the ground. Coming out from behind the woodpile, Cioma told the boy's father that he was a political refugee from Germany. Friends in Berlin had told Cioma not to say he was Jewish: the Swiss might send him back. Then, thinking of all the lies he'd told in the last few years, all the evasions, prevarications, stories and deceptions, all the efforts he'd made to convince people he was other than what he was, Cioma admitted he was Jewish. He was free. He wanted to be himself for a change.

The boy's father tried to ease Cioma's concerns: "I've seen many Jews come through here. I don't think they'll send you back." But the father was an ordinary resident of a small town in a small corner of a small country. He had no power and no authority. All he wanted to do was calm this scared stranger who had come from the other side of the stream. As a father, perhaps he could see that under the façade of this brash young man was a boy who was scared, lost, and not sure what would happen to him next.

The father invited Cioma to his house for the night. He gave him dry clothes, a hot meal, and a warm bed, and the next day, a policeman took Cioma by train to Schaffhausen, a town fifteen miles away. In a prison where Germans who'd crossed the border were kept until their status was determined, a policeman refused to believe Cioma was Jewish or that his real name was "Schönhaus," as Cioma kept insisting. "You're really a German war criminal," the officer barked, "and you're trying to worm your way in here."

This went on until Cioma blew up. "I've had enough of this crap," he yelled. "Send me back if you want to. I didn't think Switzerland would be like this." Relenting slightly, Cioma offered to pay for some phone calls so the policeman could reach his contacts in Switzerland who would confirm that he was who he claimed to be. "Save your money for something more important," the officer told Cioma.

On his own dime, the policeman called one of Cioma's contacts—Karl Barth, an internationally renowned theologian who was living in Basel. Barth had taught at several universities in Germany, where he hadn't endeared himself to the Nazis. Even before Hitler came to power, Barth opposed the future führer's intentions to use churches as cover for his hate and bile. The Nazis had it with Barth in 1934 when he rejected replacing Jesus with "other lords" and turning churches into "organs of the state." Barth also refused to take the loyalty oath to Hitler required of all university professors unless he could amend it with "to the extent that I am responsibly able to as

a Protestant Christian." Hitler and his gang didn't need all this pro-
testing. They kicked Barth out of Germany.[1]

Barth had heard about Cioma from Kurt Müller, the pastor
Cioma had visited in Stuttgart. Impressed, Barth told the police to
let Cioma stay in Switzerland. They did.

Cioma may have been in a refugee camp in Schaffhausen, but he was
determined to make the best of the place. He made friends, a skill that
rarely failed him: he was good company and enjoyed people as much as
they enjoyed him. The mutual rapport was almost immediate, quickly
establishing trust and a certain intimacy. That's why a German Jew
who'd just arrived mystified Cioma.

"I know you," Cioma said.

"I never saw you before in my life," the newcomer replied.

"Well," Cioma repeated, "I know you, and I know you very well."

"I still say I've never seen you. I don't know who you are."

The next day, Cioma told the stranger, "I know why you look
familiar. I forged the Nazi insignia over the photo on your ID. I stared
at your photograph for two hours."

The stranger, Walter Joelson, was the same age as Cioma. In Berlin,
they'd been in different chapters of Hashomer Hatzair, the Jewish
youth group that gave Cioma a greater sense of community and gave
Joelson the confidence to take a train heading south from Berlin, get
off near the border with Switzerland, and stumble, in the middle of
the night, through woods and fields into the country he hoped would
give him sanctuary. Swiss police found him sleeping on a park bench.
They took him to Schaffhausen, where he met the young man who'd
saved his life.[2]

Joelson eventually settled in the United States. Cioma spent the
rest of his life in Switzerland, a life that was rewarding and gratifying,
although without Karl Barth, who'd persuaded the Swiss authorities
to let him stay, it almost certainly would have taken Cioma longer to

create a new life for himself. Without Barth, Cioma might have been sent back to Germany and had no life at all.

Barth and Cioma met once—the day after Christmas 1943 at Barth's home in Basel. Cioma brought a small gift for Barth's assistant, a lovely theologian thirteen years younger than Barth. Charlotte von Kirschbaum had been living in Barth's home since 1929. The rest of the world called her Barth's researcher and collaborator. Barth's five children called her "Aunt Lollo." Barth's closest friends called her Barth's lover. Cioma knew nothing of this and handed Kirschbaum a small bowl he'd carved from cherrywood. (In German, *Kirschbaum* means "cherry tree.") While Cioma had unintentionally slighted Barth's wife by not bringing her a gift, he had reason to show his gratitude to Kirschbaum: since he'd arrived in Switzerland, she and Barth had become his guardians and protectors, helping him with finances, his education and, of course, assuring he didn't go back to Germany.

On December 26, Barth was waiting for Cioma in his study. Looking up from a leather chair, Barth sized up this kid he'd heard so much about. He liked him. At Barth's invitation, Cioma filled him in about life in Berlin and explained how he'd made his forgeries on jerry-rigged equipment and, of course, described his bike ride that everyone said he'd never finish. A smorgasbord of smells blended in the air: the sweet tobacco from Barth's pipe, the sap and the needles from the Christmas tree in the next room, the pungent meat Barth's housekeeper was roasting for dinner. This would be one of Cioma's most relaxing nights since he'd left Berlin. Maybe the most relaxing since the war began.

Before dinner, Cioma couldn't resist taking a playful jab at Barth. How, he asked, could Barth—intelligent, humane, well educated—believe anything in the Bible? So much of it was just plain silly, like the story about the serpent speaking to Adam and Eve in the Garden of Eden. Snakes don't talk. People don't talk back to them. Didn't Barth have anything better to do than read these goofy fairy tales?

What Cioma didn't know was that, for Barth, Scripture wasn't a bedtime story for little children. Barth looked beyond history and beyond reason into the spirit of the Bible, a spirit that lifts us toward God: ineffable, unknowable, perplexing, enriching. Barth explained to Cioma that what was most important wasn't "how we should talk with God, but what He says to us; not how we find our way to Him, but how He finds His way to us." The means of communication were beside the point. The fact that God even bothered to communicate with us was essential and humbling. With that in mind, Barth told Cioma, with humor and affection, "Young man, what matters is not whether the snake spoke or not. It's about *what* the snake said."[3]

That apparent contradiction frustrated Cioma. It had to. Cioma and Barth were speaking different languages. Barth's God was endless, deathless, and a puzzle for anyone who tried to sort Him out: a conundrum of faith, humility, eternity. Cioma's God didn't speak like Barth's. Cioma's God couldn't. Cioma's God died in Auschwitz.

After a fine dinner, Barth returned to Cioma's doubts about faith by telling him "a little story that shows what unconditional faith really means," a story about a tightrope walker who stretched his rope from the tower of a city hall to the spire of a nearby church. Balancing from one end of the rope to the other, the tightrope walker pushed a wheelbarrow in front of him. Climbing down to the street, he passed his hat around to collect money from his audience, pausing to ask one man, "Do you think I can repeat what I just did?" "Yes, of course," the man replied. "In that case," said the tightrope walker, "climb that tower with me and get into the wheelbarrow."

"You see, my dear Schönhaus," Barth continued, "whoever sits down in the wheelbarrow *really* believes." The depth and strength of that belief is "where the extraordinary begins, and where there is forgiveness and salvation. It's where we know that faith itself is a miracle."[4]

Somehow, Cioma and Barth were ignoring the miracle that was right in front of them: a young man who had biked through the middle of Nazi Germany, his spirit still intact, his heart still open and still loving. Cioma's story was one God might have included in the book to which Barth was so devoted. After all, Cioma's tale was as improbable as the Bible stories that he dismissed as silly stories for silly people.

Cioma was transferred to a work camp in Lostorf, fifty miles west of Schaffhausen, then to one in Muhlin, fifty miles north of Lostorf. Meanwhile, Charlotte von Kirschbaum wrote to Jewish and Christian refugee groups, learning how Cioma could receive a study permit and a residential permit, apply to an art school in Basel, and acquire money for tuition and living expenses. Contributions came from several individuals and organizations; Barth himself provided sixty Swiss francs a month for half a year. Von Kirschbaum assured everyone to whom she wrote that Cioma was "a talented young graphic artist." She also asked her contacts in the anti-Nazi church in Germany who knew Cioma to confirm by mail that he was Jewish. "Since he does not look Jewish at all," she wrote, "some people have voiced doubts about him. We must dispel those doubts."[5]

The doubts were dispelled. Aiding that were hints about Cioma's forging in Berlin. Hints because you couldn't be too specific in letters German censors might open.

Cioma would go on to college, and hone his art and his life, and begin to remember who he had been, and decide what he might become. When he graduated in 1948, the director of the art school praised him for being "industrious," "serious," and approaching his education with "great zeal." It was time for Cioma to begin his new life.[6]

Despite the fine recommendations Cioma received from his art school, he was told there were few jobs in Switzerland for someone with his skills. It might be best, he was told, for him to emigrate, maybe to New Zealand, where he had relatives, or to Israel, where he'd help build a new country and be part of the Jewish community. Conceivably persuading him not to go to Israel was remembering how disastrous Palestine had been for his parents the one year they'd been there. He didn't want to relive that.

Cioma stayed where he was, married a Swiss woman, had children, started his own graphic design firm, and in 1955 became a Swiss citizen. He also had a frequent visitor from Germany: Helene Jacobs. Cioma and Helene had been resisters, friends, conspirators, and lovers. In 1946 Cioma wrote to Helene, using the address for the apartment she'd had during the war: Bonner Strasse 2. When Helene wrote back, Cioma was "ecstatic": "In my view, you have risen from the dead and probably went through hell." She had: two years in a Nazi prison were hell. But she hadn't changed. She was working in an office in Berlin that was providing aid to Jews who were still living in Germany.

Cioma told Helene how scared he'd been for her when she didn't return after a member of Franz Kaufmann's circle phoned, claiming he needed to meet her, and he told her about his bicycle ride to Switzerland, which had amazed his friends and defied the Nazis, and about his life as a graphic artist: "One of the few creative professions that still exist in this quasi-normal world." Most important was that it would give him an opportunity to provide a "face" to peace and to war. He was too familiar with both not to do this.

Cioma assured Helene that his esteem for her had never waned: "In my eyes, you are a true hero. Most likely, I will never find such a noble individual as you." He'd told many people about her: friends in art school, guests at a Christmas party, and someone else: his fiancée—Rosmarie-Susanne. They'd met in art school and were "very much in love." Telling Helene about Rosmarie was "difficult," but Cioma wanted her to know "everything." If he hurt her, he apologized: "You really deserve the opposite." He hoped they would remain friends, and write to each other, and visit each other.[7]

Helene did visit, sometimes every year, sometimes every other. Helene never married nor, as far as we know, did she ever have a lover. Her few months with Cioma as he hid in her apartment during the summer of 1943 were almost certainly the romantic apex of her life—incomparable to anything else that might come along, though it seems nothing else did. On her visits, Helene and Cioma reminisced about the war and about their friends, and she told him which buildings in Berlin were still standing and which had been reduced to rubble and still were. Helene's empathy impressed Cioma's son, Michael, eight years old at the time. Years later, he would remember Helene telling him she'd sent food and clothing to Jews in "camps" for the simplest of reasons: they were human, just like her. There was nothing complex about that. Even Helene's appearance impressed Michael. "Her plainness," he said years later, "masked her courage."[8]

Cioma's graphic design firm—Cioma Schönhaus, A.G.—did well, with commissions from Swiss Air; Perilli vermouth; and Kaloderma Gelee, a moisturizing hand cream. These were among brands and products that promised a new life, a better life. Cioma's designs were whimsical and playful except for a black-and-white poster he designed for a 1963 referendum that would ban nuclear weapons from the Swiss army—exactly how Cioma had anticipated his life as a graphic artist, giving a "face" to peace and to war. His poster was a benediction for peace.[9]

Cioma's firm prospered, with as many as ten employees at a time, and occasional interns from high school or college. The experience deeply affected Roger Le Marie, who was then fifteen years old. Cioma, he said, was "calm, clever, meticulous and well organized." At the end of Roger's internship, Cioma had a long talk with him about his interests and his future. "Cioma took me seriously as a human being. I didn't understand why he spent so much time with a teenager. Only later did I learn about his life during the war. Certain people who have gone through tragedies are warm in the heart. Cioma was one of them."[10]

Cioma's professional life was booming as his marriage was falling apart. He and Rosmarie-Susanne divorced in 1956. The very qualities that had served him well during the war could now be wearisome, to Rosmarie-Susanne and to their children. "To him," said one son, "*everything* was possible. He faced reality in his own way.

That could be difficult, sometimes. This worked to his advantage under the Nazis, but it needed to be moderated now. The story he had lived created his character. Occasionally, he could have benefited from having a different character." [11]

Cioma's optimism brooked no dissent, especially if it advanced another perspective, one he didn't see because he couldn't. That's why Michael, Cioma's oldest son, was "kicked out" of his father's design firm after working there for eight years: "When I would tell him that some things were *not* possible, he'd say, 'Why not?'"

Cioma's refusal to consider what was not possible spilled over into his life beyond the office.

When Michael was ten years old, his father rented a sailboat on Lake Neuchâtel, one of Switzerland's largest lakes. Aboard were only Cioma and Michael. Cioma hadn't been on a sailboat since he'd left the *Comrade* tied up at a dock in Berlin just before leaving the city. That didn't matter. "I know how to do this," he told Michael. He didn't. At first, the water was placid and flat, almost like a mirror. Then the wind picked up, the boat almost keeled over, and water poured through its portholes. Michael, belowdecks, tried to bail it out; Cioma, on the deck, tried to right it. Two hours later, they returned to where they'd rented the boat. Cioma never stepped foot on a boat again.

Cioma remarried in 1963, this time to a woman named Rigula. She was Catholic; Rosmarie-Susanne had been Protestant. Neither practiced the faith they were born into, and neither they nor Cioma raised their sons—two from his first marriage, two from his second—as practicing Jews. Cioma had soured on Judaism years ago, blaming it for his parents' deaths: if Fanja and Boris hadn't been Jewish, he reasoned, they wouldn't have been killed. Their God hadn't saved them; their faith hadn't saved them. To Cioma, their deaths were still fresh, and always would be. Rare was the day when he didn't think about his parents, often crying when he did. His tears became a link to Fanja and to Boris.

Cioma's sons' knowledge of Judaism was largely limited to history and folklore and the peppy klezmer music, which originated among Jews in Eastern Europe, that Cioma's younger sons, the two from his second marriage, performed in a group they called Beit Jaffe, Hebrew for "beautiful house," which is also English for "Schönhaus." Cioma loved the success of Beit Jaffe: its music resonated with the songs he'd learned from his father and grandmother as a child. He was less disposed toward the resurgence of Judaism that it vaguely hinted at. True to the conversations he'd had with Helene Jacobs while hiding in her apartment during the war, he preferred that there be one world culture and one world religion, not specific faiths called Judaism, Christianity, Hinduism, Buddhism, nor any of the many others that had inspired or, Cioma would say, had afflicted humanity. His would be a world in which identities blurred and blended, where no one was pitted against anyone else, where various religions didn't divide people into camps and factions and blocs. In Cioma's dream world, there would be no dogmas. There would only be humanity: united and whole. In his eternal optimism, he believed it could be possible.

Cioma was one of the more improbable Holocaust survivors: a connoisseur of outrageous, life-saving, and totally original gestures. A bon vivant, if you will, among the Nazis: proof that optimism and courage can surface in the least expected moments, and in the least expected individuals. Surviving as he did was a miracle, one that might have sustained his faith in God—if he'd been so inclined. Instead, Cioma placed his faith in himself, and he was not mistaken.

In time, Cioma's animosity toward Germany softened, mostly because of the Germans he'd known who'd resisted Hitler, whether it was Helene Jacobs, Ludwig Lichtwitz, or the unknown parishioners at St. Anne's Church who had provided all those IDs for him to work with. Their tenacity and their decency prevented him from condemning a whole people. In 1997, for his seventy-fifth birthday, Cioma's sons took him to Berlin. They visited some of the sites that had been important to him years ago: the grave of his paternal grandfather, and the dock at Lake Stössensee where he'd kept the *Comrade*, though, of course, it wasn't there, and no one who worked there knew where it was: abandoned sailboats weren't kept at their moorings for seven decades. They visited the apartment building at Sophienstrasse 32–33, where Cioma and his parents had lived. The façade was the same as when the Schönhauses resided there. Much of the rest of the building, wrecked by bombs in 1942, had been rebuilt after the war. On the sidewalk in front of Sophienstrasse 32–33 were two *stolpersteine* (stumbling blocks)—small brass plaques embedded in pavements all over Berlin in front of buildings where the Nazis' victims had lived. The plaques in front of Sophienstrasse 32–33 memorialized Cioma's parents:

HERE LIVED

BORIS SCHÖNHAUS

YEAR OF BIRTH—1898

DEPORTED JUNE 13, 1942

SOBIBOR MAJDENAK

EXTERMINATED AUGUST 16, 1942

HERE LIVED

FANJA SCHÖNHAUS

YEAR OF BIRTH 1899

DEPORTED JUNE 13, 1942

SOBIBOR

EXTERMINATED AUGUST 18, 1942

Cioma Schönhaus died on September 22, 2015—six days short of his ninety-third birthday. Spry, stubborn, and armed with a terrific memory, Cioma conveyed the same pluck that had saved him during the war. Also remaining was his charm. He was so charming, in fact, that it was tempting to indulge in a fleeting fantasy when meeting him, an imagining that if others had biked along with him in 1943, there might have been a lengthy caravan of the young, the old, and the hopeful: a long line of freedom-seekers stretching from Berlin to Switzerland—from one horizon to the next. In this pleasing fantasy, Cioma's high spirits buoyed a continent that suffered under dark clouds, gray skies, and tomorrows that never seemed to come. Alas, there was no line of bicyclists. There was only one: Cioma Schönhaus.

Yom Kippur fell on the same day Cioma died. On Yom Kippur, Jews atone for their sins and their misdeeds. Not Cioma, even if he'd had the strength to repent. His faith in Judaism had shattered long ago. We know, however, that not long before he died, one of Cioma's sons asked him, "How can one be sure if a decision is right or wrong?" Cioma's answer could have inspired several sermons for Yom Kippur: "Everything that leads to life is good," a succinct summary of his lifelong quest for decency and dignity; an assurance that the good is worth pursuing, every day and in every way; and that as Fanja, Cioma's mother, believed, no one, not even the Nazis, can stop the sun—the sun of our own goodness—from shining, brightening, and warming this place we call home.[12]

Fanja was no fool. Neither was Cioma. With full faith in him and with full contempt for the Nazis, she was sure Cioma would survive. She knew his wily ways, his appetite for exciting and wondrous escapades, all of them delighting in the magic that's beyond the ordinariness of more narrow and less adventurous lives.

Acknowledgments

This book, as are most books, especially nonfiction, is the fruit of a collective, one that's invisible to its readers, but held dear and close and deeply appreciatively by its author. A collective that's generous with its time, knowledge, and patience; polite when it's apparent that the American standing in front of them speaks no more than six words of the language in the country where he finds himself; willing to walk blocks out of their way to show the newcomer how to traverse from Point A to Point B or instruct him in negotiating a transit system that's simple to a child but befuddles the alleged adult from far away. The collective includes cashiers, waiters, waitresses, hotel clerks, and staff in museums, libraries, and archives who are good at spotting a guy who doesn't know what the hell he's doing.

To this small army of kind people I met while working on *Two Wheels to Freedom*: your kindnesses are much appreciated.

So much for anonymity. Now I'll salute many others, old friends and new, by name:

Most importantly, Cioma Schönhaus, who devoted many hours over several days to interviews with me at his home near Basel. His remarkable openness, generosity, candor, and humor were living proof of how he'd masterminded his singular adventures during the war and, indeed, how he'd survived that horrible conflict.

Rob Kanigel for shop talk, bicycle talk, and coffee talk, and recommending his agent, Michael Carlisle of Inkwell Management. With great alacrity, Michael took out my proposal for *Two Wheels to Freedom*. With equal alacrity, Jessica Case, deputy publisher of Pegasus Books and my editor, accepted the proposal and backed this project, at every stage, fully, astutely, and enthusiastically. Kudos to copyeditor Jessica L. Bax and proofreader Stephanie Marshall Ward for their eagle-eyed attention to details, large and small, that eluded me.

Uta Larkey, translator extraordinaire who stoically tolerated my sometimes vague requests about what I hoped was in a language that was jabberwocky to me. Prost, and schnapps when we meet again!

Uta, in turn, directed me to Marion Ehrlich, and Marion, in her turn, directed me to Karen Joelson. Marion's late father, Gerd, and Karen's late husband, Walter, lived in Berlin for most of the war, then escaped to Switzerland, where they lived in the same refugee camp as Cioma. They told me stories they'd heard about the Nazis, and about Stella Kubler, and about the refugee camp in Switzerland where Cioma stayed. Karen also gave me the photo of Cioma, Gerd, and Walter that appears in this book.

Bravo to the interlibrary team at the library of the University of Baltimore—Tammy Taylor, Sean Hogan, Delores Redman, and Erin Toepfner—who tirelessly located the most obscure articles, books, pamphlets, and monographs in places I didn't even know existed.

Michael Schönhaus, one of Cioma's sons, kindly provided memories and insights of his father, hours of interviews, and thoughtful permission to use rare photos of Cioma.

Jurgen Hartmann and Daniel Hoffman offered details on the labor camp in Bielefeld where Cioma worked in 1941; Roger Le Marie provided an intern's view of Cioma's graphic studio in Basel; Ryan Long, archivist with the Bicycle Museum of America in New Bremen,

Ohio, researched bicycle costs and models; and the Reverend Christine Schlund, pastor of Sophien Church (across the street from Cioma's family's apartment on Sophienstrasse), was an invaluable source of information on theology, church history, and its congregants and ministers' resistance to Hitler. Such rare courage is needed, always.

In Wittenberg, two municipal historians—Tim Lehmann and, especially, Desiree Baur—were of immense aid. From Desiree came history, maps, photos, hunches, and determined sleuthing. She's tenacious and indefatigable.

Malte Zierenberg, a professor at Humboldt University, knows Berlin's black market during the war years so well that he could have scored anything he desired—if it hadn't folded eighty years ago. And Jochen Heller was an invaluable resource about Lake Stössensee, where Cioma sailed.

Martina Voigt, historian extraordinaire in Berlin's Silent Heroes Memorial Center, interviewed Cioma in the 1980s, when hardly anyone knew of him or cared about those who resisted the Nazis quietly, unobtrusively. For two days, Martina guided me through neighborhoods, buildings, and streets that figured into Cioma's life in Berlin; piled me with books, articles, and knowledge; discussed Cioma's forging technique, amorous adventures, life on the run, places where he could have sought shelter, and more. I'm indebted to her encyclopedic appreciation of Cioma.

Erika Otto deserves a medal for helping me jump-start this project early on. Danke for impeccable translations that provided rich insights into Cioma's story, for your excitement when we found the stream where Cioma crossed into Switzerland, and for convincing me there's more to German beer than foam and bubbles.

Tanja Mancinelli boosted my spirits while poring over musty archives and mind-numbing translations. Her jokes and laughter ricocheted off so many walls in so many institutions that we were lucky not to be thrown out. But stay we did, later treating ourselves to fine dinners, tea with our favorite mother superior at a certain Catholic convent, and sugary desserts in a former castle. With Tanja, there's always an appreciation of the now—this now—and of *joie de vive*. And who doesn't want *joie* in their life?

Illustration Credits

Cioma, page xiv: © Swiss Federal Archives, E4264 #1985/196#22584*, Ref. N14825, Schoenhaus, Samson, 28.09.1922, 1943-1955

Arranged in order of layout in image insert:
Cioma in sailor suit: Courtesy, Michael Schönhaus
Hackescher Market: © Mitte Museum, Bezirksamt Mitte von Berlin. With museum's permission, this photo has been slightly cropped to eliminate writing along its right margin.
"Hitler Pledged" headline: public domain
Book burning, Berlin: public domain
Helen Keller's typing: public domain
Gestapo HQ exterior: public domain
Stumbling blocks: author
Lotte Windmüller: Courtesy, Daniel Hoffmann
Dorothee Fliess: © Stadtarchiv Detmold
Klepper family: Private reproduction/German Resistance Memorial Center
Edith Wolff: © United States Holocaust Memorial Museum. Provenance: Jizchak Schwersenz
Jizchak Schwersenz: © United States Holocaust Memorial Museum. Provenance: Gad Beck
Esplanade dining room: © Seuddeutsche Zeitung Photo/Alamy Stock Photo
Lake Stössensee: public domain

Rev. Vogel: © Dr. Christoph Vogel

Franz Kaufmann: Private collection/German Resistance Memorial Center

Helene Jacobs: Private collection/German Resistance Memorial Center

Stella Kubler: Landesarchiv, Berlin C Rep 375-01-07, Nr. 1

Cioma wearing tie: © Swiss Federal Archives, E4264 #1985/196#22584*,
    Ref. N14825, Schoenhaus, Samson, 28.09.1922, 1943-1955

Heinz Geutzleff's fake ID: © German Resistance Memorial Center/Edith
    Hirschfeldt Collection

Tintentod: © German Resistance Memorial Center BEGUM

Pouch, map for Cioma's bike ride: Courtesy, Jewish Museum of Switzerland,
    JMS 2060-1, photographer Elwira Spychalska

Nazi rally, Wittenberg: public domain

Pigs, Wittenberg church: author

Kurt Müller: public domain

Karl Barth, Charlotte von Kirschbaum: Courtesy, Karl Barth Archives, Basel

Schaffhausen refugee camp: Courtesy, Karen Joelson

Cioma's Swiss ID's: © Swiss Federal Archives, E4264 #1985/196#22584*,
    Ref. N14825, Schoenhaus, Samson, 28.09.1922, 1943-1955

Cioma with first wife: Courtesy, Michael Schönhaus

Cioma, 2004: © Dominik Plüss

Cioma on bike with son: Courtesy, Michael Schönhaus

Notes

A Note from the Author

1 **Sixty-five thousand**: Beate Kosmala, "The Rescue of Jews, 1941–1945," in *Nazi Europe and the Final Solution*, ed. David Bankier and Israel Gutman (Jerusalem: Yad Vashem, 2003), 95–96. **Seven thousand, two thousand**: Email from Martina Voigt, October 25, 2023.

Prelude

1 **Peter Schönhausen**: "Interim Investigation by German State Police re: Gunter Rogoff, Aug. 31, 1943," in *Der Passfalscher*, by Cioma Schönhaus (Frankfurt: Scherz, 2004), 228. *Der Passfalscher* is the German edition of Schönhaus's memoir. The English-language translation—*The Forger*—does not include this police report.

2 **Nobody would**: Author interview with Cioma Schönhaus, July 28, 2012.

3 **Mahogany**: Cioma Schönhaus, *The Forger* (New York: Da Capo Press, 2007), 127.

4 **Pillows**: Schönhaus, *The Forger*, 134.

Chapter 1. "You Better Go Back"

1 **Brooch, ninety guests, shoes**: Martina Voigt interview with Cioma Schönhaus, November 17, 1988. **Nineteen months older**: Calculated from "Boris Schönhaus," www.stolpersteine-berlin.de/biografie/620, and from "Fanja Schönhaus geb. Bermann," www.stolpersteine-berlin .de/biografie/619.

2 **Four percent of the city's population**: Sabine Hake, *Topographies of Class* (Ann Arbor: University of Michigan Press, 2008), 47. **Thirty**

thousand Jews: Malte Zierenberg, *Berlin's Black Market, 1939–1950* (New York: Palgrave Macmillan, 2015), 234. **Yellow caps and kerchiefs**: "History of the Jews in Belarus," Wikipedia, January 13, 2022, https://en.wikipedia.org/wiki/History_of_the_Jews_in _Belarus. **Eighty-eight percent, largest industries, synagogues and schools closed, grazing fields, disenfranchised**: Elissa Bemporad, *Becoming Soviet Jews* (Bloomington: Indiana University Press, 2013), 19, 31, 34.

3   **Largest industrial city, largest tenement, 2,153 square feet**: Harald Bodenschatz, *Berlin Urban Design* (Berlin: Dom Publishers, 2010), 7, 13, 14.

4   **Forty thousand**: Sanders Isaac Bernstein, "Berlin's Vanished Jewish Quarter," Slow Travel Berlin, September 25, 2021, www.slowtravel berlin.com/berlins-vanished-jewish-quarter/. **Nineteen prayer rooms**: "Jewish Migrants from Eastern Europe in the 1920s," Jüdisc Museum Berlin, hes www.jmberlin.de/en/exhibition-berlin-transit. **Scale model**: Joseph Roth, *What I Saw: Reports from Berlin, 1920–1933* (New York: W. W. Norton, 2003), 43.

5   **Lawyers, doctors**: Beate Kosmala, "The Rescue of Jews, 1941–1945," in *Nazi Europe and the Final Solution*, ed. David Bankier and Israel Gutman (Jerusalem: Yad Vashem, 2003), 93.

6   **Persons who left, unprotected, outlaws**: P. Weis, *The Problem of Statelessness* (London: British Section of the World Jewish Congress, 1944), 8, 4, 13.

7   **Few dozen, pestilence, concentration camp**: Hitler's September 18, 1922, speech, "Adolf Hitler, Collection of Speeches, 1922–1945," http://nseuropa.org.

8   **Ten thousand unemployed, one Jew killed, 129 injured, one thousand shops**: Bernstein, "Berlin's Vanished Jewish Quarter."

9   **Destroyed twice**: "History of Jerusalem," Wikipedia, https://en .wikipedia.org/wiki/History_of_Jerusalem.

10   **Moved in 1926**: "Fanja Schönhaus geb. Bermann," www.stolper steine-berlin.de/biografie/619. **1,373 Jews, twenty-three Muslims**: "British Mandate Palestine Census," https://kehilalinks.org/rishon _lezion/census.asp. **Seventy names**: Lawrence A. Hoffman, *Israel: A Companion for the Modern Jewish Pilgrim* (Woodstock, VT: Jewish Lights Publishing, 1998), 43.

11   **Wild country**: Aliza Fuss quoted in Tal Alon-Mozes, "Perceptions of Landscape among *Hachshara* Members," in *Jewish Horticultural Schools and Training Centers in Germany and their Impact on Horticulture and Landscape Architecture in Palestine/Israel*, ed. Irene Aue-Ben-David

Mozes and Joachim Wolschke-Bulmahn (Munich: AVM-
Akademische Verlagsgemeinschaft, 2020), 73. **Between your teeth**:
Martina Voigt interview with Cioma Schönhaus, November 17, 1988.
12   **If you want**: Martina Voigt interview with Cioma Schönhaus,
November 17, 1988.

Chapter 2. "In Earlier Times, They Would Have Burned Us"

1   **Würzburger, Sophienstrraße**: "Fanja Schönhaus geb. Bermann,"
www.stolpersteine-berlin.de/biografie/619.
2   **Seven workers, three coachmen**: "Boris Schönhaus," www
.stolpersteine-berlin.de/biografie/620; "Fanja Schönhaus geb.
Bermann," www.stolpersteine-berlin.de/biografie/619. **White-
lacquered, pink curtains, crystal bowl, plums**: Cioma Schönhaus,
The Forger (New York: Da Capo Press, 2007), 2.
3   **1,200 rooms**: "The Interior," Association Berliner Schloss, https
://berliner-schloss.de/new-palace/architecture-concepts/. **Simple life**:
Martina Voigt interview with Cioma Schönhaus, March 14, 1989.
4   **Hitler's friends, friendship**: "Hitler Sweeps to Power," *Syracuse
Herald-Journal*, January 31, 1933, 1. **Little apprehension,
surrounded, free agent**: "Washington Is Not Worried Over Hitler,"
Syracuse Herald-Journal, January 31, 1933, 2. **Hitler pledged,
promises to govern, will seek**: "Hitler Pledged to Rule Sanely,"
Boston Herald, January 31, 1933, 1.
5   **Playing soldier**: Interview with Cioma Schönhaus, July 28, 2012.
6   **You must be a Nazi**: Interview with Cioma Schönhaus, July 28, 2012.
7   **Beer-inspired, student zeal**: Christian Zentner and Friedemann
Bedurftig, eds., *The Encyclopedia of the Third Reich* (New York:
Macmillan, 1991), 100. **Only our books**: Leonidas E. Hill, "The Nazi
Attack on 'Un-German' Literature, 1933–1945," in *The Holocaust and
the Book: Destruction and Preservation*, ed. Jonathan Rose (Amherst:
University of Massachusetts Press, 2001), 17. Sigmund Freud should
have taken the book burnings more seriously given the title of one of
his books: *Civilization and Its Discontents*. With the book burnings,
and worse, the discontents of civilization were pouring out of their
dungeons.
8   **History has taught you nothing**: Helen Keller, "To the Student
Body of Germany," letter, May 9, 1933. Courtesy of Helen Keller
Archives, American Foundation for the Blind. The book burnings in
Nazi Germany are often linked to Heinrich Heine's warning, "Those
who burn books will in the end burn people." Heine wrote that after
German students burned books in 1817, mostly books by French

authors after France's occupation of Germany's Rhineland ended, and by Jews because Jews allegedly had an outsized influence on Germany, though one scholar says they were "so marginalized at the time, they were basically invisible." While there's no credible argument that Heine anticipated the Holocaust, it's not too great a leap from eliminating the ideas in books to eliminating the people who wrote them. **"So marginalized"**: Shlomo Avineri, "The Tale of Two Book Burnings: Heine's Warning in Context," Central European University, March 13, 2014, https://www.ceu.edu/article/2014-03-13/tale-two-book -burnings-heines-warning-context#:~:text=Heinrich%20Heine's%20 ominous%20sentence%2C%20%22those,century%20history%20 of%20German%20Jewry.

9　**English way of life**: Christian Adam, *Bestsellers of the Third Reich* (New York: Berghahn Books, 2021), 21.

10　**Never know, no matter, listen, sniff, nose to ground, murdered**: Felix Salten, *The Original Bambi*, ed. and trans. Jack Zipes (Princeton, NJ: Princeton University Press, 2022), 15, 17, 32–33, 68. Sigmund Salzman used "Felix Salten" as a pseudonym to, in his word, "unmark" himself as a Jew.

11　**Marx, Engels, Polgar, *Die Weltbuhn*, just having books**: Schönhaus, *The Forger*, 2.

Chapter 3. Hitchiking on the Autobahn

1　**Meet other children, little more left**: Martina Voigt interview with Cioma Schönhaus, March 14, 1989.

2　**Progressive, revolutionary, clean**: No author, *Pioneer Saga: The Story of Hashomer Hatzair* (New York: Hashomer Hatzair Organization, 1944), 16, 20, 22.

3　**Ten and eight million**: William L. Shirer, *The Rise and Fall of the Third Reich* (New York: Touchstone, 1990), 252–54.

4　**Hitchhiking**: Author interview with Cioma Schönhaus, July 28, 2012. **In prison, Hitler's roads**: Thomas Zeller, *Driving Germany* (New York: Berghahn Books, 2007), 63.

5　**Must write, schizophrenia**: Martina Voigt interview with Cioma Schönhaus, November 17, 1988.

6　**Reimburse, streets, children, benches, midwives, rubble**: Renata Stih and Frieder Schnock, *Places of Remembrance* (Berlin: Bezirksamt Schoeneberg von Berlin, 1998), 12–13. In the years after Cioma tried to escape to Belgium, new laws forbade Jews from leaving their apartments after 8:00 P.M., owning radios, receiving ration cards for clothing, riding public transportation during peak hours, using private or public telephones or public libraries, or buying soap, shaving cream, books, magazines, newspapers, cigars, cigarettes, eggs, meat. or fresh milk. Moreover, they could buy food—the little they were allowed to buy—only between four and five o'clock in the afternoon.

7   **Can only tell you**: Dagmar Buchwald and Martin Decker, "The Jewish Camp Schlosshof 1940–1943," in *Der Schlosshof*, ed. Barbel Sunderbrink (Bielefeld, Germany: Tpk-Regionalverlag, 2012), 115.

8   **797 Jews**: "Bielefeld," Destroyed German Synagogues and Communities, germansynagogues.com/index.php/synagogues -and-communities?pid=63&sid=243:Bielefeld. **129,000**: "Bielefeld," Wikipedia, https://en.wikipedia.org/wiki/Bielefeld.

9   **Agreement**: Buchwald and Decker, "The Jewish Camp Schlosshof," 118.

Chapter 4. "This Business Could Have Gone Very Badly"

1   **Palace Garden, dance floor, mothers, bunk beds**: Cioma Schönhaus, *The Forger* (New York: Da Capo Press, 2007), 3–5.

2   **Ping-pong, parties, Sabbath, piano, door is still open**: Daniel Hoffman, "Forced Labor and Leisure Time: Paul Hoffman's Youth in Work Camp Schlosshof," in *Der Schlosshof*, ed. Barbel Sunderbrink (Bielefeld, Germany: Tpk-Regionalverlag, 2012), 147.

3   **Are you blind, who's Lotte**: Schönhaus, *The Forger*, 5.

4   **Have a sweetheart**: Cioma Schönhaus, *Der Passfalscher* (Frankfurt: Scherz, 2004), 14. **To you**: Hoffman, "Forced Labor," 151.

5   **Training, hangers, barracks**: Henry L. deZeng IV, "Luftwaffe Airfields 1933–45," www.ww2.dk/lwairfields.html.

6   **Do you know, my dear Schönhaus**: Schönhaus, *The Forger*, 11–12.

7   **Twenty-two bombers, ten killed, twenty-one injured, slight damage**: Nicholas Stargardt, *The German War* (New York: Basic Books, 2017), 111.

8   **Three and a half million**: Stargardt, *The German War*, 158. **153 divisions; 600,000 vehicles; 3,580 tanks, artillery, airplanes; 10,000 warplanes, 600,000 and 665,000 prisoners**: Joachim Fest, *Hitler* (Harcourt Brace & Co., 1974), 648, 650–51, 653. **Lost forever, practically lost**: Klaus Reinhardt, *Moscow—The Turning Point: The Failure of Hitler's Strategy in the Winter of 1941–42* (Providence, RI: Berg Publishers, 1992), 34.

9   **Let you out of prison**: Schönhaus, *The Forger*, 3.

10   **Not own mill, never convert, not godfather, parents' deaths**: Jurgen Hartmann's emails to author, June 4, 2022, June 17, 2022. **Certificate, wedding**: "Lotte Windmüller und Paul

Hoffmann," Deportation Nach Auschwitz / Bielefeld, www.dfb.de
/Auf-den-Spuren-von-Julius-Hirsch/58.

Chapter 5. "Nothing Ever Happened except One Kiss"

1   **Jonny Syna, Wolfgang Pander, 98 feet x 164 feet,
     Westerfeldhausen**: Cioma Schönhaus, *The Forger* (New York: Da
     Capo Press, 2007), 12–13.

2   **Over five hundred**: "Girls from the Lenore Goldschmidt School
     Celebrate the Birthday of [first name unidentified] Schlesinger,"
     United States Holocaust Memorial Museum, https://collections
     .ushmm.org/search/catalog/pa1175585.

3   Descriptions of students at the Goldschmidt School gleaned from
     viewing film footage of the school shot in 1937 by the American
     photographer Julien Bryan, United States Holocaust Memorial
     Museum, https://collections.ushmm.org/search/catalog/irn1000956.

4   **Unfortunately, we cannot**: Nicholas Stargardt, *The German War*
     (New York: Basic Books, 2017), 29–30.

5   **Intelligent eyes, bow legs**: Schönhaus, *The Forger*, 15.

6   **You're a Jew, except for a kiss**: Martina Voigt interview with Cioma
     Schönhaus, March 14, 1989. **Admiringly**: Schönhaus, *The Forger*, 17.

Chapter 6. The Butter Conspiracy

1   **Audubon Avenue**: *Fragebogen* ("questionnaire") Cioma submitted to
     Swiss authorities, January 1, 1944. **Twenty years older**: Calculated
     from 1940 US census, which lists Morris's birth year as 1892.

2   **Thirty thousand Reichsmarks, laborer**: "Boris Schönhaus," www
     .stolpersteine-berlin.de/biografie/620.

3   **Half**: Interview with Malte Zierenberg, September 10, 2022.
     Rations: Roger Moorhouse, *Berlin at War* (New York: Basic Books,
     2010), 84. Clever waiters were adept at evading rules about scarcity
     of certain wines. If you served customers in top-drawer restaurants
     delicacies they never expected, kindnesses were shown your way, like
     the waiter who bought a farm in the country with the generous tips
     he received for "finding" bottles of a rare Moselle wine. "Finding" was
     another word for ignoring rationing. **Waiter**: Earl R. Beck, *Under the
     Bombs* (Lexington: University Press of Kentucky, 1986), 146.

4   **Beuthen, pounds, and prices of butter**: "Reichsjustizministerium,"
     Bundesarchiv, Berlin, 3001/23426. **Notebook**: Author interview
     with Cioma Schönhaus, July 28, 2012. Every German was
     rationed 116 grams (or four ounces) of butter per week. To
     compensate, the Nazis accelerated their efforts to develop a

greasy substitute—margarine—with Hitler ordering Göring to find a reliable supply of animal fat for margarine. Margarine manufacturers relied on whale blubber for their cheapest, most plentiful supply of fat, and Norway controlled the largest supply of whale blubber from the North Atlantic. To find another source, Göring sent an expedition to Antarctica in 1938 to determine if a base should be established there to slaughter whales and render their fat into margarine. The ship returned to Germany with inconclusive data. Göring now turned to Arthur Imhausen, a German already experimenting with synthesizing margarine from coal. There was a problem: Imhausen was half Jewish. When he emerged from his lab with an ersatz margarine, Imhausen and his family were made honorary Aryans, with all the privileges of real Aryans. **Never rationed, Imhausen**: "Hitler and the Secret 'Margarine Whale Plan,'" *The Fantastic History of Food* (podcast), February 21, 2020, https://podcasters.spotify.com/pod/show/foodhistory/episodes /10---Hitler-And-The-Secret-Margarine-Whale-Plan-eavmii.

5   **1938**: Arvind Narrain and Clifton D'Rozario, "Lawyering in Impossible Times," *Leaflet*, April 4, 2022, www.theleaflet.in /lawyering-in-impossible-times-remembering-nazi-germanys -treatment-of-lawyers.

6   **Two of us**: Cioma Schönhaus, *The Forger* (New York: Da Capo Press, 2007), 18.

7   **Yiddish, screaming**: Schönhaus, *The Forger*, 32.

8   **Soul, exploiting, comfortably**: "Reichsjustizministerium," Bundesarchiv, Berlin, 3001/23426.

Chapter 7. An Act of Lunacy

1   **Welfare services, hugged, bed**: Cioma Schönhaus, *The Forger* (New York: Da Capo Press, 2007), 19–20.

2   **A bomb, destroyed**: Schönhaus, *The Forger*, 20.

3   **Bakers, prostitution, mother**: Schönhaus, *The Forger*, 41–43.

4   **Where'd it land**: Schönhaus, *The Forger*, 21.

5   **Lunacy**: Sebastian Haffner, *The Meaning of Hitler* (Cambridge, MA: Harvard University Press, 1979), 117, 120. **Puzzling**: Ian Kershaw, *Fateful Choices* (New York: Penguin, 2007), 382. "Lunacy" because Hitler did not understand America's strength or its determination to defeat him. Nor did he consult with military advisers before declaring war on the United States. In fact, until three days before Pearl Harbor—December 7, 1941—Germany wasn't obliged to join Japan against the United States. On December 4, Hitler promised Japan

he'd side with it if there was a war with the United States, no matter who started it. This replaced the 1940 Tripartite Pact, which was essentially a defensive pact between Germany, Italy, and Japan.

6   **Poststrasse 6, ninety-six Jewish tailors, Gunther**: Schönhaus, *The Forger*, 22–23.

7   **Four hundred Jews, Kyffhauser, tram no. 3**: Bernd J. Wagner, "13 December 1941: Deportation of Jews to Riga," www.historischer-rueckklick-bielefeld.com.

8   **March 2, 1943**: "Lotte Windmüller und Paul Hoffmann," Deportation Nach Auschwitz / Bielefeld, www.dfb.de /Auf-den-Spuren-von-Julius-Hirsch/58.

9   **February 26, suitcase with papers, rings, books, socks**: Bernd J. Wagner, "March 2, 1943: Jewish People Were Deported from Bielefeld to Auschwitz," www.historischer-rueckklick-bielefeld .com/2018/03/01/01032018/.

10 **Happy, resolute, Johanna**: Bernd J. Wagner, "March 2, 1943: Jewish People Were Deported from Bielefeld to Auschwitz," https ://historischcherer-rueckklick-bielfeld.com/2011/12/01/01/01122011 /comment-page-1/.

11 **Number 104951**: "Deportations from Westphalia to Auschwitz in 1943," www.statistik-des-holocaust.de/list-ger-wfn-43a.html. **Death march, escaped**: Daniel Hoffman, "Forced Labor and Leisure Time: Paul Hoffman's Youth in Work Camp Schlosshof," in *Der Schlosshof*, ed. Barbel Sunderbrink (Bielefeld, Germany: Tpk-Regionalverlag, 2012), 147. **Married, children**: Email from Daniel Hoffman to the author, July 25, 2022.

Chapter 8. "Do Not Shed Too Many Tears"

1   **Glamorous, wouldn't pinch, come along**: Cioma Schönhaus, *The Forger* (New York: Da Capo Press, 2007), 23.

2   **You're crazy**: Author interview with Cioma Schönhaus, July 28, 2012.

3   **Don't want to believe, stay with your father**: Martina Voigt interview with Cioma Schönhaus, March 14, 1989.

4   **Impossible for a normal person**: Schönhaus, *The Forger*, 29.

5   **Forty-eight women, four men, tea, coffee, if a bullet, Levi, Wiesner, stand fast**: Schönhaus, *The Forger*, 37, 40–41. **Coffee disappeared**: Pamela E. Swett, *Selling under the Swastika: Advertising and Commercial Culture in Nazi Germany* (Stanford, CA: Stanford University Press, 2014), 189.

6   **Evchen**: Schönhaus, *The Forger*, 30–31.

7   **Some kind, terrible shame, amusing thing**: Schönhaus, *The Forger*,
     34–35. If the Nazis had a better sense of aesthetics and of the
     value of fine art, they might not have been so quick to call modern
     art "degenerate." In time, work by the "degenerate" artists in that
     gallery's back room would be worth a fortune, with work by Max
     Pechstein, Max Beckmann, and Oskar Kokoschka selling for up to
     $22.5 million. Wikipedia entries for "Pechstein" and "Beckmann,"
     October 16, 2022.

8   **Jewish Council told**: Danny Orbach, *The Plots Against Hitler* (New
     York: Houghton Mifflin, 2016), 152–53. In 1933, hearing that the
     German government was about to ban all Jewish lawyers from
     the bar, Fliess had urged the ministry of justice to allow exceptions
     for Jews who'd fought in the last war. His argument was that if they
     were good enough to fight for Germany, they were good enough to
     serve as lawyers now. Appealing to the past to save Jewish lawyers
     proved ineffective. In November 1938 every Jewish lawyer in
     Germany was expelled from the bar.

9   **Four hundred Dutch Jews**: Orbach, *Plots Against Hitler*, 150,
     147–48. In 1939 Canaris had even saved the head of the
     Lubavitch Hasidic group, Rabbi Yosef Yitzhak Schneerson, who
     was trapped in Warsaw as the German army conquered Poland.
     Learning of the rabbi's plight, American Hasidim asked the US
     Department of State for help. American diplomats recruited a
     high-level Nazi who was opposed to the war—diplomatic channels
     were still open. This was before the United States entered the war.
     The Nazi, in turn, recruited Canaris, who sent three German
     intelligence officers to Warsaw to hunt for Schneerson. Meanwhile,
     American diplomats and politicians secured visas for the
     rabbi from the State Department in Washington and from Latvia,
     where Schneerson held citizenship. Two months later, German
     agents found Schneerson in Warsaw, and he traveled to Berlin,
     Latvia, Sweden, and finally the United States. **Schneerson**: Orbach,
     Plots Against Hitler, 147–48.

10   **Eichmann warned**: Orbach, *Plots Against Hitler*, 153.

11   **One million dollars**: Orbach, *Plots Against Hitler*, 156–57. Hitler
     unknowingly helped Operation 7 along. Furious that the few spies
     the Abwehr had smuggled into the United States were caught
     almost immediately, Hitler called Canaris to his office. Raging
     that the Abwehr hadn't carefully screened the spies it was sending
     abroad, Hitler claimed they were traitors. If not, they wouldn't

have been caught so easily. "If that's the quality of your work," Hitler yelled, "employ Jews or criminals." On their way out of the Chancellery, Canaris whispered to a colleague who was in on Operation 7, "Did you hear? Jews or criminals." They knew exactly which Jews they'd send on the mission Hitler had inadvertently authorized.

That million-dollar withdrawal doomed the organizers of Operation 7. A few weeks after Operation 7's 14 Jews entered Switzerland, Nazi officials discovered the illegal transaction. Initially, they suspected the funds had been embezzled for personal use. Investigations led them to Dohnanyi. While Dohnanyi's office was being searched, a Gestapo agent saw a colleague of Dohnanyi's hide a piece of paper in a jacket pocket. It was a list of all the conspirators in Operation 7, including Dohnanyi and his brother-in-law, the theologian Dietrich Bonhoeffer. Dohnanyi and Bonhoeffer were arrested. In February 1944, Canaris was fired from the Abwehr; in July he was arrested because of his close association with the perpetrators of the July 20 plot to kill Hitler, though no evidence proved he was involved in it. In April 1945, Canaris, Dohnanyi, and Bonhoeffer were hanged—a month before the war ended. **Employ Jews, did you hear**: Orbach, *Plots Against Hitler*, 157.

12   **Never can tell, secret**: Schönhaus, *The Forger*, 36–37.
13   **September 30, five months**: Orbach, *Plots Against Hitler*, 157.

Chapter 9. A Night on the Town

1   **Our turn, look confident**: Schönhaus, *The Forger* (New York: Da Capo Press, 2007), 38.

2   **Shoe tree**: William P. Powell, "Why I Like Berlin," *New Yorker*, October 3, 1931, 77. **Göring wedding**: Adam Bisno, "Hotel Berlin: The Politics of Commercial Hospitality in the German Metropolis, 1875–1945" (PhD diss., Johns Hopkins University, 2017), 319.

3   **Riefenstahl, monstrous losses, not enough, five of seven**: Bisno, "Hotel Berlin," 305, 311. By ceding the hotel to Hitler, the Kaiserhof's board of directors essentially ruled that the Kaiserhof was off-limits to Jews. Meinhardt fled to the United Kingdom and, in 1941, began coordinating relief efforts through the Association of Jewish Refugees in Great Britain. In November 1943, the Kaiserhof burned down during a British bombing raid.

4   **Paintings, wood panels**: Bisno, "Hotel Berlin," 330. **Whiskey, fjord**: Schönhaus, *The Forger*, 38–39. **Visible pain**: Roger Moorhouse, *Berlin at War* (New York: Basic Books, 2010), 86.

5 **Twelve-hour shifts**: Schönhaus, *The Forger*, 45. **4.5 miles**: Leonard Gross, *The Last Jews in Berlin* (New York: Touchstone Books, 1999), 52.

6 The S-Bahn was a tinderbox for small incidents that revealed the chasm between Nazism and many Germans. For example: riding on the S-Bahn, a mother saw whom her daughter was sitting next to and loudly said to her, "Lieschen, sit somewhere else. Don't sit next to a Jew." Hearing that, another passenger made his seat available to the Jew, declaring as loudly as the mother had to her daughter, "And I don't have to sit next to Lieschen." **Lieschen**: Albert Meirer, "Berlin's Jews: Deprived of Rights, Impoverished and Branded," in *Jews in Nazi Germany: From Kristallnact to Liberation*, ed. Beate Meyer, Hermann Simon, and Chana Schutz (Chicago: University of Chicago Press, 2009), 98.

7 **Same ones**: Schönhaus, *The Forger*, 46, 51.

8 **Fine art**: Schönhaus, *The Forger*, 52.

9 **Creating too much**: Schönhaus, *The Forger*, 58–59.

Chapter 10. The Kindest Nazi Fanja Ever Met

1 **So lucky**: Cioma Schönhaus, *The Forger* (New York: Da Capo Press, 2007), 40.

2 **Family man, you know all the Jews**: Schönhaus, *The Forger*, 48. The Grunewald station became the Nazis' central depot for deporting Jews from Berlin.

3 Deportations from the synagogue on Levetzowstrasse had begun during the fall of 1942. Over four days, four thousand Jews had marched from Levetzowstrasse to the station in Grunewald. Sixteen thousand more would march in the next few months, past homes, schools, and cafés where patrons, sipping their ersatz coffee, would stoically note the lines of Jews marching down the middle of the street. The Nazis had seized the synagogue on October 1, 1941, as Yom Kippur, the holiest day of the Jewish year, ended. Almost overnight, they ripped out its 2,120 seats and filled the floor of the empty space with straw so Jews could sleep there. By 1945, more than fifty thousand Jews would leave from Grunewald for "the east." Orders for those deportations had come from the second floor of Burgstrasse 28, where a kind Gestapo officer had wished Fanja "all the best" on her journey to "the east."

4 **Certify**: Schönhaus, *The Forger*, 53.

5 **He's going, exempt, my girl, rescue us**: Schönhaus, *The Forger*, 67, 69. **Of course**: Author interview with Cioma Schönhaus, July 29, 2012.

6 **Very undramatic**: Martina Voigt interview with Cioma Schönhaus, November 17, 1988.

7   **Same mistake, sacrificing, don't draw attention**: Martina Voigt
     interview with Cioma Schönhaus, November 17, 1988.
8   **Colleagues, arrived safely**: Schönhaus, *The Forger*, 68, 72. Boris
     was murdered at Majdanek on August 16, 1942. The date of Fanja's
     murder at Sobibor is not known.

Chapter 11. A Brainless Hitler and a Stupid Joke

1   **Pigs, out of our ears, Borchardt, sausages**: Roger Moorhouse, *Berlin
     at War* (New York: Basic Books, 2010), 91–94.
2   **Soulless existence**: Danish journalist Paul von Stemann in
     Moorhouse, *Berlin at War*, 346–67.
3   **Untrue, champanzees, guillotined, suicide, glass eye, vacation,
     3,744**: Rudolph Herzog, *Dead Funny* (New York: Melville House,
     2011), 41, 66–67, 86, 167–68, 188–89, 208–10. **Herring**: Schönhaus,
     The Forger, 86.
4   **Six hundred, cows, divine protection**: Daniel B. Silver, *Refuge in
     Hell* (New York: Mariner, 2004), 19, 29, 156, 193.
5   The last three hundred residents of the Jewish nursing home were
     sent to Theresienstadt in June 1943. The Gestapo gave the staff two
     hours to get them ready. Patients were barely dressed and many were
     swaddled in diapers, which had to be changed more often than usual
     because of the stress and commotion. Urine and shit were everywhere.
     When a Gestapo officer demanded to know why the trucks with the
     elderly hadn't left already, he was told the old people were having
     trouble climbing into the vehicles. "Give them a kick in the ass," the
     officer yelled. "That'll speed things up." **Three hundred, two hours,
     diapers, kick in ass**: Silver, *Refuge in Hell*, 152–53.

Chapter 12. He Took the Job

1   **Benefits**: Email from Martina Voigt, December 3, 2022.
2   **What are you up to**: Cioma Schönhaus, *The Forger* (New York: Da
     Capo Press, 2007), 75.
3   **Abraham, Kaiseralle 79**: Schönhaus, *The Forger*, 77. Most
     improbably, two Theodore Wolffs worked at the *Berliner Tageblat*—
     one was the top editor, the other a reporter. Perhaps because he was
     better known, Editor Wolff is often identified as the father of Edith
     Wolff. But Theodore Wolff's daughter was named Lilly, not Edith.
     Neither of the Theodore Wolffs survived the war. Editor Wolff,
     seventy-five years old and ill, was transferred to the Jewish Hospital
     in Berlin in September 1943. He died three days later. Reporter
     Wolff, Edith's father and the Wolff who would have been home when
     Cioma visited Edith, was killed at Auschwitz on July 20, 1943.

4   Friedenau was a contraction of two German words: *frieden* ("peace") and *au* ("plain"). Together, they alluded to the "plain of peace" that might flower in Friedenau: a plain of solace, of quiet reflection. Noble aspirations during a war.

5   Schwersenz's original forename was Heinz-Joachin. He changed this to Jizchak—often mistaken for Yitzhak—of his own volition, possibly in the late 1930s when he became active in Zionist youth groups.

6   **Ten thousand**: Moorhouse, *Berlin at War*, 285. **Letters, tracts, aunt removed**: Marion Kaplan, *Between Dignity and Despair* (New York: Oxford University Press, 1998), 215.

7   **Elegant clothes**: Edith Wolff's testimony to Yad Vashem, Jerusalem. Once a merchant specializing in handkerchiefs and fine embroidery, Albert Kleinberger, like his wife and like almost every Jew in Berlin, was working in a factory in early 1943. They'd watched numerous relatives depart—a few to safety, like their daughter, Lotte, who'd emigrated to England; most, the Kleinbergers suspected, to their murders. The Kleinbergers figured it was too late for them to escape from Berlin, and they had no idea how to hide. Ill, frail, alone, and aged, they fled by "escaping into death," as suicide was becoming known.

8   **Thirty-three out of forty**: Karen Notzel, "The Only Jewish Underground Youth Group Was Founded in Friedenau," *Berliner Woche*, March 4, 2019.

9   **What good, hikes, sports, box office, classes, Havdalah, prayers for dead, air raids**: Kaplan, *Between Dignity and Despair*, 196, 212–13, 262. Chug Chaluzi was smartly organized. Members rarely went out in groups of more than two; if they did, they pretended not to know each other. Little stopped them, not even bombs. If there was an air raid, they gathered for meetings or classes within an hour after the all-clear signal.

10   **What good, sweet child, married Heinz**: "Zionism Underground in Berlin," excerpted from Jizchak Schwersenz's memoir, in *Daring to Resist: Jewish Defiance in the Holocaust*, ed. Yitzchak Mais (New York: Museum of Jewish Heritage: 2007), 31–32.

11   **Small, radiant, penetrating, control, I'll try, Taunussatrasse 79, great demand**: Schönhaus, *The Forger*, 77–78.

Chapter 13. The Yard Sale of the Century

1   **You can have the room**: Cioma Schönhaus, *The Forger* (New York: Da Capo Press, 2007), 79–80.

Chapter 14. The Reluctant Forger

1   **Fortunate position, go and see, still correct German**: Cioma Schönhaus, *The Forger* (New York: Da Capo Press, 2007), 92–93.

2   Often, it's said that Franz Kaufmann's parents converted him and his two brothers to Christianity when they were young. Not so, said a family member who should know. In a 1979 interview, Kaufmann's nephew, Walter Kaufmann, then a retired professor from Princeton University, said the three brothers had all "converted to Protestantism when they were roughly twenty years old." Over time, this family was awash in conversions—Jewish to Christian or Christian to Jewish. When he was eleven years old, Walter (Franz's nephew) converted to Judaism, unable to accept the Holy Ghost or the divinity of Jesus. Walter dedicated his book, *The Faith of a Heretic*, to his uncle Franz: "A devout convert to Christianity, shot by the Secret Police in 1944 for gallantly helping others in obedience to conscience." **Roughly twenty**: Trude Weiss-Rosmarin, "An Interview with Walter Kaufmann," *Judaism* 30 (Winter 1981): 122. **No one should**: Robert L. Kehoe III, "Left for Dead," *Los Angeles Review of Books*, September, 23, 2019. **Devout convert**: Stanley Corngold, *Walter Kaufmann: Philosopher, Humanist, Heretic* (Princeton, NJ: Princeton University Press, 2018), 4.

3   **Three tenths:** Christoph David Piorkowski, "Anti-Semitism and the Culture of Remembrance," Tagesspiegel, April 28, 2020, https://www.tagesspiegel.de/wissen/die-grosste-luge-der -bundesrepublik-4163017.html. The same article cites current Germans' distortions of their relatives' history during the Nazi era, claiming that 29 percent helped victims, 70 percent of their ancestors were not among the perpetrators, and 36 percent were certain their ancestors were victims. These Germans who are alive today inherited the country they imagine, and the history they wish for. **Lawyer**: Schönhaus, *The Forger*, 152. **World falling apart**: Jacobs quoted on "Helene Jacobs," Yad Vashem, www.yadvashem.org/de/righteous /stories/jacobs.html. **Did it for humanity**: Jacobs in Gay Block, *Rescuers: Portraits of Moral Courage in the Holocaust* (Santa Fe, NM: Radius Books, 2020), 186.

4   **Person in photo**: Interview with Helene Jacobs, Yad Vashem, March 22, 1967.

5   **Fingerprints**: Jane Caplan, "'Ausweis Bitte!': Identity and Identification in Nazi Germany," in *Identification and Registration Practices in Transnational Perspective: People, Papers and Practices*, ed. Ilsen About, James Brown, and Gayle Lonergan (New York: Palgrave Macmillan, 2013), 232–33.

6   **Mills**: Martina Voigt to the author, January 3, 2023.

7   **Old friend**: Schönhaus, *The Forger*, 96–97. Meyer and his wife, Lotte, were deported to Theresienstadt on June 30, 1943. On September 29, 1944, they were sent to Auschwitz, and soon killed.

Chapter 15. Better Than Dueling with Sabers

1   **Sideshow**: Anne Dreesbach, "Colonial Exhibitions, 'Völkerschauen' and the Display of the 'Other,'" European History Online, May 3, 2012, http://www.ieg-ego.eu/dreesbacha-2012-en. **Rough as sea, Assyrian palace**: Barbara Wunnenberg, "The Weimar Experience in British Interwar Writing" (PhD diss., King's College, London, and Humboldt University, Berlin, 2020). Luna Park was one of seventy-seven amusement parks that were built around the world, mostly from 1902 through the 1920s. They remain in Buenos Aires, Mumbai, and Melbourne. Essentially, "Luna Park" is shorthand for "You Will Have Fun Here," as upbeat a slogan as Disney World's claim that it's "The Happiest Place on Earth" is bogus.

2   **Duel**: John Toland, *Adolf Hitler* (New York: Anchor Books, 1992), 138. **Pahl**: "George Pahl," Wikipedia, https://en.wikipedia.org/wiki /George_Pahl. **Beers, blows**: Thomas Friedrich, *Hitler's Berlin* (New Haven, CT: Yale University Press, 2012), 35–38. With his driver pushing Hitler's twenty-horsepower Selve—an auto that a small company in Hameln had been producing for the last four years—on that trip to Berlin, Hitler passed through Communist strongholds in Saxony and Prussia. Police stopped the car once. Hitler later said if they'd realized who he was, "They would have had my head." In Berlin, Hitler raised funds for the nearly bankrupt Nazi Party, visited the war memorial, and admired Rembrandt's *Man in a Golden Helmet* in the National Gallery, assuring his entourage that, "in spite of the many pictures Rembrandt painted in Amsterdam's Jewish quarter, at heart he was a true Aryan and German." **Twenty horsepower**. "Selve," https://de.wikipedia.org/wiki/ DSlve (German-language edition of Wikipedia). **Had my head, Rembrandt**: Toland, *Adolf Hitler*, 138. Hitler couldn't keep his face out of the papers the next fall. Pahl spotted Hitler at a parade in Nuremburg, clicked his shutter, and ran before Storm Troopers, or Hitler himself, could nab him. Soon, the first images of Hitler were in papers all over Germany.

3   **Safe when they're stopped**: Cioma Schönhaus, *The Forger* (New York: Da Capo Press, 2007), 98.

4   **Good idea**: Schönhaus, *The Forger*, 104–5.

5   **Fail to keep, lost ID**: Schönhaus, *The Forger*, 99, 102.
6   **Grandmother, Schönhausen**: Schönhaus, *The Forger*, 99, 103, 111.
7   **Showy, stunning, fantastic, bad end**: Schönhaus, *The Forger*, 100.

Chapter 16. "You Shall Be the Emperor of My Soul"

1   **Coat rack, undressed, bore me**: Schönhaus, *The Forger* (New York: Da Capo Press, 2007), 109.
2   **Show-off**: Schönhaus, *The Forger*, 109.
3   **Passengers, carpet, guards**: Aram Bakshian (as told to by Robert Stolz), *The Barbed Wire Waltz* (Melbourne: Robert Stolz Publishing Co., 1983), 167–68, 201–2.
4   **Oysters, Gewürztraminer, wallet, until Monday**: Schönhaus, *The Forger*, 115.
5   **Auschwitz, Hirschfeld, Sheuer, Dimsack**: Martina Voigt email to the author, February 17, 2023.
6   **Military secret**: Schönhaus, *The Forger*, 107.
7   Without Pelikan's Tintentod, Cioma couldn't have removed those incriminating "Sarah's" and "Israel's" from Jews' IDs. But Pelikan wasn't a benign company. Its owner, Fritz Beindorff, joined a dozen German industrialists who signed a letter in 1932 asking President Hindenburg to appoint Hitler chancellor, convinced his economic "genius" would rescue Germany from "decay and misery." Beindorff eventually used several thousand prisoners of war and forced laborers in Pelikan's workforce. One of the inks they produced—a carbon-based black ink, often called Indian or India ink—was used to tattoo numbers onto the left forearms of prisoners at Auschwitz.

Chapter 17. Cioma, the German Nobleman

1   **Twenty-three million, Winter Garden, cherubs**: Friedemann Kreuder, "Hotel Esplanade: The Cultural History of a Berlin Location," *PAJ: A Journal of Performance and Art* 22, no. 2 (May 2000): 23.
2   When the Nazis took over Germany, they planned to demolish the Esplanade: the memory of Jews and monarchists who frequented the place was too much for them. Quickly, Albert Speer, Hitler's chief architect, requisitioned much of the hotel as a guest house for honored visitors of the Third Reich. Among them was William Dodd, the new US ambassador, who stayed with his family in a six-room suite when they arrived in Berlin in 1933. Within weeks, a confidante of Hitler introduced the führer to Martha, the ambassador's daughter, telling the blonde, vivacious, twenty-six-year old, "Hitler needs a woman.

Hitler should have an American woman—a lovely woman would change the destiny of Europe. Martha, you are the woman." Martha didn't think so. Meeting Hitler was a letdown. She wrote he had a "weak, soft face," "deep pouches under his eyes," and a "bony facial structure." Only his eyes were memorable: "Unforgettable, intense, unwavering, hypnotic." Rather than marry Hitler, Martha had an affair with Rudolf Diels, the head of the Gestapo. **Needs a woman, weak, pouches, bony, unforgettable**: "Martha Dodd," Traces, https://usgerrelations.traces.org/marthadodd.html.

3   **Good idea, slurping, consul general**: Author interview with Cioma Schönhaus, July 29, 2012.

Chapter 18. Cioma's Comrade

1   **Sunny**: Cioma Schönhaus, *Der Passfalscher* (Frankfurt: Scherz, 2004), 228. *Nomen est omen*: Cioma Schönhaus, *The Forger* (New York: Da Capo Press, 2007), 129.

2   **Child's play**: Schönhaus, *The Forger*, 128.

3   **Tacking**: Schönhaus, *The Forger*, 133.

4   **Moved like a dancer**: Schönhaus, *The Forger*, 133–34. **Cioma offered**: Author interview with Cioma Schönhaus, July 29, 2012. **Frick offered**: Nicholas Stargardt, *The German War* (New York: Basic Books, 2017), 262. Pressing his luck, Jochen asked Frick to help get his Jewish wife out of Germany, as well as Renate. Frick said he no longer had the authority to protect even one Jew these days. For now, Joanna, Klepper's wife, was protected by her marriage to an Aryan. But if efforts for forced divorces between Jewish and Christian couples became legal, Jews like Joanna, now saved by her marriage to Jochen, would be immediately deported. Just as Jochen tried to save Joanna, she tried to save him. A divorce, she told him, would let him live, and write, in peace. Jochen refused. "Purchasing" a career like this, he wrote in his journal, "would seem to me as if one betrayed the word of God."

5   **Not finally**: Stargardt, *The German War*, 262. The Kleppers' suicides shook Berlin. Some said the deaths were cruel and heartless. Good parents don't kill their children, and Renate was a victim of her parents' refusal to obey the state, and the state always knew what was best. Others said the suicides were a sign that the Third Reich had exhausted God's infinite patience and love. A neighbor of the Kleppers wept that if "a man like Klepper who was so imbued with the gospel, a man who could write, write, write, and flee life [through death], then one could only think that God is leaving us to hell, to pain, to misery." Though Nazism was built on slaughter and

extermination, suicide was different from other ways of leaving this world. To the Nazis, every human body belonged to the Reich. Since Hitler embodied the Reich, every body belonged to him, and suicide was an insult to the man who'd given Germans hope. The Kleppers didn't care about that. They were through living amid people who worshipped this false god. **If a man**: Gerlof Homan, "A German Mennonite Affirmation of Jochen Klepper in Nazi Germany," Historical Committee & Archives of the Mennonite Church, http ://www.mcusa-archives.org/MHB/Homan-GermanMennonite.html. **Suicide was different**: Robert N. Proctor, *The Nazi War on Cancer* (Princeton, NJ: Princeton University Press, 1999), 120.

Chapter 19. The Tide Turns

1 **Vodka, Moet et Chandon, actors**: Cioma Schönhaus, *The Forger* (New York: Da Capo Press, 2007), 131.
2 **Foolish, feelings for me, apart from her looks**: Author interview with Cioma Schönhaus, July 29, 2012.
3 **Progressively loses**: Primo Levi in Judith Butler, *Parting Ways: Jewishness and the Critique of Zionism* (New York: Columbia University Press, 2012), 191.
4 **Criminal, telling**: Schönhaus, *The Forger*, 135–36.

Chapter 20. Don't Show Your Face in Public

1 **Forty-six stations**: Email to author from Berliner U-Bahn-Museum, May 6, 2022.
2 **Dark**: Interview with Martina Voigt, September 5, 2022.
3 **Ruth, friends, why do you always, police**: Cioma Schönhaus, *The Forger* (New York: Da Capo Press, 2007), 145.
4 **Markelstrasse, Südwestkorso, Hohenzollerndamm, Auguste-Viktoria-Strasse.** Schönhaus, *The Forger*, 146.
5 **Photos,** *Police Gazette,* **not show face**: Schönhaus, *The Forger*, 146.
6 **Respectable**: Jeremy Noakes, *Nazism, 1919–1945*, vol. 4 (Exeter, UK: University of Exeter Press, 1988), 632. Popitz wanted to preserve the Germany he'd known. For several years, he'd secretly met with other Germans opposed to Hitler: high-level civil servants, intellectuals, professors. This all-talk-no-action group plotted ways to topple Hitler: a coup d'etat, an arrest, an assassination. All they agreed on was that Hitler was a disaster. In 1939 Popitz drew up a "Provisional Basic Law" intended to slightly tame the Nazis. Under the proposal, every German had to "comport himself [so] the good of the community is not affected and no damage done to the good name

of Germany." "Good" wasn't defined. Every German was entitled to "a way of life worthy of a human being," to an old-age pension and health and unemployment benefits, and to decent housing if they "did their duty to the people and the state." "Duty" wasn't defined. Popitz's law would dissolve the SS and the Gestapo and suspend, not abolish, Hitler's worst anti-Jewish laws and policies. Popitz wanted Jews to "disappear from the life of the state and the economy," preferably by permanently exiling them. **Duty, way of life, disappear:** Peter Hoffman, *The History of the German Resistance, 1933–1945* (Cambridge, MA: MIT Press, 1977), 180–82.

7   **True:** Schönhaus, *The Forger,* 148.

8   **By no means safe:** Helene Jacobs testimony, Yad Vashem, March 22, 1967. **Need him:** Schönhaus, *The Forger,* 148.

9   **Slid down the railing, ran down side streets, Bonner Strasse 2:** Schönhaus, *The Forger,* 151.

Chapter 21. "Simple Is What You Are, Schönhaus"

1   **Worry:** Cioma Schönhaus, *The Forger* (New York: Da Capo Press, 2007), 151.

2   **People are human:** Interview with Michael Schönhaus, May 31, 2023.

3   **I will deal:** Zephaniah 3:19, Holman Christian Standard Bible, https://read.csbible.com/?book=zephaniah&chapter=3. **United more firmly:** 1982 exhibit, "On the Way to the Responsible Community," Martin Niemoller Peace Center, Berlin: www.niemoeller-haus-berlin.de/ausstellung/tafe35.html.

Chapter 22. Hiding, Loving, Fleeing

1   **Stayed on bus:** Cioma Schönhaus, *The Forger* (New York: Da Capo Press, 2007), 51.

2   **Three quarters:** Roger Moorhouse, *Berlin at War* (New York: Basic Books, 2010), 209.

3   **Come on:** Schönhaus, *The Forger,* 155. **Not allowed:** "Nazis Put New Curbs on Jewish Workers," *New York Times,* April 3, 1941, 4.

4   **Head down, rely, have you done:** Schönhaus, *The Forger,* 156.

5   **Message, Feuerbachastrasse, agents:** Gerda Szepansky, *Frauen leisten Widerstabnd: 1933–1945* (Frankfurt: Taschenback, 2018), 75–76.

6   **Pancakes, champagne, longest hours, mad, calm, rational:** Schönhaus letters to Jacobs, May 14, 1946, August 27, 1946.

7   **Don't worry, if you ask, interest you, dreamed:** Schönhaus, *The Forger,* 57–58, 162, 176.

Chapter 23. "The Lifeboat Is Full"

1 **Religiously, understanding**: Beate Kosmala, "The Rescue of Jews, 1941–1945," in *Nazi Europe and the Final Solution*, ed. David Bankier and Israel Gutman (Jerusalem: Yad Vashem, 2003), 101.

2 **Rely on me, notebook is safe, fifty people, sentenced**: Cioma Schönhaus, *The Forger* (New York: Da Capo Press, 2007), 156–57, 210.

3 **Likeable, Moabit**: Gestapo interrogation of Franz Kaufmann, Stapo IV D1-1715/43 g., August 19, 1953.

4 **Young man, Schönhausen, accompanied, stopped**: Interim Investigation by German State Police re: Gunter Rogoff, August 31, 1943, in Cioma Schönhaus, *Der Passfalscher* (Frankfurt: Scherz, 2004), 228.

5 **Two and a half years, Sachsenhausen**: Kosmala, "The Rescue of Jews," 101.

6 **Clouds, gladness, not to yodel**: Mark Twain, *A Tramp Abroad* (New York: Library of America, 2010), 170, 176. Twain's dislike of cuckoo clocks was similar to Harry Lime's, a character in the 1947 film *The Third Man*, played by Orson Welles. In lines that Welles improvised, Lime questioned what really went on in Switzerland, and toward what aim: "In Italy for thirty years under the Borgias, they had warfare, terror, murder, and bloodshed, but they produced Michelangelo, Leonardo da Vinci, and the Renaissance. In Switzerland, they had brotherly love, and they had five hundred years of democracy and peace, and what did that produce? The cuckoo clock."

7 Switzerland hewed to neutrality partly to avoid another humbling defeat, partly to maintain domestic harmony. Its war with France in 1515 had almost torn the country apart. Swiss in the north favored the Duke of Milan, on whose side Switzerland was fighting; Swiss in the south preferred the duke's enemies, the French, who would soundly defeat the Swiss army. Four centuries later, different parts of Switzerland supported different sides during World War I. Swiss in the west backed France; those in the east favored Germany. The Swiss were slow learners when it came to a national consensus.

8 **Foreign influence**: Independent Commission of Experts—Second World War, *Switzerland and Refugees in the Nazi Era* (Bern: BBL/ EDMZ, 1999), 84.

9 **Nineteen thousand**: Clive H. Church and Randolph C. Head, *A Concise History of Switzerland* (New York: Cambridge University Press, 2013), 210. **Star of David**: Independent Commission, *Switzerland and Refugees in the Nazi Era*, 73. **Banned kashrut**:

Jacques Picard, *On the Ambivalence of Being Neutral: Switzerland and Swiss Jewry Facing the Rise and Fall of the Nazi State* (Washington, DC: United States Holocaust Memorial Museum, 1998), 9. Switzerland actually banned Jewish slaughtering ninety years before Germany did. In April 1933, a Nazi law banned kashrut, though it didn't use that term. Rather, the law prohibited killing animals for food if they hadn't been stunned or anesthetized first. Since kashrut requires that animals be conscious when they are killed, it automatically violated the law.

10   **Two centimeters**: Independent Commission, *Switzerland and Refugees in the Nazi Era*, 80. The Swiss were fine with the consequences of that even after Ernst von Weizsacker, Germany's ambassador to Switzerland, threatened that, if Switzerland or other countries didn't take in Germany's half a million Jews, they'd "face extermination." Not until July 1944 did Switzerland fully open its borders, even to Jews (Independent Commission, *Switzerland and Refugees in the Nazi Era*, 99).

11   **Isn't overflowing**: Independent Commission, *Switzerland and Refugees in the Nazi Era*, 95.

12   **Blackouts**: Christian Leitz, *Sympathy for the Devil: Neutral Europe and Nazi Germany in World War II* (New York: NYU Press, 2001), 19–20, 22. The percentage of Swiss exports sold to Germany increased throughout the war: 14 percent of all exports went to Germany in 1939, 42 percent in 1943. Much of this was armaments: in the first half of 1942, Switzerland sold Germany 250 million Swiss francs worth of material that a Swiss politician claimed had "very great importance to the [German] war effort"—arms, munitions, fuses, ball bearings. Similar exports worth only 13.8 million Swiss francs went to the Allies. **Fourteen percent, 42 percent, 250 million, 13.8 million**: Leitz, *Sympathy for the Devil*, 31, 33.

13   **Washing up, dogs, Singen**: Alfred G. Frei, "In the End, I Just Said OK: Political and Moral Dimensions of Escape Aid at the Swiss Border," in *Resistance Against the Third Reich, 1933–1945*, ed. Michael Geyer and John W. Boyer (Chicago: University of Chicago Press, 1994), 85, 87.

14   **Twenty-seven thousand, 51,000, 2,592, 1,404**: Georg Kreis, "Swiss Refugee Policy, 1933–45," in *Switzerland and the Second World War*, ed. Georg Kreis (London: Frank Cass, 2000), 118. Not until 1979 did Swiss laws allow asylum for anyone persecuted for religion or race. See Kreis, "Swiss Refugee Policy," 106.

15   **We're heading**: Schönhaus, *The Forger*, 165.
16   **Chambermaid**: Schönhaus, *The Forger*, 113–14.
17   **Gets caught, reliable, my fate**: Schönhaus, *The Forger*, 169.

Chapter 24. The Great Balancing

1   **Scrap metal**: Cioma Schönhaus, *The Forger* (New York: Da Capo Press, 2007), 162.
2   **So, we want**: Schönhaus, *The Forger*, 162–63. To indicate how much Cioma overpaid for his bike: in 1940, Victoria bikes, one of Germany's top brands, sold for between eighty to two hundred Reichsmarks—thirty-seven times less than what Cioma paid three years later. Bikes' rarity during the war inflated their price, and Cioma's desperation inflated whatever Hans might have been ready to ask for a bike. Author interview with Malte Zierenberg, October 6, 2022. "Victoria Markenrad Preisliste 1940," Velopedia, https://velopedia.online/Document/Show/1323. It's impossible to precisely convert the three thousand Reichsmarks Cioma paid into foreign currency like US dollars or British pounds: the war suspended all trade between Germany and the Allies. The best we can do is convert Reichsmarks into British and American currency shortly before each nation's conflict with Germany began. Since in 1939, 11.5 Reichsmarks equaled one British pound, Cioma would have paid about 260 pounds for his bike had he bought it that year. And since 2.5 Reichsmarks equaled one US dollar around the same time, his bike would have cost $1,200 in American currency. However it was calculated, neither of these was a minor expense in war-torn Berlin. Nor would what Cioma paid have been a negligible expense in the United States, though it was a more affluent country than Germany. For his bike, Cioma paid sixteen times more than the price of a Schwinn Paramount, the most expensive model Schwinn (then the premier bike manufacturer in the United States) sold in 1940. But when you buy a bike on the black market during a war, you expect to be gouged. Cioma was gouged. All prices from email to author from Bicycle Museum of America, January 26, 2022.
3   **More black market deals**: Malte Zierenberg, *Berlin's Black Market, 1939–1950* (New York: Palgrave Macmillan, 2015), 84. During the war, Zierenberg writes, 17 percent of arrests for trading on the black market in Berlin occurred in Mitte. The next highest percentage of arrests—eleven—was in Charlottenburg, a neighborhood four miles west of Mitte and much more well-to-do.

4   **Three hundred thousand members, five thousand chapters, largest workers' club, twenty thousand bikes**: https://de.wiki.org/wiki /rad_Kraftfahrbund_Solidarity.

5   **Solid**: Email to author from Bicycle Museum of America, January 26, 2022. **Fewer vibrations**: "Balloon Bikes," https://www.schwalbe.com /en/balloonbikes, January 25, 2022. Tires also affected the scarcity of bicycles in Germany. There'd been a rubber shortage in Germany since the war started. In 1939 synthetic rubber accounted for 22 percent of Germany's rubber supply; by 1943, this was up to 90 percent. Tires for civilian cars were rare. For bicycles, they were almost impossible to find. Cioma was lucky Hans found a bike for him that had any tires. That he found one with tires that were ideal for a long trip—balloon tires—bordered on the miraculous. **Twenty-two percent, 90 percent**: John Tully, *The Devil's Milk: A Social History of Rubber* (New York: NYU Press, 2011), 295.

6   **So comfortable**: Author interview with Cioma Schönhaus, July 29, 2012.

7   **Truth, despair, weakness, instant**: No author, *Pioneer Saga: The Story of Hashomer Hatzair* (New York: Hashomer Hatzair Organization, 1944), 21–22.

Chapter 25. Pigs to Avoid

1   **Burkhardt**: Helene Jacobs, "Illegality and Responsibility," *Unterwegs*, March 1947, 17. **Eighteen, cork, overprotected**: Cioma Schönhaus, *The Forger* (New York: Da Capo Press, 2007), 167, 170–71.

2   **Flat, cobbled**: Karl Baedeker, *Germany: A Handbook for Railway Travelers and Motorists* (New York: Charles Scribner's Sons, 1936), xl. From their beginning, the autobahns were shrouded in myth. Three examples: *Myth*: Hitler dreamed up the autobahns while imprisoned in 1923. *Fact*: In 1927, Fritz Todt, an engineer, drew up plans for a twenty-mile freeway from Munich to Lake Starnberg, Germany's largest body of fresh water. It was never built. By April 1933, Todt had expanded his plan into a national network of roads. Hitler used the scheme to convince Germans that a new infrastructure was being built that would make their lives better and the world envious. Todt, a devoted Nazi (he joined the party in 1922), let Hitler take credit for the autobahns. They advanced the cult of the führer. *Myth*: The autobahns were the first superhighways of their day. *Fact*: In 1924 the Italian engineer Piero Puricelli built the twenty-two-mile intersection-free autostrada near Milan. By 1935, the autostrada had expanded to almost 300 miles. Though these were toll roads and the

autobahns were free, the autostradas were functioning eleven years before the first cars sped along the autobahns. *Myth*: The autobahns were indispensable for Germany's automotive mobility. *Fact*: Among the major nations, Germany was one of the least reliant on automobiles. In 1935 there were 204 vehicles per one thousand people in the United States; in France, 49; in the United Kingdom, 45; in Denmark, 41; in Switzerland, 21. Germany had merely 16 vehicles per one thousand people. This was more than only Italy (9.5) and the USSR (1.5). See Thomas Zeller, *Driving Germany: The Landscape of the German Autobahn, 1930–1970* (New York: Berghahn Books, 2007), 63, 48, 52–53.

3   **Murderer**: Cioma Schönhaus, *The Forger* (New York: Da Capo Press, 2007), 180.

4   **RAF bombing**: www.berlinluftterror.com/raids. **Never go into**: Schönhaus, *The Forger*, 176.

5   **Childish delusion:** Sir Arthur Harris, *Bomber Offensive* (London: Greenhill Books, 2005), 52.

6   **Seventy-six degrees Fahrenheit**: "September 1943 Berlin Weather," Germany Weather Records, Extreme Weather Watch, https://www .extremeweatherwatch.com/countries/germany. **New start**: Schönhaus, *The Forger*, 176.

7   **Nobody stopped**: Cioma Schönhaus letter to Helene Jacobs, August 27, 1947.

8   **Thank God**: Cioma Schönhaus to Helene Jacobs, August 27, 1948.

9   **Straw, milk**: Heidrun Robing, *Lutherstadt Wittenberg: A Walking Tour of the City* (Lindenberg, Germany: Kunstverlag Josef Fink, 2018), 36. Judensau, or "Jew's pig," began appearing on churches in Europe in the fourteenth century. Gradually after World War II, most were removed, although in 2020 more than twenty remained in various European countries, including Germany. At first, Martin Luther was sure droves of Jews would convert to Christianity after hearing about his new theology. Furious in his later years that Jews had rejected the gift he offered them, Luther raged that Christians should burn Jews' homes, schools, and synagogues; destroy their prayerbooks; and steal their money and jewels.

10   **Train station, signs**: Ronny Kabus, *Juden der Lutherdstadt Wittenberg im Dritten Reich* (Norderstedt: Auflage, 2015), 2015.

11   **Forced laborers, seventy Jews**: Interview with Desiree Baur, September 10, 2022. **Shanghai, Palestine, suicide**: https://de .wikipedia/org/wiki/Liste_der_Stolpersteine_in_Lutherstadt _Wittenberg.

Chapter 26. "I'm Crossing My Fingers for You, Schönhaus"

1   **Can't you see**: Cioma Schönhaus, *The Forger* (New York: Da Capo
     Press, 2007), 178.

2   **Hotel food, lungs**: Schönhaus, *The Forger*, 181.

3   **Traitors**: "Hitler Makes Caustic Attack on Italian Leaders,"
     Adelaide Mail (Australia), September 11, 1943, 2. Cioma incorrectly
     wrote that the diners in Hotel Bamberger heard Hitler announce
     that commandos had rescued Mussolini from his prison in Italy.
     German radio did air a speech by Hitler on September 10, 1943, as
     Cioma recalled, but it didn't mention the rescue. It couldn't. The
     raid didn't occur until September 12, and then it was announced
     by a communique from Hitler's headquarters. Not by a live radio
     broadcast by Hitler. Instead, Hitler devoted his September 10
     speech entirely to his fury that Italy had surrendered to the Allies
     two days before. His only mention of Mussolini was calling him a
     "great, true man" and "my friend."

4   **Just a German**: "Hitler's Speech about Italy Was a Record," *Adelaide
     Mail* (Australia), September 11, 1943, 1.

5   **Stuttgart**: Karol Baedeker, *Southern Germany* (New York: Charles
     Scribner's Sons, 1929), 255, 263, 164–67.

6   **That's why, looking forward, most people, God watch**: Schönhaus,
     The Forger, 183, 184, 187.

Chapter 27. "I Only Want to Warn You"

1   **Where are you going, carry on**: Cioma Schönhaus, *The Forger* (New
     York: Da Capo Press, 2007), 170, 188.

2   **Dimensions of Lake Constance**: Karol Baedeker, *Southern Germany*
     (New York: Charles Scribner's Sons, 1929), 237.

3   Cioma went to Feldkirch in Austria. Not the Feldkirch in Germany.
     Germany's Feldkirch, slightly north of the western end of Lake
     Constance, was a unique little town. So small (roughly four hundred
     people) that it wasn't on most maps and so close to France—only
     four miles—that its residents' German was peppered with French
     inflections, French words, and French idioms. This Feldkirch
     would have been worthless to Cioma. It wasn't served by trains,
     and without a train, Cioma couldn't hop aboard a freight into
     Switzerland.

4   **Exactly as Claus**: Schönhaus, *The Forger*, 188.

5   **Very attractive, hotel room, handbag, stupid**: Schönhaus, *The Forger*,
     189–90.

6   **Only want**: Schönhaus, *The Forger*, 190.

Chapter 28. No More Hopeless Plans

1 **Young man, all in order**: Cioma Schönhaus, *The Forger* (New York: Da Capo Press, 2007), 192–93.

2 **Jewish population, census, SS, Gurs**: "Wangen am See," www .judische-gemeinden.de/index.php/gemeinden/u-z/2179-wangen-am -see-baden-werttemberg.

3 **Since September 14**: "Sonderausgabe zum Deutschen Kriminalpolizeiblatt," in Cioma Schönhaus, *Der Passfalscher* (Frankfurt: Scherz, 2004), 235.

Postscript: "I Know You. I Know You Very Well"

1 **Other lords, organs of the state**: "Barmen Theological Declaration," Widerstand!?, https://en.evangelischer-widerstand.de/html/view .php?type=biografie&id=1&l=en. **Responsibly am able**: "Karl Barth Biography," Center for Barth Studies, Princeton Theological Seminary. https://barth.ptsem.edu/biography.

2 **I know you, Hans Klausner, park bench**: Interview with Karen Joelson, December 15, 2021.

3 **How we should talk**: Karl Barth, "The Strange New World within the Bible," *NAMENSgedächtnis* (blog), 2016, https://jochenteuffel .wordpress.com/2016. **Young man**: Martina Voigt interview with Cioma Schönhaus, November 17, 1988.

4 **Cherry bowl, glasses, smells, what snake said, tightrope walker**: Ciona Schönhaus, *Der Passfalscher* (Frankfurt: Scherz, 2004), 65–66.

5 **Talented, dispel**: Charlotte von Kirschbaum letter to Pastor Karl Vogt, January 19, 1944.

6 **Industrious**: B. V. Grunigen letter to Cioma Schönhaus. January 14, 1948.

7 **Ecstatic, creative professions, in love, difficult, deserve**: Cioma Schönhaus letters to Helene Jacobs, May 14, 1946, August 27, 1946. Cioma's loyalty to Helene never wavered. In 1987 he wrote to Yad Vashem, Israel's memorial to the victims of the Holocaust, that she "is one of the few people I could consider a hero." She helped Jews "with great energy," "managed every situation thoughtfully and often even with a little bit of humor," "did not squeal on me" during her Gestapo interrogations, and "deserves every honor." Helene received one of those honors in 1983 when Yad Vashem declared her a Righteous Gentile, a Christian who helped save Jews from the Holocaust. **One of the few people**: Cioma Schönhaus letter to Yad Vashem, November 29, 1967.

8   **Human, plainness**: Interview with Michael Schönhaus, May 31, 2023.
9   The referendum not to provide nuclear weapons to Swiss troops
     prevailed, 62–37 percent.
10   **Calm**: Interview with Roger Le Marie, February 19, 2023.
11   **Everything possible**: Interview with Michael Schönhaus, May 31, 2023.
12   Judaism traditionally teaches that anyone who dies on Yom Kippur
     after fully and sincerely repenting dies without sin. Had Cioma
     repented, he'd have died at one with himself, with others and with
     God. Ketubot 103b, The William Davidson Talmud, www.sefaria
     .org/william-davidson-talmud.